MARK O'ROWE

Plays: One

The Aspidistra Code
From Both Hips
Howie the Rookie
Made in China
Crestfall

with a Foreword by the author

NICK HERN BOOKS

London
www.nickhernbooks.co.uk

A Nick Hern Book

Mark O'Rowe Plays: One first published in Great Britain as a paperback original in 2011 by Nick Hern Books Limited, 14 Larden Road, London W3 7ST

This collection copyright © 2011 Mark O'Rowe
Foreword copyright © 2011 Mark O'Rowe

The Aspidistra Code copyright © 1999, 2011 Mark O'Rowe
From Both Hips copyright © 1999, 2011 Mark O'Rowe
Howie the Rookie copyright © 1999, 2011 Mark O'Rowe
Made in China copyright © 2001, 2011 Mark O'Rowe
Crestfall copyright © 2011 Mark O'Rowe

Mark O'Rowe has asserted his right to be identified as the author of these works

Cover image © Ros Kavanagh
Cover design by Ned Hoste, 2H

Typeset by Nick Hern Books, London
Printed in Great Britain by CLE Print Ltd, St Ives, Cambs PE27 3LE

ISBN   978 1 84842 160 8

Contents

Foreword   vii

The Aspidistra Code   1

From Both Hips   75

Howie the Rookie   177

Made in China   223

Crestfall   315

Foreword

I started writing plays because the idea of doing something creative for a living appealed to me, and because I had no skills or education beyond second level, and because I was probably too lazy to get a proper job – though that last isn't strictly true; I was twenty-six years old and had had several proper jobs ('proper' meaning menial and repetitive and utterly disagreeable to a poetic soul like myself), but none I wanted to continue in any longer than I had to – added to which, if I hadn't found something else to do, I might have 'had to', I feared, I mean, *really* feared, for the rest of my life, so making some kind of move in that direction was imperative really, even if only to try and fail and never to try again.

Movies would have been more my cup of tea back then, but the odds against getting a movie script produced seemed, probably were, actually, astronomical. A novel, I suppose, was another option, literature being another form I was pretty passionate about, but I couldn't get over the sheer amount of words one had to put down on paper. I reasoned that, with theatre, far less stamina was required, and less command of the English language, given that it's all only dialogue anyway, and so I could write colloquially, concealing in doing so my many grammatical shortcomings (shortcomings which I know are being cruelly exposed right now), and also that, even if nobody wanted to produce something I'd written, perhaps I could produce it myself and put it on in some local hall or whatever, with myself and my friends – or maybe *just* my friends – playing the parts.

As it turns out it didn't come to that. The finished script, *The Aspidistra Code*, was one of five selected in an initiative devised by Ireland's National Association for Youth Drama, to encourage young playwrights between the ages of eighteen and thirty. Each play chosen received a week's rehearsal followed by a reading at the Peacock Theatre in Dublin, which, though immensely rewarding, not to mention deeply encouraging for a fledgling-or-would-be writer-complete-with-poetic-soul such as myself, never led to an actual production, and to date, it remains the only play in this collection never, at least as far as I'm aware, to have received one. It's a light, funny piece, probably most easily categorised as a kitchen-sink-crime-comedy-drama, a description which could equally be applied to its follow-up, *From Both Hips*, which *did* receive a professional production, courtesy of Jim Culleton at Fishamble Theatre Company (I found some addresses in the phone book and went around town, dropping the script into letterboxes; Jim was the only one who replied), who did an excellent job and, perhaps just as importantly, gave me a relaxed and highly enjoyable first experience in professional theatre.

This, inevitably, was followed by a couple of *less* enjoyable experiences, where I wrote several things for several people, which were rejected as unfinished, or not what was asked for, or just not good enough (the word 'shit' might have been used once or twice, I'm not sure; when I look back on the whole experience, I see it, even now, through a vague red haze), and went through a crisis period, which seems to me something that happens to many writers, especially those with poetic souls, at the beginning of their careers. We become victims of the combination of our suddenly enormous, though still incredibly fragile self-belief and our lack of any kind of psychological armour to counteract the frank, wounding, insensitive, occasionally correct, though often just plain ignorant, opinions of potential employers (or even friends or peers) with *non*-poetic souls, who don't recognise a work of art when they see it. Though I have to confess that I never returned to any of these rejected pieces afterwards, the reason for which might be that, either I was so deeply traumatised by their rejection that I just couldn't face them again, or that, indeed, they *were* shit all along, or if not shit then just not very good all along, certainly not producible, and that those people were right and I was wrong all along. I suppose there is that possibility. Anyway, after a year or more, consumed by self-doubt, unable to write (I would scribble out a few pages, consider them useless, dump them, scribble out a few more, consider them useless, dump them, etc., etc.) and on the verge of giving up altogether, I started a play called *Howie the Rookie*, and, astonishingly, to me at least, finished it. It was a monologue play and was inspired by my coming across, firstly, Conor McPherson's play, *This Lime Tree Bower* (you can just have an actor tell a story directly to the audience?!!!) and, secondly, Samuel Beckett's great novel, *Molloy* (you can have two lead characters who never meet and a plot which doesn't even tie itself up at the end?!!!). I found the latter fact very liberating, absolving me as it did of several literary or narrative responsibilties, though, in the end, the two lead characters in *Howie the Rookie did* meet up and the plot *did* tie itself up – quite nicely, in my opinion, which, I'll admit, is not of much value, or at least, of less than anyone else's, given the fact that I'm way too close to the play, having written it, and therefore pretty biased in its favour. The play was produced at London's Bush Theatre, directed by Mike Bradwell, and was a modest success, winning some awards and travelling to a few other countries where it was well received, and it would be remiss of me not to acknowledge that the lead performances by Aidan Kelly and Karl Shiels were extraordinary, two of the best I've seen, let alone been involved with, either before or since.

Next was *Made in China*, a dark comedy about two tough criminals fighting over the loyalty of a slightly more innocent third. It was an attempt, I suppose, to transpose the style, or if not the style, then the energy, or if not the energy, then at least the milieu of *Howie the Rookie* (though it doesn't really) into the type of play where characters actually talk to each other and not the audience – call it a proper play, or a well-made play, or a play which *aspires* to being a well-made play – and it culminates in a fight where two of the men take on the third who has the advantage of martial-arts training and the fact that he's armed with a prosthetic leg, and which really needs to be impeccably and spectacularly choreographed to work. One or two aspects of the play are a little dated now, such as the use of pagers – though, when I wrote it in 2001, pagers were already becoming extinct, which shows exactly how behind the curve (is that the phrase?) I was.

Both *Howie the Rookie* and *Made in China* were written for exclusively male casts, so I now decided, out of perversity, I suppose, or for the sake of symmetry, or maybe just to nourish the feminine side of my poetic soul, that I would write a play for a cast which was exclusively female, though it would retain the extremity and darkness and vulgarity and violence (I know, I know; all these masculine qualities), of the earlier work. This was *Crestfall*, another monologue piece, which was produced at the Gate Theatre in Dublin, whose seats I can still hear banging up one by one as people fled the theatre in horror or outrage (or boredom? or incomprehension?). It concerned three women living in a fictional town where venality, brutality and depravity are the norm, not the exception, and featured, appropriately, much that is venal, brutal and depraved, including a scene of (almost) bestiality which, most nights, now that I think of it, was where the seat-banging, sporadic up to this point, became cacophonous, or would have, had there been enough people in the theatre on any given night to actually raise a cacophony, if you see what I'm saying, which there weren't.

Now, *Crestfall* has never been published before and, in helping to put together this collection, I recently re-read it, deciding once I did, that there were some elements I wanted to rework – a final rewrite, eight years after the fact, before it's committed to print for better or worse – mostly the language, which I found too spare, too humourless, and almost wilfully contradictory in its lack of flow or rhythm. In doing so, though, and due, in fact, to a minor narrative issue that its existence exposed, I have had to excise, and with great regret, my (almost) bestiality scene. So, for those who like that kind of thing, I apologise (you didn't miss much: there was a woman and a dog, and the woman had the dog's dick in her hand – it went no further than that). The result, though, is a better play (in my opinion, and once again, what value does that have?), though how much better, I can't really say. A little better, anyway. Maybe. Or not much worse, in any case.

So I hope you enjoy the plays in this collection and will end this foreword by making a request, from one poetic soul to another, presuming you *are* a poetic soul (and if you're not, that's okay, the request is still made to you, though with slightly less hope of a sympathetic response), that you try to forgive its shortcomings, of which there may be many, and also try to appreciate its accomplishments, of which there may be some.

Mark O'Rowe, 2011

THE ASPIDISTRA CODE

The Aspidistra Code was first presented as a rehearsed reading as part of the National Association for Youth Drama's Stage IT! Young Playwright's Project at the Peacock Theatre, Dublin, on 2 December 1995, directed by Gerard Stembridge.

Characters

JOE

BRENDAN

SONIA

RONNIE

DRONGO

CRAZY HORSE

*An average-sized living room. A couple of armchairs on either side
of a coffee table. Television, down left. Large window at back and a
few feet in front, a sofa. At left, a hallway leading to the front door.
At right, a doorway leading to kitchen. Beside this doorway, a phone
on the wall. Down right, a dining table and chairs. Sitting at this
table are* JOE *and* BRENDAN. *There are playing cards scattered
across the table.* BRENDAN *is picking them up and putting the deck
back together.*

JOE. Imagine, right? We're in a... One of those... Say, for instance,
you're...

BRENDAN *tries to interrupt.*

No. Hang on. Hang on. You're in... Hold your horses. Say you're
in Las Vegas, right?

BRENDAN. No, no...

JOE. You're in Vegas, playing at one of those crap tables. Or a...
No. You're playing cards.

BRENDAN *tries to interrupt.*

Stop it, will you? You're at the card table and you're playing for
high stakes against James Bond and a Venetian, say, property
dealer and the... Who else? All these rich fuckers. The Duke
of... The Duke of Venice. Hang on. The Duke of Venice and his
six muscley bodyguards. They look like the Chippendales, only
with tuxedos, right? You're playing for chips. This is just for
instance, now. You've a tuxedo as well.

BRENDAN. Tuxedo?

JOE. This'd be the class of people you're playing against. They're
all rich fuckers, all right? Now, you lose the game and you lose
all your chips. That's all you had and now it's gone. You've
nothing. Now, you're safe enough. You're not lacking for a place
to stay or anything, you're booked in somewhere. *But...* That's
all you have. *Now...* You get a yen for something, I don't know.
For a glass of wine or champagne. You want something to eat.

BRENDAN. Cigarettes.

JOE. Right. We'll say cigarettes. You have a yen for a smoke. The excitement. You know the way, sometimes, like after a good game, you fancy a smoke.

BRENDAN. Yeah.

JOE. And, you're broke, now. So what are you going to do? Are you going to go up to the Ayatollah of, of fucking Iraq...? for a few quid, a few dollars for twenty cigarettes? You can't get tens there. Of money of what he just won from you? Because if you do that, all you're saying is, effectively, like, gimme some of my money back. Is he going to give you something?

BRENDAN. No.

JOE. That he just won off you? 'Cos he won it. The rules are strict. It's not yours any more, it's his.

BRENDAN. I know.

JOE. Is he going to return some of your, which is now his, money to you?

BRENDAN. Of course not.

JOE. Probably have you thrown out of the place or something. Get one of his Chippendales to give you a good hiding.

BRENDAN. Mmm.

JOE. Do you see?

Pause.

BRENDAN. What if...

JOE (*interrupting*). No, no, no...

BRENDAN. He could be a nice bloke.

JOE. No, Bren. It's not like that. It doesn't work that way. He probably is a nice bloke and all. Most people are. Thing is... What I'm trying to get across to you... Do you understand?

BRENDAN. Yeah.

JOE. You...

BRENDAN. I understand.

JOE. It's against the rules to give you money back. Even if he wanted to throw you a few... something for cigarettes. Etiquette demands that he refrain from such, you know, shows of emotion or good fellowship. And that's the rules. He can't do it if he takes his gambling seriously. We all do. We have to. And if you're going to take it seriously, you have to follow the rules. Do you think I'm greedy? 'Cos I'm trying to make you understand I'm not. Ciga... Something small even. It doesn't matter the size of the thing. I have to obey the etiquette of the table.

Pause. JOE *leans back in his chair and lights a cigarette.* BRENDAN *watches.*

BRENDAN. Play another hand.

JOE. With what? You've none left. And we're not playing for money.

BRENDAN. Play for 10ps.

JOE. No, Bren. No money. The game's over. Sorry that has to be the way, but... Money's out. We've what? (*Looks at watch.*) Half an hour. Relax.

Pause.

BRENDAN. Half an hour.

JOE. Relax. (*Pause.*) What are you worried about?

BRENDAN. A lot of things.

JOE. Relax.

Pause.

BRENDAN. I'm...

JOE. Relax.

BRENDAN. Who knows...? You see, who knows what way it's going to go?

JOE. Nobody knows, so relax.

Pause.

BRENDAN. Anything could...

JOE (*interrupting*). Hey, hey, fuck's sake, we've got the Crazy Horse, haven't we. All right, you're nervous, but we... Whatever happens with him, we can... Even the worst isn't going to be that bad, all right? Calm down. So calm down and relax. Take it easy.

BRENDAN. Okay. (*Shuffles the cards*.)

Pause.

JOE. Bit of trivia, Bren.

BRENDAN. What?

JOE. English, right...?

BRENDAN. Yeah?

JOE. ...the language, contains twice or more, I don't remember, as many words as a language, say, like French.

BRENDAN. Twice, yeah?

JOE. Or more.

Pause.

BRENDAN. So, English would be a fairly hard language to learn. If you had to learn it. Say, if you were foreign.

JOE. Oh, definitely. Definitely.

Pause.

BRENDAN. So, there's... Are there things the French don't have a word for?

JOE. No, they've a word for almost everything. Maybe you wouldn't think so.

BRENDAN. Yeah.

JOE. They don't have as *many* words. But the words they *do* have are better put to use. D'you know what I mean? For example, one word might have anything from fifty to a hundred meanings, depending on which way you say it.

BRENDAN. Pronunciation.

JOE. Yeah. Or what context. You say something with a deep voice and it means something completely different from the exact same word. Exact same. Same spelling, everything, only...

BRENDAN (*interrupting*). Wait, wait, listen.

Pause. They listen.

JOE. What?

We hear footsteps descending stairs.

BRENDAN. Sonia. (*Looks at watch.*) Shite!

JOE. What?

BRENDAN. Supposed to…

SONIA *enters.*

Hey, hey!

SONIA (*sleepily*). Hey.

BRENDAN. All right?

SONIA. Mmm-hmm.

BRENDAN. We were playing cards.

SONIA. It's okay. What time is it? (*Yawns.*)

BRENDAN. Almost twenty to. We were… Got a bit caught up. Sorry. (*To* JOE.) How long was it?

JOE. A while, Bren. Good game it was.

BRENDAN (*to* SONIA). How are you feeling?

SONIA. Bit sleepy. Tea?

BRENDAN (*getting up quickly*). No, no, no. Sit down, sit down.

He hustles her towards an armchair.

Get you a cup of… (*To* JOE.) Tea, Joe?

JOE. I wouldn't say no, Bren.

BRENDAN (*to* SONIA). Sit down. You're staggering around like a… Sit.

SONIA *sits.*

Good. (*Exiting to kitchen.*) I'll get it.

Silence.

JOE. You know something, Sonia?

SONIA. What?

JOE. The French language, beautiful and all as it is, contains only half as many words as English.

SONIA (*not really interested*). Really?

JOE. They've got no word for the word 'splash'. If they want to say 'splash', they have to say something like 'the sound that water makes when something hard hits it'. Hard to believe, isn't it.

SONIA. Mmm.

JOE. Or they could go 'pffshhh!'

SONIA (*absently*). They could.

Pause.

JOE. Why don't you go next door?

SONIA (*suddenly coming to life*). No, I... Joe! No. Brendan and I already spoke about this.

JOE. But this isn't your business. Well, it is your business, it's your house and all, but it's not, like...

SONIA (*interrupting*). I'm not going next door.

JOE. You should go in and sit down and have... (*Sighs.*) It's not really your business being here. Not business. That's not... But, you know...

SONIA. Joe. I'm not going next door. We... We...

JOE. You shouldn't be here.

SONIA. ...We already spoke about this, Joe. The discussion's over. It happened before you got here. I'm staying with my husband.

JOE. This isn't for ladies.

SONIA. This isn't for anyone.

JOE. *Particularly* for ladies. I don't want to see you... I want to shield you from things your eyes shouldn't be, you know, tainted with. You're not doing yourself any good.

SONIA. Don't worry about me.

JOE (*casually*). Oh, I'm not. (*Then, seriously.*) Come on, Sonia. (*Imitates her.*) 'Don't worry about me.' You know what that is? You know what you're doing there...?

The telephone rings. JOE *leaps up.*

I'll get it, I'll get it, let me get it. Could be... (*Picks up.*) Hello? (*Pause.*) Yes. Just hold the line one moment, please.

JOE *holds the phone out for* SONIA. *She takes it from him and he sits back down. As* SONIA *speaks,* BRENDAN *peeks his head in the door and aims a quizzical look at* JOE. JOE *shakes his head.* BRENDAN *disappears back into the kitchen.*

SONIA (*into phone*). Hello? No, everything's fff... No, we should... He's... (*Pause.*) No, thanks a lot, no. I'm sure. (*Pause.*) No, I'll... No, really. Thanks a lot all the same. Yeah, thanks a lot. (*Pause.*) Okay. (*Pause.*) All right, bye-bye. (*Hangs up. To* JOE.) I don't know.

JOE. Why do you talk to her?

SONIA. I don't know. Ah, she...

Pause.

JOE. What did she want?

SONIA. She wanted to know if she could be of any assistance. Was there anything I needed.

JOE. About what?

SONIA (*sitting back down*). What?

JOE. About this?

SONIA. She asked me if... Yeah. She was offering...

JOE. Why? 'Cos of this?

SONIA. She... Yeah. Why else?

JOE. Ah, Sonia.

SONIA. She was only...

JOE. You told her.

SONIA. Yes.

JOE. Ah, Sonia.

SONIA. What?

JOE. That wasn't the best of moves, now.

SONIA. It's Karen. What's the problem?

JOE. You just said you don't like her.

Pause.

SONIA. Right.

JOE. So, why are you going around telling her what's going on?

SONIA. I'm not 'going around'.

JOE. You *told* her.

Enter BRENDAN.

BRENDAN. Who was that?

SONIA. Karen. The phone? Karen.

BRENDAN. Karen?

JOE. She knows.

BRENDAN. Who's Karen?

SONIA. Karen next door.

JOE. She knows.

BRENDAN. Knows this? What does she know?

JOE. About this. That was her.

BRENDAN. On the phone.

JOE. Asking if she could be of assistance.

Pause.

BRENDAN. Who? (*To* SONIA.) Sonia!

SONIA. I told her yesterday. I'm sorry, but I told her. What difference can it make? The only difference is she wants to help. At least she gives a shit.

Pause.

BRENDAN. I don't like her. I'm sorry, Sonia. I know she's your friend and you like her and all...

SONIA. I don't like her.

BRENDAN. She's your friend.

SONIA. But I never said I liked her.

JOE. On the contrary.

BRENDAN. But the way it...

SONIA. I never said I liked her.

Pause.

BRENDAN. So you *don't* like her.

SONIA. Not really. No.

Pause.

BRENDAN. Neither do I.

JOE. Some tea, there, Bren?

BRENDAN (*remembering*). Oh, yeah.

BRENDAN *exits to the kitchen again. He returns with a tray of tea, cups, condiments. He puts it on the dining table. They sit down and start pouring, milking, sugaring, etc. The telephone rings again.* JOE *jumps up and answers it.*

JOE (*into phone*). Hello? Hey, how are you? You, you… (*Pause.*) Okay. No, no, no, not at all, no. Yes, that's… No, that's… (*Short pause.*) I don't know. Whatever you want. (*Short pause.*) Yes. (*Looks at watch.*) Okay. Hurry if you can, could you? If you *can*. (*Pause.*) Okay. I'm sorry. I'll see you then. All right. Goodbye. What? (*Pause.*) No, I… No, I said 'Good*bye*'. Yeah. All right. See you soon. (*Hangs up. To others.*) Thought I was calling him a good boy.

BRENDAN. That him?

JOE (*imitating whoever was on phone.*) 'You patronising me?'

BRENDAN. Joe.

JOE. That was him.

BRENDAN. The Crazy Horse?!

JOE. That was the Crazy Horse.

SONIA. What did he say?

BRENDAN. Is he coming?

JOE. He'll be here soon.

Pause.

BRENDAN (*to* SONIA). Why don't you go next door.

SONIA. No, Bren. I already told you I don't like her. I'm not going in there.

JOE. Why don't you just stay here.

BRENDAN. 'Why don't you'…? All right, just… I'm worried.

SONIA. So am I.

Pause. They drink their tea contemplatively. There is a deep, foreboding silence.

I was thinking, maybe…

BRENDAN. What?

SONIA. You know the chair?

JOE. Lovely tea, Bren.

SONIA. The old… My grandmother's chair. The chair my grandmother left me.

BRENDAN. The chair upstairs.

SONIA. It's worth money.

BRENDAN. That *chair*? That *eyesore*?

SONIA. The chair upstairs. It must be worth…

BRENDAN. That fucking *thing*!

SONIA. The money. We could use it, you know, to… You know.

BRENDAN. With the Drongo.

SONIA. Yes.

BRENDAN. It's an *eye*sore.

JOE. Which chair is this?

SONIA. It's an eyesore, I know, but he could… We could give it to him to sell.

BRENDAN. Where would he sell it?

SONIA. I don't know. At a market. In one of those things.

JOE. At an auction.

SONIA. At a, yeah. People could bid for it.

BRENDAN. The Drongo deals in… He doesn't deal in antiques. Hard cash. The Drongo is a hard-cash man. What the hell would he want with a chair?

SONIA. It's an antique.

BRENDAN (*to* JOE). Will you give me a cigarette?

JOE. Sorry, Bren.

BRENDAN. Just a... *One*!

JOE. Bren. You know I can't. You know the rules, there's no refunds. I won these. It'd be ethically wrong. Tomorrow, maybe.

BRENDAN (*sulkily*). Tomorrow.

SONIA. I'm going to bring it down.

SONIA *exits the living room and goes upstairs.*

BRENDAN. Give me a cigarette.

JOE. No.

BRENDAN. I need one.

JOE *lights a cigarette for himself.*

JOE. All this talk of cigarettes. Christ. (*Pause. Exhales smoke.*) Another bit of trivia for you, right? In the future. Not in our life. In the distant future... There'll be a brand of cigarettes which, when we inhale, will purify our bodies' innards, and which, when we exhale, due to the mixing of the special tobacco and the oxygen in our lungs, will promote rainforest growth and ozone-layer repair. (*Takes a drag on cigarette.*)

BRENDAN (*not really listening*). Imagine. (*Looks at watch.*)

JOE. Also... (Not tryin' to torture you or anything.) They also say that... You listening?

BRENDAN. Mmm.

JOE. Skyscrapers won't be made from steel and cement any more, but from foliage and, and mud and, like, things that nature has provided. They'll still be the same things; big buildings. Still serve the same uses. But they'll be built from the gifts, say, of the earth, which'll be... *the tobacco*. This special tobacco will enhance the growth of all good things. So, we can all smoke if we want to. And have big buildings, and...

BRENDAN. Very nice.

JOE. This is what they say, now. I myself... (Not trying to torture you, Bren.) (*Takes a long drag on cigarette. Exhales.*) I like a good smoke.

The telephone rings again and JOE *jumps up to answer it.*

(*Into phone*.) Hello? Is this... You're the... (*Pause*.) No, everything's fine. I'm, yes. I'm Brendan's brother. (*Pause*.) I supp... No, it's okay.

Pause.

As JOE *speaks, we can hear something heavy bumping down the stairs.*

Listen, could... Yes. There's just... Could you please... Could you... We're waiting for an important call. (*Pause*.) Yes, so... (*Pause*.) Yes, *we'll* get on to *you*. (*Pause*.) Yes, we'll get on to you. Right. (*Hangs up*.)

SONIA *enters, lugging the antique chair behind her.*

SONIA. Who was that?

BRENDAN. Your 'friend'.

JOE. Jesus Christ. Look at that. Who in their right... Is that it?

SONIA. Yeah.

JOE. That's the chair, the... The special chair.

BRENDAN. The magic chair.

SONIA. The an*tique* chair. That was my grandmother's chair.

JOE. That's a travesty.

SONIA (*to* BRENDAN). Who was it? Karen?

BRENDAN. She's checking up.

SONIA. I'm not going over there.

JOE. Fuck her.

BRENDAN. Just leave it there, Sonia.

SONIA. I'll... It might...

BRENDAN. Could be.

SONIA. ...It might come in useful.

JOE. That's a bloody disgrace.

BRENDAN. Leave it there.

SONIA *leaves the chair beside one of the other armchairs. It now looks like a hideous part of the sitting-room furniture. She sits back down.*

Won't be long now.

The lights of a passing car shine through the window. Everybody stiffens. The car continues on its way. They relax.

(*To* JOE.) What about the Crazy Horse?

JOE. What about him?

BRENDAN. Do you know him well?

JOE. I already told you, Bren.

BRENDAN. Remind us.

SONIA. Yeah.

JOE. I know he's crazy.

SONIA. Crazy?

JOE. Well, he's the Crazy Horse.

BRENDAN. But he's a friend of yours.

JOE. No, he's... No.

BRENDAN. Well, what is he? You *know* him.

SONIA. He's not your friend, Joe?

BRENDAN. Is he coming?

JOE. Wasn't he just on the phone, Bren.

BRENDAN. That doesn't mean he's coming.

SONIA. And you don't *know* him.

JOE. I *do* know him. He's someone I know but I wouldn't call him a *friend* of mine.

SONIA. He doesn't like you?

BRENDAN. Is he coming?

JOE. Yes. He's coming.

SONIA. Why doesn't he like you?

JOE. It's not that he doesn't *like* me. He's just not a friend of mine.

SONIA. Why not?

JOE. Because… I don't know. He's a bit difficult to get on with. He has problems with certain things, social things, hence his fucking… his occupation. His ideas are different to most people's. They're different to mine, anyway.

BRENDAN. How, different?

JOE. And that's why I don't hang around with him.

SONIA. And we're letting him in our house?

JOE. He's not…

BRENDAN. He's problems?

JOE. He has a few problems. Nothing.

BRENDAN. Could he do something?

JOE. Something, what?

BRENDAN. Is he dangerous? That's what I'm… As Sonia said. We don't want…

SONIA. That's right. In the house. I mean, who knows…?

JOE. He's…

BRENDAN. Yeah. In our home. Would it be stupid?

JOE. He *is* dangerous, yes, but…

BRENDAN. And he's going to… You've…

JOE. He's…

SONIA. In our house?

JOE. He's… Hold your horses, for Jaysus' sake, *yes*, he is dangerous, but he's… Hang on, he's a channelled, a controlled danger. He's on our side, for fuck's sake. He's coming here to help us. He's not an animal.

Pause.

BRENDAN (*to* SONIA). Maybe you should go in to Karen.

SONIA. Fuck off, Bren.

JOE. He's here to… Calm down, Bren, will you? For fuck's sake relax, the two of you. When I said he has problems, I meant he's annoying, right? He's not a monster, he's just a bit strange. His real name's Al, sure. I mean, the worst thing he'll do is get on your nerves, all right? There's no problem whatsoever about having him in your house. (*Pause.*) Okay?

Pause.

BRENDAN. If you say.

JOE. I do.

SONIA (*to herself*). 'The Crazy Horse.'

There is a thunderous knocking on the front door. Everybody jumps.

BRENDAN. God!

JOE (*getting up*). Relax.

JOE goes out to answer the door.

RONNIE (*offstage*). How's it going?

JOE (*offstage*). What's up, there, Ronnie?

RONNIE (*offstage*). Can I come in?

JOE (*offstage*). Yeah. Come on in.

We hear the front door shut and JOE and RONNIE enter the living room. RONNIE is from the country and speaks with a very heavy accent.

BRENDAN. What's up, Ronnie?

RONNIE (*dejectedly*). Ah.

BRENDAN. You all right?

SONIA. What is it?

RONNIE. I… (*Sighs.*)

BRENDAN. What's wrong?

RONNIE. The feckin'… (*Pause.*) Ah, you know, I just…

Pause.

SONIA. Ronnie?

RONNIE. Feckin' Karen! Do you know what…? I'm botherin' you, amen't I? You've got this thing happening and I'm in your way, amen't I?

SONIA. No.

RONNIE. 'Cos the feckin' hooer. I'm supposed to come in and see
you're all right. I know you don't want, you, you don't need me
here. Can't tell her that. Sent me in, she did.

BRENDAN. Do you... (*To* SONIA.) Get Ronnie a glass, a drink,
will you, Sonia? (*To* RONNIE.) What do you want, Ronnie?

RONNIE. 'Go in, go in.' 'No,' I say. 'All right, then,' she says.
'That's it.' 'What?' says I. 'If you don't go next door, then that's
a month.' D'you know what a month is?

BRENDAN. What?

RONNIE. I don't get me hole for a month. She doesn't let me, I'm
sorry, Sonia, shag her for a month. This is the thing, now. This is
the new business. Before... Last time it was dinner. Now, I'm a
hard-working man. I need my grub. Now it's sex. She won't...
That's her new thing, now, for getting what she wants.
Withdrawal of favours, the slut! One year we're married.
Withdrawal of favours. Who the devil does she think she is? One
month if I don't come in. I'm sorry. I'm supposed to be, I don't
know, protecting you or something. What the hell good am I?

JOE. Exactly.

RONNIE. What the hell can I do? One month, can you believe that?
Who would belie... (*Notices the antique chair.*) Where the hell
did you get that thing?

Pause.

SONIA. It's my grandmother's. Was.

JOE. It's an antique.

BRENDAN. What do you want to drink, Ronnie?

RONNIE. Would you believe it, Brendan? What would you do if...?
A month. Four weeks. What gives her the right? Using her
whatsit? Using her... Who gave her the right? A month of
wanking, excuse me, like a thirteen-year-old. 'Scuse me, Sonia.

SONIA. It's all right, Ronnie.

RONNIE. Give us... Give us a... What have you got?

BRENDAN. We've got some whiskey. (*To* SONIA.) Have we
whiskey?

SONIA. Paddy's.

BRENDAN (*to* RONNIE). Or a nice cup of...

RONNIE (*interrupting*). Paddy's'll do. I could use a glass. Straight. How are you, Joe? No, with ice.

JOE. How are you, Ronnie?

RONNIE. Unbelievable. That's... (*To* JOE.) No, but isn't it? Isn't it beyond belief? (*To* BRENDAN.) Would you believe it, Brendan?

SONIA *exits to get the drink.*

JOE. Relax, Ronnie. Calm it. Sit down. (*Pause.*) Sit down and relax.

RONNIE *sits.*

That's... Yeah.

Pause.

RONNIE. Hooer.

JOE. Relax.

Pause.

BRENDAN. Have you got a cigarette, Ronnie?

RONNIE. Suppose.

RONNIE *gives* BRENDAN *a cigarette.* BRENDAN *looks at* JOE.

JOE. What?

BRENDAN (*lighting cigarette*). Nothing a-tall, Joe.

SONIA *re-enters and gives* RONNIE *his whiskey.*

SONIA. There you go.

RONNIE. Thanks.

SONIA. So, how is Karen, anyway?

RONNIE. How's...? *Fuck* Karen!

SONIA. Ronnie. I was only...

RONNIE (*interrupting*). *Shag* her. Thinks she can control me. First food. Then sex. I go out and earn the bread, so I do. I earn the crust. You don't see her makin' demands of a Friday night, *do* you? On *pay* day. Pay day's 'be nice to Ronnie' day.

JOE. What does she look like?

RONNIE. You met her before, Joe.

JOE. Did I?

RONNIE. We were over here once for… Remember the party you had for… The party Brendan and Sonia had for little Jason's communion. Where *is* Jason?

SONIA. My sister's.

RONNIE. Good idea. Keep him out of danger. (*To* JOE.) For Jason's communion. You remember her.

JOE. No, I…

RONNIE. We were here. Hatchetface. She was with me.

SONIA. She's not a hatchetface, Ronnie.

RONNIE. She's not. She's a good-looking woman.

JOE. Yeah?

RONNIE. I have to admit, now. (*To* BRENDAN.) Brendan?

BRENDAN. Yeah, she's…

RONNIE. She's grand.

BRENDAN.…She's an attractive woman.

RONNIE. But she's a hooer.

JOE. What was she wearing?

RONNIE. I don't know. Some yoke.

SONIA. She was wearing a brown suit.

JOE. Ah, yeah. Now, I… That was the night Pebbles…

SONIA. Oh, Jesus, yeah.

JOE. She…

SONIA. Yeah.

JOE.…He pissed on your woman's lap. Carole Stewart.

BRENDAN. Typical.

SONIA. That was funny, now…

JOE. Poor bitch.

SONIA. ...wasn't it.

JOE. What was it she...?

SONIA. That devil dog.

JOE. That's it. 'Your devil dog.' (*To* RONNIE.) And Karen was... I remember her. The brown suit.

RONNIE. Brown suit. Says something, doesn't it. A brown power suit and the perfect colour for her.

BRENDAN. Why?

RONNIE. Colour of shite.

JOE. She doesn't drink.

RONNIE. Doesn't do anything.

SONIA. ...So *funny*!

RONNIE. Doesn't do anything. Trying to, now... This is the... A man can't live without a bit of drink once in a while, now, can he?

BRENDAN. What's she...?

RONNIE. Yeah, she's...

BRENDAN. ...She's...

RONNIE. Yes. That's another, the latest... Trying to *wean* me. Trying to get me off, the bitch. (*To* SONIA.) I'm sorry.

SONIA. It's all right.

RONNIE (*to himself*). The hooer! (*Pause. Looks at chair.*) That's some chair.

SONIA. That's an antique. It's worth a lot of money.

RONNIE. I'd like to ram it down her fecking gullet...

JOE. It's an appeasement.

RONNIE. ...Strangle her. A what?

JOE. An appeasement.

SONIA. It's for the Drongo, Ronnie.

RONNIE. This the...

JOE. Yeah. They call him the Drongo.

RONNIE. What's he going to do with it?

JOE. He can sell it. Who knows? It's worth a lot of money.

RONNIE. How much?

SONIA. Over two thousand pounds.

RONNIE. Yeah? And how much do you owe?

SONIA. Six hundred and fifty.

RONNIE. He might take it. That's worth a lot of money, that chair.

JOE. Do you know that the word 'drongo' is actually a derogatory term?

BRENDAN. Is it?

JOE. Mmm-hmm.

SONIA. Meaning?

JOE. I'm not sure. But something bad, I think.

RONNIE. A drongo.

SONIA. It means something bad?

JOE. Yeah.

SONIA. Does *he* know this?

JOE. Jesus, I don't know, but… (*Pause. Looks at her.*)

SONIA. Right. No. Of course.

JOE. Okay?

SONIA. Yeah.

RONNIE (*holding out empty glass*). Thanks, Sonia.

SONIA. You're welcome.

She takes the glass, but stays where she is for the time being.

JOE. Listen, Ronnie. As long as you're staying here…

RONNIE. No fecking choice, have I?

JOE. Right. Well, as long as you're here: when the Crazy Horse comes, could you just talk as little as possible, okay?

RONNIE. 'The Crazy Horse'?

JOE. Just sit down and be quiet and pretend you're not here. You can't do anything to...

RONNIE (*interrupting*). The Crazy Horse is coming here?

JOE. Yeah.

RONNIE. Here?

JOE. Yes. (*Pause.*) You know him?

RONNIE. I heard about him.

JOE. He's a friend of mine. *Well...* What did you hear about him?

RONNIE. Do you know him personally?

JOE. I do.

SONIA. What did you hear, Ronnie?

RONNIE. Heard he did something to a dog once.

SONIA (*to* BRENDAN). Pebbles!

BRENDAN. Ssshh.

JOE. What did he do, Ronnie?

RONNIE. Well... (*Pause.*) Some fella did something on some fella. I don't know what. Something bad. So the fella that had something, the thing done to him, knew the Crazy Horse. Or knew how to get in touch with him, anyway. So, he asked him for some assistance. I think it's something like the Crazy Horse won't help you unless he feels it's...

JOE. To see that it's ethically right that he help you.

RONNIE. Yeah, ethically... yes. He won't help... Is that right? He won't help just anyone.

JOE. That's correct. He has to decide...

RONNIE. Right. If the people are deserving.

JOE. Right.

RONNIE. Anyway, this man, he decided, was. So what it was was, he was being persecuted for something and the thing was to stop the fella, you know, the other lad from persecuting him. So the Crazy Horse drops down to your man's house. This is the... the...

BRENDAN. The bloke who was doing the persecuting.

RONNIE. Yeah. The fella doing it. His house. And he kicks him around a bit and he ties him to a chair and says to him, 'Who dies?' Which I hear is a typical thing he does. 'You make the decision who dies and who lives.'

SONIA. Between who?

RONNIE. It was… He had to decide between his… This… What kind? A… A… The little…

JOE. A Jack Russell.

RONNIE. Yeah?

JOE. Yeah.

RONNIE. Little… The little mutt. Between… Or this bag of… This moggie. A cat he had. Now, anyone with a bit of common sense… Which one are you going to choose?

SONIA. The dog.

RONNIE. The d… To live?

SONIA. Yeah. The dog to live.

RONNIE. Right. Who the feck'd pick a cat over a dog? Cats, they're treacherous little… hooers. Bit of common sense, you're going to pick the dog. So he picks the dog.

JOE. And the Crazy Horse kills the dog.

RONNIE. Yeah. He lets the little ball of shite live and kills the dog.

JOE. Tell them how he does it.

BRENDAN. No, hold on. I don't think… (*To* SONIA.) You don't want to hear this, do you?

SONIA (*to* RONNIE). No, go on.

BRENDAN. Is this going to…

SONIA. I want to hear it.

BRENDAN. …To upset you, or…?

SONIA (*to* RONNIE). What happened the dog?

RONNIE. Right. Well, first he tied your man up and taped his eyes open. Then, he put the dog in a see-through plastic bag and hung it out of the light. So your man had to sit there with his eyes taped open and watch his dog suffocate. (*Pause.*) So the dog's hanging

there and your man's watching it 'cos he can't do anything else.
Just watch it. And the bag's going in and out, in and out, slower
and slower with, you know… as the dog breathes. And it's getting
slower and slower, in and out, in and out, slower and slower, and
the man's watching it, and the bag's all fogged up, now, so all we
can see is the movement of the bag, in and out, and slower and
slower and slower… (*Pause. Then, matter-of-factly.*) and the
doggie croaked. Doggie dies and all this while, the feckin' moggie
is skulking around the room and pissing on the floor while man's
best friend is taking his last. Few. Breaths… Ever.

BRENDAN. Jesus Christ.

SONIA. Pebbles.

BRENDAN. Shut up, will you? *Fuck* Pebbles.

JOE. He's on our side, Sonia.

RONNIE. But, he's a good lad, I hear. He's decent in that he's… He
goes around doing good deeds. He helps people less fortunate. Or
the downtrodden.

   SONIA *notices that she still has the empty glass in her hand. She
   exits with it to the kitchen.*

JOE. They say that if you die in your home, a dog will stay by your
side the whole time and die with you. He'll remain loyal and true
and die with his master. But a cat'll, as soon as he sees you're
helpless, he'll eat you. A cat's got neither morals nor ethics.

RONNIE. Doesn't surprise me, Joe. Some women are like that, too,
and I'm not talking about your Sonia, Brendan. If you know what
I mean. I'm talking about someone else.

   SONIA *re-enters.*

BRENDAN (*to* SONIA). He all right?

RONNIE (*half to himself*). Someone near*by*, though.

SONIA. She's asleep. Poor little thing.

BRENDAN (*nervously*). How much longer? Jesus. I just wish it was
over. (*Pause.*) Get it over with.

   Pause.

JOE. Relax.

   Pause.

BRENDAN. Need a… (*Sighs.*) Can I have another cigarette, Ronnie?

RONNIE. Sorry, Brendan. Five left.

BRENDAN. Well, give me one, will you?

RONNIE. Five *left*, Brendan. That's all I have till tomorrow. I gave you one.

BRENDAN. Five, so give me one and then you'll have four.

RONNIE. Sorry, Brendan. From… I calculate. From now until I go to bed, I'll smoke exactly five cigarettes.

BRENDAN. Smoke four.

RONNIE. No.

JOE (*to* BRENDAN). Play him for one.

BRENDAN. With what?

JOE. I don't know, with… What have you got?

RONNIE. What's this, now?

BRENDAN. Emmm…

RONNIE. What's this? Poker?

JOE. Play him for the chair. The chair against a cigarette.

RONNIE. Poker, is it?

SONIA. That chair's an antique. (*To* BRENDAN.) And you should be more worried about the Drongo.

SONIA *exits to the kitchen.*

RONNIE. I don't normally gamble.

JOE. Karen cure you of that already, Ronnie?

RONNIE. Very funny. Whatsit? Poker?

BRENDAN. Yeah.

Pause.

RONNIE. What have you got?

BRENDAN. I don't know. I'll play you for…

JOE. Play him for the chair.

RONNIE. I don't want the chair.

BRENDAN. I've got... I'll play you for 10ps. 20ps. A twenty against a cigarette.

Pause.

RONNIE. An aspidistra.

BRENDAN. One of *my*...

RONNIE. A cigarette against an aspidistra.

Pause.

BRENDAN (*not too pushed on the idea*). Ehhmm...

JOE. That's a good bet.

BRENDAN. Yeah, but... My aspidistras, you know...?

JOE. That's a good bet, Bren.

RONNIE. That *is* a good bet.

BRENDAN. ...They're my pride and joy.

RONNIE. A cigarette versus an aspidistra.

BRENDAN. What the hell do you want with my aspidistras?

RONNIE. I like them.

BRENDAN. You like them.

RONNIE. I've seen them over the back wall. They're gorgeous.

Pause.

BRENDAN. Two cigarettes versus one aspidistra.

RONNIE. Two?!

BRENDAN. Two. I'm not going any lower.

JOE. You'd better hurry.

Pause.

RONNIE (*to* BRENDAN). All right.

JOE (*looking at watch*). You'd better hurry, lads.

BRENDAN. All right. (*To* RONNIE.) We'll just play one hand, without sees and bluffs and stuff. Just the... We pick up and then we show our hands. Make it quicker, all right?

JOE. That's not poker.

BRENDAN. It's just a short wager.

JOE. That's not how you play the game.

BRENDAN. We haven't got time to play a proper game. I haven't
got the nerves. (*To* RONNIE.) Right, Ronnie?

RONNIE. Right.

> BRENDAN *and* RONNIE *sit down at the table.* BRENDAN
> *picks up the deck of cards.*

JOE. You're prostituting the art, you fool. You're bastardising it.
You don't bastardise the skill and the art.

BRENDAN (*ignoring him*). Okay. Aspidistra versus cigarettes. Two
cigarettes. Let's go. You shuffle, Joe?

JOE. I'm not going to aid in the tainting of those cards.

BRENDAN. You want to shuffle, Ronnie?

RONNIE. All right.

> RONNIE *shuffles and deals.*

BRENDAN (*looking at hand*). Okay. Gimme… Gimme… What do
you want?

RONNIE. What do *you* want?

BRENDAN. Gimme three.

> BRENDAN *throws down three and* RONNIE *gives him three
> from the deck.*

RONNIE. Three. And I'll have… two.

> *He throws down two and takes two from the deck.*

> All right?

BRENDAN. Yep.

RONNIE. What have you got?

BRENDAN. What have *you* got?

RONNIE. You go. Show me your hand.

BRENDAN. You first.

RONNIE. Dealer has choice, Brendan. Go.

BRENDAN. What choice? Dealer goes first.

RONNIE. Dealer doesn't go first.

BRENDAN. Dealer goes first.

RONNIE. Dealer *says* who goes first.

BRENDAN. Joe. What's the rule?

JOE. You *broke* all the rules.

BRENDAN. Who shows their hand first?

RONNIE. Dealer has choice. And it doesn't matter anyway.

JOE. Congratulations, lads. Anarchy. Anarchy in poker.

BRENDAN (*to* JOE). Who shows first?

RONNIE. It doesn't matter a whit, Brendan.

BRENDAN. It doesn't matter?

RONNIE. Not a whit.

BRENDAN. Well, it matters to me. You show.

    RONNIE *sighs. Then lays down his cards.*

RONNIE. Three Jacks.

BRENDAN (*laying down cards*). Balls! Two sixes.

RONNIE. One aspidistra, *s'il vous plaît.*

    Pause.

BRENDAN. Another hand.

RONNIE. That's it. No, no. That's it. One hand. We played it and I won. I'm sorry for your loss.

BRENDAN. Fuck off.

RONNIE. No, I am. (*Pause.*) I know how much they mean to you.

BRENDAN. Yeah, well…

RONNIE. And I'll take good care of them.

BRENDAN. I hope so. It.

RONNIE. Sorry. It.

JOE. Hundreds of years of tradition and ancestry, destroyed over bloody cigarettes.

RONNIE. And the plant, Joe.

JOE. Yeah. And a bloody plant.

RONNIE (*to* BRENDAN). An extremely well-cultivated plant.

BRENDAN. Thanks.

JOE. You shouldn't be allowed to play if you can't show deference or respect to the game.

The telephone rings. JOE *jumps up and answers it.*

(*Into phone.*) Hello? (*Pause.*) Yes, he's… Is this important? (*Pause.*) No, no, no, I'm not being… I thought I already told you that… All right, right, right, here he is. Yes. I'm sorry. Here you go.

JOE *holds the receiver out to* RONNIE. RONNIE *takes it from him.* JOE *sits back down.*

RONNIE (*into phone*). Yes? Yes, I'm here. No, nothing's… Everything's… (*Pause.*) He's fine. (*Pause.*) No, they're all… It's just us. Yes, I'm… (*Pause.*) Yes, I'm doing what I can. Guess what I just did? Just now. I won one of Brendan's aspidistras off him. Yep. I… (*Pause.*) Yes, you… Okay, I will. Yes, I will. *Now.* Okay. (*Pause.*) Right, bye-bye. I lo… I love you too. Yes, that much. And more. Bye. (*Hangs up.*) Jesus!

BRENDAN. They should be…

SONIA *enters.*

SONIA. Who was that?

RONNIE. My… bane.

SONIA. Karen again?

RONNIE. The hooer.

BRENDAN. Shouldn't…? He's late.

JOE. They're both late.

Pause.

SONIA. Who won?

BRENDAN. He did.

SONIA. Well done, Ronnie.

RONNIE. Yeah. Listen, Brendan.

BRENDAN. What?

RONNIE. She says I have to see it.

BRENDAN. See what?

RONNIE. My aspidistra.

BRENDAN. Now?

RONNIE. Yeah.

BRENDAN (*getting up*). Jesus.

JOE (*looking at watch*). You'd better hurry, Bren.

BRENDAN. Right. Right.

   BRENDAN *goes out the door to the kitchen.*

RONNIE. Sure he's loads anyway, hasn't he?

JOE. He does, Ronnie. You won it fair and square.

   We hear the back door open.

BRENDAN (*offstage*). Sonia!

SONIA. What?

BRENDAN. The fucking dog! For fuck...!

SONIA. You let it in, Bren. If you let it in, you've to put it out.

BRENDAN. I'm trying to do... For fff...!

   We hear a scuffle. Then the back door opens and closes.
   BRENDAN *re-enters with an aspidistra.*

SONIA (*to* BRENDAN). All right?

RONNIE. Oh, my God.

BRENDAN (*giving aspidistra to* RONNIE). There you go.

RONNIE. Oh, Jaysus. Thanks very much, Brendan.

BRENDAN. Now, do you know how to take care of it?

RONNIE. Oh, I do. I do. It's a beauty.

BRENDAN (*to* SONIA). Bloody mutt.

SONIA. She's not a mutt.

RONNIE (*of aspidistra*). And it's mine, you know?

BRENDAN. That was the best one.

RONNIE. I don't believe you, Brendan, and I don't care. It's gorgeous.

BRENDAN. Good.

Pause.

SONIA (*to* BRENDAN). Should we not leave that phone off the hook?

RONNIE. Good idea. If she's going to ring again, I don't want to talk to her.

BRENDAN. No. What if…? In case the Drongo or the Crazy Horse rings.

SONIA. No. Yeah. You're right.

RONNIE (*admiring his aspidistra*). Still…

BRENDAN. Leave it the way it is.

SONIA. You're right. Yeah.

Pause.

JOE. Thing about phones. Interesting…

They are interrupted by a loud knocking on the door. Everybody is silent. Expectant.

Lights down.

Lights up.

Moments later. All present with one addition. The DRONGO. *A powerful, dangerous-looking character. He sits in the antique armchair like a king and speaks with a strong Australian accent.* RONNIE's *aspidistra sits on the coffee table.*

DRONGO. Not on your nelly. Not. On. Your. Nelly. I came here… And I can see that you're not bad people. Fair dinkum. But I can see you're not fighting to keep your heads above water either. I came here alone as opposed to sending some of my mates, because I wanted to see for myself what kind of a situation we have. Now, maybe Raymond Murphy was a good man. He *was* a good man. Personally, I don't think this business is the *right* business for a good man. And I believe that that's the essential reason he failed in this business. Perhaps the next... Who knows? Now, he might have been the type of bloke you could go up to and say, 'Sorry, mate. Bit short today. Next week?' And he'd say, 'No problems.' But, therein I believe to be the genesis of his insolvency; his downfall. He was too bloody nice. Well, now I own your debt. And I'm sorry, but I can't allow... My good business sense, my instinct for survival tells me I can't allow... can't offer leniency in payments. Regarding neither time nor amount. I can't allow it.

Pause.

SONIA. We have... We...

DRONGO. Wait, now. Just wait a minute. I'm not finished talking yet. When I finish talking, then we can all talk. All right?

SONIA. All right.

DRONGO. Don't interrupt me again.

SONIA. I'm sorry.

Pause.

DRONGO. Do you... About leniency. Have you understood what I just said?

SONIA. Yes.

BRENDAN. Yes.

DRONGO. Good. Now, I'm sure you've heard certain stories about me. Certain myths or legends... Urban legends which have been passed around in one way or another. Things I did or threatened to do. Horror stories? Let me tell you, mates... They're all true. I collect on time always. I collect or I do something. I don't have a set rule for punishment or *prompting*. Like that term, 'prompting'? Prompting. A prompter. To prompt. I don't have a set rule. I just do whatever comes into my head at the time. It's been said I have a good imagination. I collect or I do something. Remember that. Now, I came here alone as a gesture of... not goodwill, 'cos I don't have any. As a gesture of trust. If you have any thoughts on getting out of this not corresponding to my rules, dismiss them now. If something should ever happen to me, you will be found and killed. Did I just say 'killed'? You're damn right I did. This was just a little chat to... set forward, to give you a little knowledge of the situation. Do you understand?

BRENDAN. Yes.

SONIA. Yes.

DRONGO. Now, we'll discuss how to *deal* with the situation. (*Indicates* JOE.) Who's this?

BRENDAN. My brother.

DRONGO. Don't see much resemblance there. Same father?

BRENDAN. Yes.

DRONGO. Mother?

BRENDAN. Yes.

DRONGO. Hmm. (*Indicates* RONNIE.) And this?

BRENDAN. That's Ronnie. Next-door neighbour.

DRONGO. And what's he doing here?

BRENDAN. We were playing cards.

DRONGO. Yeah? Who won?

BRENDAN. He did.

DRONGO (*to* RONNIE). How much did you win?

RONNIE. I won an aspidistra.

DRONGO. A what?

RONNIE (*points at aspidistra*). There.

DRONGO. Yeah, yeah. I know what it is. Beautiful species. Beautiful. Sad to lose it, Brendan?

BRENDAN. Yeah.

DRONGO. High bloody stakes.

BRENDAN (*gloomily*). Yeah.

RONNIE (*simultaneously; happily*). Yeah.

DRONGO. Not much luck tonight, Brendan?

BRENDAN. Not much.

DRONGO. And this is your lovely sheila. (*To* SONIA.) What's your name?

SONIA. Sonia.

DRONGO. Nice. You could almost *be* a sheila.

SONIA. Eh… Thanks.

DRONGO. A *lovely*-looking sheila.

SONIA. Thank you.

DRONGO. All right. Now that we all know each other, let's get down to business. You owed Mr Murphy, and now me, six hundred and fifty pounds to be repaid at a rate of seventy pounds per week?

BRENDAN. That's right.

DRONGO. One hundred pounds a week now. All right? It's nicer to round these things off, I think. Seventy pounds. That's a disgustingly *odd* amount. One hundred pounds a week?

BRENDAN. Eh…

DRONGO. A nice figure?

BRENDAN. Yeah.

DRONGO. All right. Now. Since Mr Murphy went out of business, so to speak, you've missed a week's payment…

SONIA. That's… But…

DRONGO. …through, settle down, through no fault of your own. I understand. That's all Mr Murphy's fault. I'm not blaming you. But you know that you now owe me two hundred pounds. Is that right? That's the correct figure?

Pause.

SONIA. We don't have it.

DRONGO (*to* SONIA). Excuse me. (*To* BRENDAN.) What?

BRENDAN. We don't have it.

DRONGO. The money.

BRENDAN. Yes.

DRONGO. At all.

BRENDAN. We have… How much? Sixty-five pounds.

Pause.

DRONGO. That's not much.

BRENDAN. No.

DRONGO (*to* JOE *and* RONNIE). What about you? None of you any?

JOE. That includes what I added.

SONIA. We weren't given any time.

DRONGO. You poor people. You poor people. (*Pause.*) Hmm.

BRENDAN. Could we not...

DRONGO. No. No. I'm sorry.

BRENDAN. No chance of a...

DRONGO....No.

BRENDAN....Of an extension? A few days or...?

DRONGO. I'm sorry, Brendan.

Short pause.

BRENDAN. At all?

Pause.

DRONGO. At all.

Pause.

BRENDAN. We don't have it. I... Ronnie!

DRONGO. Ronnie?

RONNIE. No.

BRENDAN. At all?

RONNIE. I'm as smashed as you are. I've got... (*Roots in his pocket and takes out some money.*) twelve pounds fifty. Here.

BRENDAN. No, it's all right.

RONNIE. Go ahead. I'll manage.

BRENDAN. No, keep it.

RONNIE. No. Go on. Don't worry.

BRENDAN. It won't make any difference.

DRONGO. That's right.

SONIA. Couldn't we... Is there no other way to... That we could, like... Something here.

BRENDAN. Something here?

SONIA. Here. Like the television or...

BRENDAN. The telly?

SONIA. Yes.

BRENDAN. I *need* the telly.

DRONGO. I think there are certain things you should be more concerned about at this moment than watching football, Brendan.

Pause.

BRENDAN. Will you take it?

DRONGO. No.

BRENDAN. Well, is there...?

DRONGO (*interrupting*). I deal in cash, mates. I'm not in the flogging business. Now, I appreciate your telly's *worth*. But I'm not going to waste my time.

Pause.

SONIA. We've got that chair you're...

BRENDAN. Sonia!

SONIA. That chair you're sitting in is worth thousands of pounds. We'll give you that.

BRENDAN. *Cash*, Sonia.

SONIA. You'll get... If you sell it, you'll get over five times what we owe you. Well, not five, but close enough. Surely it'd be worth the hassle to...

DRONGO (*interrupting*). And would that be fair on you?

SONIA. ...Over two thousand pounds.

Pause.

DRONGO. And would that be fair on you?

SONIA. We don't mind.

DRONGO. But I do. I'm not having that on my conscience. 'Preciate the offer. Cash. (*Pause*.) Cash, cash, cash. You don't have it.

BRENDAN. No.

SONIA. I can't understand why you...

DRONGO (*interrupting*). Shut up. (*Pause. To* BRENDAN.) You don't have it.

BRENDAN. No. We've got sixty-five pounds.

RONNIE. Seventy-seven. Seventy-seven fifty, if it makes any difference.

DRONGO. It doesn't, mate. Keep it. (*Sighs*.) This is what happens. (*Pause*.) You see, mates, we've got rules here. Rules are what keep society in shape, keep it from getting flabby. Rules are what prevent anarchy. Rules are the only thing preventing the extinction of the wallaby. Life is rules and rules are what sustain the eh... (*Pause*.) And what are we if we break them? Hm? Who are we *to* break them? Nobody. What are we worth *if* we break them? Nothing. We are people without laws and without a code. We're animals.

JOE. That's right.

DRONGO. What?

JOE. A code.

DRONGO. That's right. (*To* BRENDAN.) We are without a code. Without moral values, ethics, eti*quette*, principles, we are without rules. I have to do my job. I have to do my job and I'm sorry, mates. I'm sorry for you. But if I don't stick to my rules, then what am I? (*Pause*.) Does your phone work?

BRENDAN. Em...

DRONGO. Your phone.

BRENDAN. Y... Yes.

SONIA. Who are you calling?

DRONGO. The prompters.

SONIA. Surely there's... Bren!

BRENDAN. Surely there's...

DRONGO. Shut up.

The DRONGO *goes to the phone. Before he reaches it, it rings. He picks it up.*

(*Into phone.*) Hello? (*Pause.*) Yes. Yes it is. Would, would, would you mind, please? Ron? Yes, he's fine. Would you mind... Would you mind fucking off please? (*Pause.*) Yes, thank you. Stay off the line, please.

He hangs up and begins dialling.

Your sheila, Ronnie.

RONNIE. So I gathered.

SONIA. Bren!

DRONGO. Sounds like a bit of a cunt.

SONIA. Joe!

RONNIE. She's a hooer.

DRONGO (*into phone*). Hello? Yeah. It's the Drongo. The job. What do you think? (*Pause.*) Nice people, yeah. No, nice. (*Pause.*) Really? Strewth! Ed and Mannix there? Good. Bring 'em. (*Pause.*) If you... Yeah, if you want. (*Pause.*) Hang on. (*Takes a notebook from his pocket. Opens it. Reads.*) 10 Oak Lawns.

SONIA (*becoming more and more terrified*). Bre... Joe!

DRONGO (*into phone*). Te... In Springfield, you dafty.

SONIA. Joe, for God's sake!

DRONGO (*into phone*). Yes. Okay. See you in a while. Hurry up. (*Hangs up.*)

SONIA (*hysterically*). Joe! Where's the Crazy Horse?!!

There is a knock on the door. Everybody falls silent. Seconds pass.

DRONGO. Get it, Sheila. Sonia.

SONIA *goes out to the front door while everybody else sits in suspense. She returns, with the* CRAZY HORSE *leading the way. He is carrying a bag on his shoulder. He practically saunters into the room.*

CRAZY HORSE. Who's the bloke? (*To* RONNIE.) You the bloke?

RONNIE. No.

CRAZY HORSE. Who then? (*To* JOE.) Heya, Joe.

JOE. How's it going?

CRAZY HORSE. Good. Very good. Who is it?

JOE *points out the* DRONGO.

This is the Drongo.

DRONGO. That's right.

CRAZY HORSE. This. Is. The. Drongo.

DRONGO. Who the fuck are you, mate?

CRAZY HORSE. So. This. Is. The. Famous. Drongo.

DRONGO. Brendan.

CRAZY HORSE. Know who I am?

DRONGO. I just asked you.

CRAZY HORSE. Know who I am?

DRONGO. *Who* the fuck are you?

CRAZY HORSE. I am Lucifer incarnate. I am the Crazy Horse.

Pause.

DRONGO. Know who I am?

CRAZY HORSE. Someone who just messed with the wrong people.

DRONGO. But, do you know who I am?

CRAZY HORSE. You're the Drongo.

DRONGO. That's right. I am the Drongo.

CRAZY HORSE. Well, I'm the Crazy Horse.

DRONGO. So I see. Go home.

The CRAZY HORSE *takes a pistol from his bag and sits down in a vacant armchair, facing the* DRONGO.

CRAZY HORSE. I'm staying here.

Pause.

DRONGO. What do you want?

CRAZY HORSE. Have you ever heard of me?

DRONGO. I've heard vague rumours.

CRAZY HORSE. So you know my reputation.

DRONGO. I've heard rumours, I said.

CRAZY HORSE. Well, they're all true.

DRONGO. Including the one, you have syphillis?

CRAZY HORSE. Very funny. (*Pause*.) I've heard about you.

DRONGO. All true.

CRAZY HORSE. Yeah?

DRONGO. Yeah.

RONNIE. Get on with it.

CRAZY HORSE. What the fff... Who's this, Joe?

JOE. The next-door neighbour.

DRONGO. Tell him to shut up.

CRAZY HORSE (*to* RONNIE). Shut the fuck up.

BRENDAN. Ronnie.

RONNIE. He's supposed to be doing something.

BRENDAN. He is.

CRAZY HORSE. I am, fuckhole.

JOE. Shut the fuck up, Ronnie.

CRAZY HORSE (*to the* DRONGO). So, we both know each other. We know of one another's... reputations.

DRONGO (*impatiently*). Oh, come on. (*To* RONNIE.) No, Ronnie. I'm sorry. You're right. (*To the* CRAZY HORSE.) Aren't you supposed to be doing something?

Pause.

CRAZY HORSE. These people owe you money.

DRONGO. That's right.

CRAZY HORSE. A load of money.

DRONGO. That's right.

CRAZY HORSE. How much?

DRONGO. Six hundred and fifty pounds.

CRAZY HORSE. Six hundred and fifty pounds.

DRONGO. That's right.

CRAZY HORSE. Well, you can strike it off your whatever. They don't owe you anything any more.

DRONGO. Is that right?

CRAZY HORSE. That's right.

Pause.

DRONGO. Do you know who you're talking to?

RONNIE. Oh, Jesus.

SONIA. Ronnie, can we get on with this?

DRONGO (*to the* CRAZY HORSE). Do you know who...? You get in my way and you'll be found. And you're not that hard to find. You'll be found and you'll be... DO YOU KNOW WHO THE FUCK YOU'RE TALKING TO?

Suddenly the DRONGO's *Australian accent sounds very Dublin-like. The angrier he gets, the less Australian he sounds.*

DO YOU KNOW HOW DEEP YOU ARE ALREADY? You're putting your own, and all these people's well-being in jeopardy. (*Then, back to Australian accent.*) You're being a... a... a dingbat!

Pause.

BRENDAN. Maybe eh...

CRAZY HORSE. Jesus Christ. Hah! Jesus Christ. You arsehole.

DRONGO. Fuck you.

CRAZY HORSE. You're not... Wait a minute. I'm looking and... I know who you are.

DRONGO. Drop it, mate.

CRAZY HORSE (*excited*). You have a scar from here to here. (*Indicates elbow to wrist.*) You've got... Lemme... Where'd you get the teeth?

DRONGO. Excuse me?

CRAZY HORSE. Where'd you get the teeth?

RONNIE. What the hell is he talking about?

CRAZY HORSE (*still to the* DRONGO). Fikey McFarlane.

DRONGO. Who's that?

CRAZY HORSE. That's fucking you.

Pause.

DRONGO. Do I know you?

CRAZY HORSE. Alan Kilby. The fucking showers, man.

DRONGO (*recognising him*). Alan. The sho… Shit!

CRAZY HORSE. Where'd you get the accent? I knew it.

DRONGO (*in Dublinese*). It's my… Al! It's my whatchamicallit.

CRAZY HORSE. Your gimmick.

DRONGO. My gimmick. How the fuck are you?

CRAZY HORSE. I'm great. Where'd you get the teeth?

DRONGO. Falsers.

CRAZY HORSE. Very nice. *Very* nice.

DRONGO. Not bad. (*Taps teeth with fingertips.*)

CRAZY HORSE. Not bad. Fucking great. Fucking great to see you.

DRONGO. Al!

CRAZY HORSE. Fikey boy! The accent.

DRONGO. My gimmick.

CRAZY HORSE. It slips.

DRONGO. Only if I lose the rag.

CRAZY HORSE. Jesus. How's the dog?

DRONGO. Dead.

CRAZY HORSE. Aww. I'm sorry.

DRONGO. He was never the same after you…

Pause. A respectful silence. SONIA *glances at* BRENDAN.

CRAZY HORSE. Sorry about that, too.

DRONGO. Agh! Water under the bridge. You use guns?

CRAZY HORSE (*brandishing his weapon*). Yeah.

DRONGO. Strictly muscle, myself. Can I have a look?

> CRAZY HORSE *hands him the gun. The* DRONGO *plays with it.*

> Nice. So, you're on the side of good.

> *He hands back the gun.*

CRAZY HORSE. The meek and indefensible.

DRONGO. Man.

CRAZY HORSE. But not law and order.

DRONGO. Fuck that.

CRAZY HORSE. Fuck the law.

DRONGO. Fucking right. You stayed true. Like the conver... Old times, Al. Shit! The showers!

CRAZY HORSE. The craic!

> *They stand there, facing each other. There is a long pause. Everybody is silent and confused.*

DRONGO (*full of emotion*). Good to see you, Al.

> *They embrace.*

CRAZY HORSE. Oh, you gobshite, you.

> *They hug for a long time.*

BRENDAN (*to* JOE). This is your... weapon?

CRAZY HORSE (*to the* DRONGO). You gobshite.

SONIA. What's going on, Joe?

JOE. The intricacies seem to have shifted somewhat here.

CRAZY HORSE (*still hugging the* DRONGO). Those fuckin' teeth!

> *Lights down.*

> *Lights up.*

> *A few moments later. Everybody sitting.*

DRONGO (*looking at the* CRAZY HORSE). Man.

Pause.

CRAZY HORSE. Man.

DRONGO. Oh, man.

CRAZY HORSE. He... Joe, he had a fight with this... He crashed... Where was it? Inchicore. Some gobshite crashed his car into Fikey's and...

DRONGO. Al! Al!

CRAZY HORSE. What?

DRONGO. I know you know me as Fikey, but would you call me the Drongo? It's a... I've kind of gotten used to it and people, you know? They know me.

CRAZY HORSE. It's your gimmick.

DRONGO. It's my, yeah. I'm the Drongo.

CRAZY HORSE. Then, well, it's only right. We'll call you the Drongo.

DRONGO. Good one.

CRAZY HORSE. And you call me the Crazy Horse.

DRONGO. You want me to.

CRAZY HORSE. Yeah.

DRONGO. 'Cos it's your gimmick too.

CRAZY HORSE. Well, no... Yeah. I'm... At the moment, I'm trying to establish it as my gimmick. I'm sort of between handles at the moment.

DRONGO. But you're trying to sway to...

CRAZY HORSE. Towards my, right, my...

DRONGO. Your gimmick.

CRAZY HORSE. ...My new handle, yeah. I'm in transition.

DRONGO. Right.

CRAZY HORSE. So it's important that people know me as the Crazy Horse...

DRONGO. Absolutely.

CRAZY HORSE. ...and hear the name as often as possible.

DRONGO. Okay. Crazy Horse.

CRAZY HORSE. Okay. So, Joe. This fella crashes into the Drongo, and the poor Drongo smashes his... (*To the* DRONGO.) Was it against the steering wheel?

DRONGO (*to* JOE). I wasn't wearing my seatbelt. (*To others*.) Should always wear your seatbelt.

CRAZY HORSE. Right. And knocks his four front teeth out. (*To the* DRONGO.) Oh, man, the difference. I'm looking at you. (*To* JOE.) His... His... (*To the* DRONGO.) You were like that for... It's difficult to get used to you now.

DRONGO. I suppose the beard too.

CRAZY HORSE. But it's good. It looks good. You look a hell of a lot more handsome now.

DRONGO. I used to think that a fearsome appearance would be more effective. Scare them with... (*To* SONIA.) Because I was a state. No teeth here... (*Indicates*.) And it was...

CRAZY HORSE. It was unattractive.

DRONGO. It wasn't una*ttrac*tive. But, for other people it was uncomfortable. So I thought I'd tone it down and offer a more sage, benevolent front. And I thought that in terms of inspiring fear and awe, that it would be...

Pause.

CRAZY HORSE. And was it? Is it?

DRONGO. What?

CRAZY HORSE. What you were going to say.

DRONGO. Effective?

CRAZY HORSE. Yeah.

DRONGO. Ask Sonia and Brendan.

CRAZY HORSE (*to* SONIA). Is it?

SONIA. Yes.

DRONGO. You think so?

SONIA. Very.

DRONGO. Thank you. Brendan?

BRENDAN. Effective?

DRONGO. Yes.

BRENDAN. Yes.

DRONGO (*to the* CRAZY HORSE). There you go.

CRAZY HORSE. Great.

Pause.

SONIA. Mister… Drongo?

DRONGO. Yes?

SONIA. What's the eh… What's the, you know? The story?

DRONGO. What do you mean?

Pause.

SONIA. The money.

DRONGO (*dismissively*). It's all right…

SONIA. Really?

DRONGO. …It's okay. This is a happy day, so…

RONNIE. This is good, now.

CRAZY HORSE (*to the* DRONGO). I'm sorry about your dog.

DRONGO. It's all right.

CRAZY HORSE. Do you miss him?

DRONGO. Yeah, I miss him. He was my friend as well as my dog, you know what I mean?

CRAZY HORSE. I'm sorry.

DRONGO. Ah, would you stop. You were some firecracker freak.

CRAZY HORSE. Yeah. It's all guns now. I like the bangs, you know? Did it ever get its hearing back?

DRONGO. No.

CRAZY HORSE. I'm sorry.

DRONGO. That's okay.

CRAZY HORSE. He was a good dog. One of the few.

DRONGO. That's okay.

SONIA (*tentatively. To the* CRAZY HORSE). Do you not like dogs?

DRONGO. Fucking hates them.

CRAZY HORSE. With a vengeance.

DRONGO. With a fucking… intensity.

CRAZY HORSE. With a rapture. All animals.

DRONGO. You liked Bubbles.

CRAZY HORSE. Bubbles was okay. She was trained well. Didn't go pissing everywhere. I like an animal I'm not afraid to touch for fear of… Aaachh! Disgusting.

DRONGO. You didn't get that with Bubbles.

CRAZY HORSE. Bubbles was clean.

DRONGO. Too right.

Pause.

CRAZY HORSE. So, how are things?

DRONGO. In general?

CRAZY HORSE. How's life?

DRONGO. Good. I'm decorating my apartment.

CRAZY HORSE. Where are you living?

DRONGO. In… Can't say in front of… (*To others.*) Sorry, everyone. You understand. Information is dangerous. (*To the* CRAZY HORSE.) We'll drop around later if you want.

CRAZY HORSE. Yeah. I'd love to.

DRONGO. Yeah?

CRAZY HORSE. Yeah.

DRONGO. It's a bit of a mess. I told you. Decorating. Give me your opinion. Or we could go out to eat.

CRAZY HORSE. We'll order something.

DRONGO. Perfect.

CRAZY HORSE. Old times.

DRONGO. Yeah.

CRAZY HORSE. The conversations. And the thing is, in effect, we stayed true to our own realities.

DRONGO. That's right. To our... Sure, look at us now. To our principles and our beliefs.

CRAZY HORSE. That's right. (*Pause*.) Man, the conversations. (*To others*.) We used to talk about...

DRONGO. Over coffee in Mulligan's.

CRAZY HORSE. Man, yeah. Used to talk about how we would do things. We thought we were bohemians.

DRONGO. We *were* bohemians.

CRAZY HORSE. About nonconformity. We would, however way, live outside what was the norm. What was considered the norm, then.

DRONGO. Still is.

CRAZY HORSE. Outside and above the law. Course we didn't know then, what our vocations would be.

DRONGO. But, we stayed true.

CRAZY HORSE. To our beliefs. Absolutely.

Pause.

DRONGO. Man. Coffee in Mulligan's.

CRAZY HORSE. Coffee and cigarettes.

DRONGO. And poetry.

CRAZY HORSE. Oh, fuck.

DRONGO. And Gauloises.

CRAZY HORSE. Oh, fuck! And Gitanes.

DRONGO. And Serge Gainsbourg.

CRAZY HORSE. Fuck!

DRONGO. Nonconformity. The buzzword of the late seventies. (*To others*.) See, that's what separates us from you. You're in prison for all intents and purposes. You don't know what freedom is. Of course if there weren't people like you, there wouldn't be people like me.

CRAZY HORSE. Or me.

DRONGO. That's right.

JOE. They say that... Just listening to...

DRONGO (*to others*). Because you're... (*To* JOE.) What?

JOE. They say that... Now this isn't me.

CRAZY HORSE. What do they say?

RONNIE. I'm going to just... (*Everybody looks at him.*) Just going up to the loo.

DRONGO. Oh, go on, yeah. Go ahead. Oh, by the... (*To* SONIA.) Sheila.

SONIA. Sonia.

DRONGO. Sonia. Sorry. Could we have some coffee?

SONIA. I don't know if we've...

DRONGO (*interrupting. To the* CRAZY HORSE). Coffee?

CRAZY HORSE. I'm more a tea man nowadays.

DRONGO. Old times.

Pause.

CRAZY HORSE (*to* SONIA). Give us a coffee.

SONIA. I don't know if we've any.

BRENDAN. There's some in the biscuit press, Sonia. Behind the... At the back.

SONIA. Two coffees. (*Exits.*)

DRONGO (*calling after her*). Black.

Pause.

CRAZY HORSE (*to* JOE). What do they say, Joe?

JOE. Oh, nothing.

CRAZY HORSE. We're interested. Come on.

JOE. Just…

DRONGO. Something about the lifestyle?

CRAZY HORSE. Fucking right.

JOE. Yeah.

DRONGO. Well, what?

JOE. They say that… Not me, now… That people like you… You said we were in a prison because we're, I suppose you mean… Because we obey the law and worry about mortgages and whatever. The children. School and shit. We're in a prison.

DRONGO. Yeah.

JOE. But conscience, they say. Because your actions and what you do…

The DRONGO *makes to interject.*

Hang on. Conscience. Because what you do is against the law and against the norm and… not very nice. Then you're in a prison. The prison of your conscience. Because however free you are, physically, to do stuff, you're bounded by your guilt and your conscience. Say you… Say the bloke who crashed you. To get revenge. Whatever it is you do. You hurt him…

DRONGO. Pulled his teeth out.

The CRAZY HORSE *laughs.*

JOE. Okay, you… What?!!

DRONGO. With a fucking pliers.

The CRAZY HORSE *laughs.*

Pause.

JOE. Jesus.

CRAZY HORSE. Go on, Joe.

Pause.

JOE. Okay, well I think you get the idea. You pull his teeth out. Later, you think to yourself, 'I'm not very nice, 'cos I've hurt someone.' Unconsciously, now. Your conscience forces you to think these things. So, these thoughts become a prison. A different type of prison, but a prison all the same.

Pause.

CRAZY HORSE. Jaysus' sake!

JOE. No?

DRONGO. Fucking stupid! If I hurt someone, it's for one of two reasons. One: revenge. In which case I've done right. Two: my job. In which case I've done right. And *him*... Except for what he did to my dog...

CRAZY HORSE. Ah, here, now.

DRONGO. I'm messing, man, Jaysus...!

CRAZY HORSE. All right.

DRONGO (*to* JOE, *continuing*)....He's on the side of law and order.

CRAZY HORSE. Hey!

DRONGO. Sorry, but on the... Justice. You fight for justice.

CRAZY HORSE. Right. (*Beat.*) Not the law.

DRONGO. Fuck the law.

CRAZY HORSE. Well... (*Pause.*) That's just what somebody once said. I heard it.

RONNIE *re-enters the room and sits down. Silence. The* DRONGO *stands up.*

DRONGO (*to the* CRAZY HORSE). Give me a look at that gun.

The CRAZY HORSE *gives him the gun. The* DRONGO *points the gun at* JOE.

(*To* JOE.) Are you making judgements?

JOE. No.

DRONGO (*going closer to* JOE). Are you sure?

JOE. Yes. Fuck.

BRENDAN. Mister... Drongo.

DRONGO (*putting gun to* JOE*'s head*). Are you positive?

JOE. Yes!!

BRENDAN. What is he… Wh… Crazy Horse?

CRAZY HORSE. Fikey! Drongo!

DRONGO. I'm only messing. (*Sits down. To the* CRAZY HORSE.) That's a great gun. Where did you get it?

CRAZY HORSE. A bloke got it for me in Hamburg.

DRONGO. Could you get me one? (*Gives the gun back to the* CRAZY HORSE.)

CRAZY HORSE. You want one?

DRONGO. Yeah.

CRAZY HORSE. I'll get you one.

SONIA *re-enters and does the business of giving out the coffee, etc.*

Coffee. Great. Thanks very much.

SONIA *is pouring his coffee.*

That's okay. (*To the* DRONGO.) You seeing anyone?

DRONGO. Like what? Love?

CRAZY HORSE. Yeah.

DRONGO. No.

CRAZY HORSE. No one special?

DRONGO. No. (*Pause.*) You?

CRAZY HORSE (*shakes his head*). It's the life.

DRONGO. Sacrifices.

CRAZY HORSE. Still. How's money?

DRONGO. Good. I'm… I told you. I'm decorating my apartment.

CRAZY HORSE. That's right, yeah.

DRONGO. You're definitely coming over.

CRAZY HORSE. Yeah. We'll go over.

Pause.

DRONGO. What about you?

CRAZY HORSE. Money?

DRONGO. Yeah.

CRAZY HORSE. I'm okay. Getting by. I don't always *take* money. Those who *have* it...

DRONGO. Right.

CRAZY HORSE. These. Brendan and Sonia, I don't take.

DRONGO. Obviously. Because their problem *is* money.

CRAZY HORSE. Exactly.

DRONGO. I understand. So, you decide between those who must pay, and those you do it for, for...

Pause.

CRAZY HORSE. I don't know. Justice?

DRONGO. Justice. (*Pause.*) I just go where the money is.

CRAZY HORSE. I know.

DRONGO. It's my job. It's the career I've chosen and I'm bloody good at it.

CRAZY HORSE. I don't doubt it.

DRONGO. But, you. Man, who would have... You're the Lone Ranger.

CRAZY HORSE. I was actually going to call myself the Lone *Wolf*.

DRONGO. Not bad. Why didn't you?

CRAZY HORSE. Crazy Horse is better. Has more punch.

DRONGO. That it does. And you get the old Neil Young connection as well.

CRAZY HORSE. Mm. (*Pause.*) Oh, that's right.

DRONGO. Yeah. You smoking these days?

CRAZY HORSE. No. Not in a while.

DRONGO. Me neither.

Pause.

CRAZY HORSE. Crazy Horse was his band, wasn't it.

DRONGO. It was, yeah. Will we have one?

CRAZY HORSE. What?

DRONGO. A smoke?

CRAZY HORSE. Why?

DRONGO. For old times' sakes.

Short pause.

CRAZY HORSE. As a nod to the old days?

DRONGO. Yeah.

CRAZY HORSE. All right.

DRONGO. Anyone got a cigarette? Brendan?

BRENDAN. No.

CRAZY HORSE. Got a cigarette, Joe?

JOE. I've none. Ronnie?

RONNIE. No, I've… (*Pause.*) Two, is it?

CRAZY HORSE. Yeah.

RONNIE *gives them each a cigarette and a light. They sit and smoke.*

DRONGO. Man, the law.

CRAZY HORSE. People. These people.

DRONGO. Fuck them.

CRAZY HORSE. They don't know, do they.

DRONGO. They *don't* know. They worry and they fret.

CRAZY HORSE. And they'll never know.

DRONGO. No.

CRAZY HORSE. It takes a certain type of person.

DRONGO. It does. Someone who'll question things.

CRAZY HORSE. That's it. To question.

DRONGO. To question.

CRAZY HORSE. To question everything.

DRONGO. Exactly.

CRAZY HORSE. To say, 'No. This is wrong, this doesn't suit me
     and I refuse to obey, to conform, to… to…'

DRONGO. To do what they want.

CRAZY HORSE. They, yes, they. I'm gonna be me. In myself.

DRONGO. As a... *As* myself.

CRAZY HORSE. As... something separate.

DRONGO. As a human.

CRAZY HORSE. A man alone.

DRONGO. As a being.

CRAZY HORSE. As something *of* itself.

DRONGO. A rock.

CRAZY HORSE. As an island. An island *unto* itself.

DRONGO. An island in the stream.

CRAZY HORSE. Precisely. Oh, man. The days.

DRONGO. We're violent? We use violent means? So be it.

CRAZY HORSE. So be it.

DRONGO. Does it shame us?

CRAZY HORSE. Course not.

DRONGO. Violence is there, is within us. It's inherent...

CRAZY HORSE. That's right.

DRONGO. ...from birth. We're pulled from the womb, kicking and screaming, aren't we...?

CRAZY HORSE. Yep.

DRONGO. Light dazzles us, blood flies...

CRAZY HORSE. I remember this... Our arse is smacked.

DRONGO. We play on man's most primordial emotion.

CRAZY HORSE. Fear.

DRONGO. Fear. And therein lies our power.

CRAZY HORSE. Our power, yes. (*Pause.*) Therein it lies. (*Pause.*) Yeah.

Pause.

SONIA. How's the coffee?

DRONGO. Good. Good. Very good.

CRAZY HORSE. Thank you, Sonia.

SONIA. You're welcome.

Pause.

CRAZY HORSE. Do you think…? No.

DRONGO. What?

CRAZY HORSE. I forgot that band was called Crazy Horse, now.

DRONGO. So? (*Pause.*) Ah, fuck that.

CRAZY HORSE. …You know? But the name's…

DRONGO. Doesn't count, man. Are you a band?

CRAZY HORSE. No.

DRONGO. No, you're a bloke. Different context. D'you get me?

CRAZY HORSE. Suppose.

DRONGO. If you were a band…

CRAZY HORSE. I get you. (*Pause.*) That's a nice chair.

DRONGO. Which? This?

DRONGO *looks at the chair without getting out of it.*

JOE. That's a horrible chair.

CRAZY HORSE. I like it. Is it old?

SONIA. Over a hundred years.

BRENDAN. It was her grandmother's.

CRAZY HORSE. It's nice.

RONNIE. I'd better go.

CRAZY HORSE. Where are you going?

RONNIE. The wife.

CRAZY HORSE. Fuck the wife. She run your life?

RONNIE. Well, actually she does, the hooer.

CRAZY HORSE. Fuck her. Hang around. You're good company.

DRONGO. That was her ringing earlier.

CRAZY HORSE. That was...? (*To* RONNIE.) Where do you live?

RONNIE. Next door.

CRAZY HORSE. And she's ringing?!

DRONGO. He doesn't like her.

CRAZY HORSE (*to* RONNIE). No?

RONNIE. Well...

CRAZY HORSE. Fuck her. Man. That is some fine chair. What do you think, Drongo?

The DRONGO *stands up and has a look at the chair.*

How would that look in your apartment?

DRONGO. It would... Jesus, actually... That's a nice chair.

BRENDAN. It's an eyesore.

DRONGO. Shut up. That's a... That's a fucking antique. That's a nice chair. (*Pause. Still looking at chair.*) I'll tell you what... (*To the* CRAZY HORSE.) What do you think of that chair?

CRAZY HORSE. It's not bad, is it?

DRONGO (*to* BRENDAN). I'll tell you what. I'll take that chair as payment for what you owe me.

BRENDAN. What?

JOE. What?

DRONGO. I'll cancel your entire debt for this chair. (*To the* CRAZY HORSE.) This chair would go beautifully with the wallpaper. We got... Did I tell you it's got wooden floors? Wooden with big rugs. Got a Persian too. This chair was *made* for my apartment.

SONIA. But you *said*.

DRONGO. Gorgeous.

SONIA. But you *said*.

DRONGO. What did I say?

BRENDAN. Sonia.

SONIA. He said.

DRONGO. What did I say?

Pause.

SONIA. You said the debt was cancelled.

DRONGO. The debt?

SONIA. You said we were all square.

DRONGO. Excuse me...

SONIA. You told us.

DRONGO. Excuse me. What did I tell you?

SONIA. I asked you about the money. I said what about the money, and you said the money was okay. We were all square.

DRONGO. No, no...

SONIA. You lied.

DRONGO. ...Excuse me, no.

SONIA. You tell us we're all square and...

DRONGO. I did not. The money...

SONIA. You told me the money was okay.

BRENDAN. Sonia.

SONIA. That's what he said.

DRONGO. Yes. I said the money was *okay*...

SONIA. Yeah.

DRONGO. ...but I didn't say your debt was cancelled. What kind of a businessman would I be if I cancelled your debt? I'd be out of business, like Raymond Murphy.

SONIA. You said.

DRONGO. Now, hold on. It's not my fault you misinterpreted what I said. I can't just cancel. Why would I say that? Why would I put myself six hundred and fifty quid out of pocket? Who'd do that? A fucking eejit would. What I meant was... The money is okay for tonight. My mates. My prompters. For tonight, I'll let you off. I'll give you another week or so to come up with the two hundred pounds you owe me *this* week. I'll give you some time.

SONIA. But…

DRONGO. What?

SONIA. We can't… (*To* BRENDAN.) Bren. We can't. Even with another week. Two hundred pounds. We can't get that amount of money.

BRENDAN (*to the* DRONGO). We can't.

DRONGO. Two hundred pounds.

BRENDAN. We can't.

DRONGO (*sighs*). Do you know what I am? I'm a loan shark. It's my job to collect what I'm owed. I use muscle. (*Pause. Looks at watch.*) I'm a violent man. But I've just met someone I haven't seen in a long time and I'm in a good mood. I'm giving you a chance. A chance you wouldn't have if it wasn't for my joy. The chair for the debt. That's a bargain. What the hell could you want with it? It doesn't match with anything in this room. In *my* apartment…

BRENDAN. It's worth a lot of money.

DRONGO. How much?

BRENDAN. Over two thousand pounds.

DRONGO. Really?

RONNIE. That thing?

Pause. The DRONGO *stares at him.*

DRONGO. That's a nice fucking chair.

RONNIE. Why don't you give it to him? That's what you were going to do in the first place. It's horrible.

SONIA. No.

BRENDAN. What?

RONNIE. Why the sudden change? That was what you were…

SONIA. He lied.

DRONGO. I told you.

SONIA. No. You led us to believe something that wasn't the truth. You said okay. (*To* BRENDAN.) He said we were all square. (*To the* DRONGO.) We can't let you have this chair. You changed the rules.

DRONGO. I didn't change any rules.

SONIA. You did. You changed the rules. You said okay. When I asked you about the money, that's what you said.

DRONGO. You misinterpreted me.

SONIA (*to* BRENDAN). He does not get that chair.

BRENDAN. Sonia.

SONIA. No. No.

DRONGO. Sonia. Think about this. I don't get this chair, something bad is going to happen to you. You just told me you can't get the money. I have to do my job. I'm offering you a way out. (*Pause.*) You don't want to be prompted.

JOE (*to the* CRAZY HORSE). What do you think? (*Pause.*) Al.

CRAZY HORSE. Crazy Horse.

JOE. Crazy Horse. What do you think?

CRAZY HORSE. He's right. She misinterpreted.

SONIA. I did not.

JOE. Did you forget why you're here?

CRAZY HORSE. The Drongo's my friend.

DRONGO. Buds, huh?

CRAZY HORSE. ...We're the buds.

JOE. But, did you forget why you're here?

CRAZY HORSE. The Drongo is my friend.

Pause.

JOE. You've no ethics.

CRAZY HORSE. Yes I do.

JOE. You're the one who lied. You were supposed to protect us. We asked you. There are no ethics there. You've no code.

DRONGO (*to* SONIA). That's a great chair. I like that chair. You don't even like it.

SONIA. That's not the point.

DRONGO. I'm taking it off your hands.

SONIA. That's not the point.

DRONGO. The fucking 'point'?

SONIA. You said we were all square.

Pause.

DRONGO. Jesus, these fucking people. (*Pause. Sighs.*) All right. I'll tell you what. I'm in a good mood. You're lucky. Here's an idea. I'll play a hand of poker with Brendan. We'll play one hand of poker. If he wins, and because of our misunderstanding, I'll absolve all debts and you can keep the chair. How's that sound?

SONIA. No. No way. We're in enough debt, Brendan. Don't start gambling what we...

DRONGO. No, no, no, no, wait a minute, wait a minute. This is the... You'll like this part. If *I* win, all right? If *I* win, I get the chair *and* I absolve all debts. See? So, whether you win or lose, your debt is still cancelled. You win simply by playing. You've nothing to lose except the chair, which you don't like anyway.

JOE. That sounds fair.

DRONGO. A better deal in this life, you'll never see.

Pause.

JOE. That's a good bet.

RONNIE. It is.

DRONGO. Well?

BRENDAN. I like it. Sonia, come on.

SONIA. How do we know he'll keep his word?

BRENDAN. He will.

SONIA. But how do we know?

BRENDAN. Sonia, will you stop making things difficult. He will.

DRONGO. There's just one more thing. Because the deal is so good, I want one thing extra.

SONIA. I knew it. You see?

BRENDAN. Sonia, come on.

DRONGO. Just a small thing. It's still a great deal.

SONIA. I knew it.

BRENDAN. Sonia. (*To the* DRONGO.) What is it?

DRONGO. If I win, I also get an aspidistra.

SONIA. Oh. Fair enough.

BRENDAN. Ah, now, hold on a sec.

SONIA. Come on, Bren.

BRENDAN. I already lost one of my aspidistras to Ronnie.

SONIA. You've loads.

DRONGO. It's still a great deal.

Pause.

BRENDAN. All right. One…

DRONGO. Just one.

BRENDAN. …Fuck's sake! (*Short pause.*) All right. Let's play.

DRONGO. Would you mind bringing my one in first? Can I see one?

BRENDAN. Why?

DRONGO. Just to see if they're any good.

BRENDAN. They *are* good. They're the best of aspidistras. (*Pointing to* RONNIE*'s.*) Sure, there.

DRONGO. I don't doubt your gardening skills, Brendan. I'd just like to see what I'm playing for.

BRENDAN (*sighs*). Sonia? Will you…?

SONIA. Yeah. (*Exits.*)

DRONGO. Okay, then. Let's get started here.

Pebbles the dog runs into the living room and behind the sofa with SONIA *in hot pursuit.*

SONIA. Pebbles!

BRENDAN. Sonia, the fucking dog. (*To everybody.*) Watch this. Watch. In behind the sofa. Straight in. Behind the sofa. Pisses. (*To* SONIA.) Sonia, the fucking dog. (*To others.*) Pisses. Every time he's let in. Why? Because he was never trained properly. I put his nose in it and give him a clatter, but what does she do? She pets him and cuddles him. Look.

SONIA *has picked the dog up and is doing just that.*

Put his nose in it.

SONIA. Leave him alone.

BRENDAN. So he doesn't learn. It'd only take a couple of days to teach him, but with her cuddling him, he just gets confused. He doesn't know, so he pisses out of confusion.

CRAZY HORSE (*contemptuously*). That's disgusting.

BRENDAN (*pointing behind sofa*). Look at that, Sonia.

SONIA. Wait. (*Exits with the dog.*)

CRAZY HORSE. I wouldn't put up with that, Brendan.

BRENDAN. What can I do? It's her dog.

CRAZY HORSE. Want me to put it out of its misery?

BRENDAN. No, no.

DRONGO. Put it out of its misery.

BRENDAN. No, please, Jesus. It's Sonia's dog. If it was mine, you know…?

DRONGO. Come on…

BRENDAN. …Be a *different* story, but…

DRONGO. …Are we playing cards or what?

CRAZY HORSE (*to the* DRONGO). Did you see what that dog did?

DRONGO. Yeah.

CRAZY HORSE. I wouldn't have it, Brendan.

BRENDAN. It has some good qualities. It's not all bad.

SONIA *re-enters with the aspidistra. She hands it to the* DRONGO.

SONIA. Here we go.

DRONGO (*examining it*). Oh, that's nice. That'll… (*To the* CRAZY HORSE.) What do you think?

CRAZY HORSE. Lovely.

DRONGO (*to himself*). That'll look great. Oh, yeah.

RONNIE *picks his aspidistra up and sits cradling it until stated.*

BRENDAN. That was the best one.

DRONGO. I'd believe it, Brendan. I'd believe it. (*Pause.*) All right. Let's play.

BRENDAN *and the* DRONGO *sit down at the table. Everybody else moves closer to watch the game. The cards are taken out.*

BRENDAN. Okay. Oooo-kay. Debt versus chair and one aspidistra. (*To the* DRONGO.) You want to deal?

DRONGO. I don't mind.

BRENDAN. Okay, I'll deal. (*Shuffles cards.*)

DRONGO. Why doesn't someone who's not playing deal?

BRENDAN. All right. Joe?

CRAZY HORSE. I'll deal.

The CRAZY HORSE *takes the cards and deals them expertly. Each player looks at his hand. Pause.*

DRONGO. I'll have three.

BRENDAN. I'll have three, too.

They throw down and the CRAZY HORSE *deals them out three cards each.*

DRONGO. Okay, I'll… Who sees first? I'll see you.

BRENDAN. Can you do that? (*To* JOE.) Who sees first, Joe?

JOE. It doesn't matter.

DRONGO. *Course* it matters.

JOE. It doesn't. It doesn't make any difference who sees who first. The bets are set. The only difference it makes is who sees first, which doesn't make any difference. If you were in Vegas, it would, because you'd be upping the bet all the time and bluffing and all. Here there's none of that. There's no tactics involved, so you're just seeing.

DRONGO. All right. (*Pause.*) Who goes first?

BRENDAN. You.

DRONGO. No, you.

SONIA. Go, Bren.

   BRENDAN *sighs. Pause. He lays down his cards.*

BRENDAN. Three fives.

   The DRONGO *lays down his cards.*

DRONGO. Two aces.

   Pause.

BRENDAN. I win.

DRONGO. What?

BRENDAN. The debt is cancelled. (*Unsure.*) Am I right?

SONIA. And we keep the chair.

BRENDAN. *And* the plant.

RONNIE (*cradling his aspidistra*). One of them.

DRONGO. I had two aces.

BRENDAN. Three fives beats it.

DRONGO. But I have aces.

BRENDAN. It doesn't matter. Three of anything beats two of
   anything.

JOE. He's right.

DRONGO. Even aces?

BRENDAN. Even aces.

DRONGO (*to the* CRAZY HORSE). Does it?

CRAZY HORSE. 'Fraid so.

   Pause.

DRONGO. Fuck.

SONIA. So our debt is cancelled.

DRONGO (*of cards*). Are you sure?

SONIA. Mr Drongo?

DRONGO. What?

SONIA. Our debt is cancelled?!

Pause.

DRONGO (*to* BRENDAN). I'll play you again.

JOE. Play him again?

DRONGO. Two out of three.

JOE. What?

SONIA. I told you, Brendan.

DRONGO. That was just a warmer-upper...

SONIA. I told you.

DRONGO. ...Get me going.

SONIA. I told you something like this would happen.

JOE. What's he...?

BRENDAN. I beat you.

JOE. Two out of three?

DRONGO. Two out of three. I wasn't sure of the rules.

JOE. Where has all the chivalry gone?

SONIA (*to* BRENDAN). I knew it.

JOE. ...The honour.

SONIA. You should have known.

BRENDAN. I beat you fair and square.

DRONGO. Two out of three.

SONIA. Fair and square. That was it. Go away.

DRONGO. Don't you get that way with me, miss. (*To the* CRAZY HORSE.) What do you think of that chair?

CRAZY HORSE (*less enthusiastically than before*). It's a nice chair.

DRONGO. It's perfect. (*To* BRENDAN.) I'll play you again.

SONIA. Why don't you go away and leave us alone?

RONNIE. Brendan won, now.

BRENDAN. I beat you.

JOE. He beat you like a gentleman. Don't disgrace yourself, Drongo. This'll look very bad.

DRONGO. Fuck you. I want that chair. I have the power.

JOE. This'll look very bad.

DRONGO. Shut up or you'll be prompted. I've lads coming who'll…

The DRONGO *goes over to the window and looks out.*

JOE. You're not staying true to your own reality.

The DRONGO *turns from the window.*

DRONGO. What's the… What?!

JOE. Think about it.

DRONGO. What the fuck are you talking about? Two out of three, Brendan.

SONIA. You're not getting that chair. (*To the* CRAZY HORSE.) Crazy Horse. You know what's right. (*Pause.*) Crazy Horse!

CRAZY HORSE (*confused*). I don't know.

DRONGO. What do you mean, you don't know? You stick with your friends.

CRAZY HORSE. I *don't* know, man.

JOE. There's a code, am I right?

DRONGO. There is no code…

JOE. There is, there's…

DRONGO. …I have the power and that's that.

JOE. What's power without a code? Know what I mean?

DRONGO. I don't… You're…

JOE. What's the sword without bushido?

DRONGO. …He's talking in riddles.

JOE. You spoke about a code.

The phone rings. The DRONGO, *who is standing next to it, picks it up.*

DRONGO (*into phone*). Fuck off! (*Hangs up.*) Crazy Horse.

JOE. Crazy Horse. You know what's right. (*To the* DRONGO.) Do you remember talking about a code?

DRONGO. I don't remember.

SONIA. Crazy Horse.

CRAZY HORSE. What?!!

SONIA. Do something!

CRAZY HORSE. 'Do something'?

JOE. Will you do something!

BRENDAN. Why don't you fucking do something!

DRONGO. I have the power!

The CRAZY HORSE *goes over to the window and looks out.*

They'll be here soon.

RONNIE (*to the* DRONGO). You're only an oul' hooer.

DRONGO. I'm a hooer? Your *wife's* a fuckin' hooer.

SONIA (*to the* CRAZY HORSE). Why don't you do something?

CRAZY HORSE (*still looking out the window*). Shut up.

DRONGO. Yeah. Shut up, you slapper. Crazy Horse. Tell them. You're the man.

The CRAZY HORSE *turns from the window. To the* DRONGO.

CRAZY HORSE. What happened to you?

DRONGO. What are you talking about?

CRAZY HORSE. What happened to you?

Pause.

DRONGO. I'm your bud, man.

SONIA. He's not your bud. He's a monster.

DRONGO. My prompters'll be here in a minute.

SONIA. He's nobody's bud.

DRONGO (*to* SONIA). Shut up. (*To the* CRAZY HORSE.) We'll deal with these fuckers and get some grub.

CRAZY HORSE. I don't know.

JOE. We hired you, you prick.

DRONGO. You don't know?

JOE. Where's your work ethic?

DRONGO. You don't fucking know? Who are you going to side with? Weakness or power?

CRAZY HORSE (*brandishing gun*). *I* have the power, Fikey.

Pause.

DRONGO. What are you... Are you threatening me? You have the power, yeah. You have the power for the moment. I know there's, like, our friendship there, and things are complicated. But fairly soon, I'm telling you... I'm telling you all... There's going to be a prompting.

CRAZY HORSE. Fikey.

DRONGO. Alan. Our friendship...

Silence. The two men stand looking at each other. Eventually, SONIA *breaks it.*

SONIA. Is someone going to do something?

DRONGO. Ah, I'm sick of this fucking shit. Fuck it. You're all dead.

RONNIE. Crazy Horse!

DRONGO. That's it. Everyone in this house, do you hear me...?

SONIA. Will you do something!

DRONGO. No one's getting out.

JOE. Make a fucking...

DRONGO....None of youse.

JOE....A decision, will you?

Tense silence. Everyone looking at the CRAZY HORSE.

CRAZY HORSE. *Am* I a Neil Young rip-off?!!

Suddenly, a car screeches into the driveway. The CRAZY HORSE *runs to the window and looks out.*

DRONGO. That'll be them, now.

Car lights fill up the room through the window.

SONIA. Brendan.

DRONGO. Youse are all…

BRENDAN. Sonia.

BRENDAN *and* SONIA *embrace*.

DRONGO.…fucking…

The car lights turn off. The CRAZY HORSE *turns from the window with a sudden movement. He slips in the dog's piss. His feet fly out from underneath him and he shoots the* DRONGO *in the chest. The* DRONGO *falls down dead.* SONIA *screams.* RONNIE, *who is now standing, drops his aspidistra. The pot shatters. From outside, we hear car doors closing and muffled voices. Slowly, the* CRAZY HORSE *emerges from behind the sofa. He takes out a second gun. He now has a gun in each hand. He exits towards the kitchen.* SONIA *and* BRENDAN *are still holding each other. We hear the back door opening, a dog barking, a gunshot…*

SONIA. Pebbles!

And then, silence. The CRAZY HORSE *re-enters the room. There is a banging on the front door. He puts his bag on his shoulder.*

You killed my dog.

The CRAZY HORSE *makes to leave the room, but just before doing so, he turns…*

CRAZY HORSE. I hate those filthy beasts!

The CRAZY HORSE *exits. We hear the front door opening, followed by shouting, gunfire, and general chaos. Tableau.* RONNIE *stands over his aspidistra.* JOE *sits.* BRENDAN *and* SONIA *hold one another. The telephone begins to ring again.*

Blackout.

The End.

FROM BOTH HIPS

From Both Hips was first produced by Fishamble Theatre Company at the Little Theatre, Tallaght, on 25 June 1997, transferring to the Project Arts Centre, Dublin, and the Tron Theatre, Glasgow. The cast was as follows:

LIZ	Marion O'Dwyer
ADELE	Clodagh O'Donoghue
PAUL	Ger Carey
THERESA	Fionnuala Murphy
WILLY	Seán Rocks
IRENE	Catherine Walsh

Director	Jim Culleton
Designer	Blaíthín Sheerin
Lighting Designer	Nick McCall

Characters

LIZ

ADELE

PAUL

THERESA

WILLY

IRENE

ACT ONE

Scene One

A sitting room in a normal, working-class house. Stage left, the hallway to the front door. Up right, the door to the sitting room. Up left, stairs leading off. A table and chairs. A sofa. LIZ sits on the sofa reading the paper. ADELE stands in the centre of the room, looking around. She exits. She returns. She exits again.

LIZ. Adele! (*Calling*.) Adele! What are you doing? C'mere!

ADELE (*entering, just inside door to kitchen*). What?

LIZ. See what it says here?

ADELE. What? (*Exits*.)

LIZ (*calling*). Where are you going? Will you stop going in and out? Come back in, will you?

ADELE (*offstage*). What?

LIZ. Come back in and sit down.

   ADELE *enters and stands there.*

   What are you doing?

ADELE. I'm looking for the ship.

LIZ. Well, just ask me. It's inside on top of the press. It's grand. Sit down.

ADELE. No, I'll stand. What does it say?

LIZ. It says… You're making me very nervous, there.

ADELE. Good. Go on. Read. Tell me.

LIZ. Something I never knew. Something very surprising. Dogs…

ADELE. Mmm?

LIZ. …Dogs. Right here, some professor. Dogs are incapable of love.

ADELE. Dogs?

LIZ. ...Some professor, here. Although they appear, he says, loving and affectionate, they actually don't have any emotions. It's all... The way they act, their behaviour. It's all instinctual.

ADELE. Yeah?

LIZ. That's not really fair, is it?

ADELE. Why not?

LIZ. Well, love's a two-way street. I wouldn't want to be giving love to something if it wasn't going to love me back.

Pause.

ADELE. Mmm.

LIZ. You know?

ADELE. Were you thinking of buying a dog?

LIZ. No, no, God!

ADELE. Well, then.

LIZ. But I know people who have dogs. Ciara and Joe have one, and thing... Theresa Nolan. She's fairly into her dog, actually. She comes out sometimes, she reeks of it, you can smell it off her clothes and all.

ADELE. Reeks?

LIZ. Bits of brown hairs on her jumper. Yeah, reeks. Ah, I'm a bit addled now, damn!

ADELE *sits down and lights a cigarette.*

ADELE. What's wrong?

LIZ. I feel like I should do something about it.

ADELE. Do some... What?

LIZ. I feel like I should tell them.

ADELE. Who? Theresa Nolan?

LIZ. She's fairly into her dog. Ciara and Joe... Who else do I...?

ADELE. Tell them what? That their dogs don't love them?

LIZ. Yeah. They should know.

ADELE. Ah, Liz.

LIZ. If I don't tell them, they could go on through life living a lie.
  Their dogs don't love them, even though they love their dogs.
  That's a lie, they're being cheated, they should be told. On the
  other hand...

ADELE. On the other hand, ignorance, Liz.

LIZ. What about it?

ADELE. Ignorance is bliss.

LIZ. It's ignorance, Adele. Nothing good comes of it. I'm saying if I
  tell, it'll hurt. It'll hurt at first.

ADELE. Could.

LIZ. Nobody likes being told they're in an unrequited relationship.

ADELE. You wouldn't call it a relationship.

  Pause.

LIZ. Are they communicating, Adele?

ADELE. I don't...

LIZ. In some way, a dog and its master, mistress. Its owner. Are
  they, like, aware of each other?

ADELE. I suppose.

LIZ. Well, then they're communicating. It's happening over a period
  of time, then it's a relationship. There's physical contact going
  on? Yes. In Theresa Nolan's case, a lot, judging from the stink on
  her, then it's a close relationship. Jesus! She feels love, the dog
  feels nothing, she's being made a fool of. Her dog's working the
  dark trick on her.

ADELE. The what?

LIZ. The dark trick. And she's not the type of girl who has many
  friends. It's probably the best friend she has. She's playing the
  fool for her dog and she doesn't even know it, she thinks it's two-
  sided and... You all right?

  ADELE *is distant.*

  ...She's getting nothing in return. Are you all right?

  Beat.

ADELE. Hmm? (*Beat*.) Yeah. I'm just… I'm kinda… I'm like… Just give me two minutes.

LIZ. Are you sure?

ADELE (*flustered*). No, no. Just gimme… I have to get my head…

LIZ. Okay.

ADELE. …Just two minutes, give me.

LIZ. Okay. You sure? Do you want me to get something for you?

ADELE. Yeah. No. I'm fine. It's just… Okay. All right. That's it.

LIZ. I'm say…

ADELE. Go on. Tell me the rest.

LIZ. I'm saying… You all right?

ADELE. Sorry. Yeah. My mind was just… This way, that, up, million directions. Go on.

LIZ. It's all right… Well… For some people, you love someone and they don't love you. But they *like* you. Some people can live with that. That's enough for them. Least there's some emotion going on, okay? But a dog… doesn't… feel… anything. What do you think?

ADELE. Well, are you sure it's true?

LIZ. It says it right here in the *Echo*, Adele.

ADELE. But, that doesn't make it…

LIZ (*interrupting, getting up*). I'm gonna ring Theresa. To hell with the other two, Ciara and… They've got each other, anyway.

ADELE. You're gonna ring, what are you gonna do?

LIZ. I'm gonna ring Theresa.

LIZ *picks up the phone and dials*. ADELE *puts her cigarette out.*

(*Into phone*.) Hello? Theresa. How are you? It's… Who d'you think it is? It's Liz. Yeah, how's it going?

ADELE *exits to the kitchen.*

Listen. What are you doing? Nothing. Good. Come over to Adele's house, will you? (*Pause*.) Because… Just come over and you'll find out. I need to tell you something. That doesn't… (*Pause*.) That's no excuse, you just told me you weren't doing anything, so come on. Half an hour or so. All right? (*Pause*.) Bit of company since you're bored. (*Pause*.) Yes, it is important. Yep. Okay. See you then.

LIZ (*calling to kitchen*). I told her to drop down. (*Pause. Calling*.) Adele!

ADELE *enters with a glass of water and a pill. She takes the pill, chases it with some water.*

Should you be taking that now?

ADELE. Just the one.

LIZ. You only took one a while ago, Adele.

ADELE. It's just the one, Liz.

LIZ. I wasn't comfortable about breaking it to her over the phone, so I asked her to drop down.

Pause.

ADELE. The dog?

LIZ. Rather in person. So if she needs a hug or something. She might need a...

ADELE. You're gonna tell her her dog doesn't love her?!

LIZ. I couldn't do it over the phone, she's on her own there. She might need a bit of support, a hug, some comforting words, someone to listen and help, to tell her...

ADELE. But, what about...?

LIZ. ...everything's...

ADELE. ...You shouldn't...

LIZ. ...everything's going to be all right. To calm down, to...

ADELE. What about...?

LIZ. ...to pull yourself together.

Pause.

ADELE. What about Paul?

Beat.

LIZ. We'll *be* here.

ADELE. *And* Theresa?

LIZ. The more, the merrier, a bigger welcome, Adele.

ADELE. He's only expecting you and me.

LIZ. He'll be delighted to see her. Paul's fond of Theresa, he'll be delighted.

ADELE. But, he's only expecting...

LIZ. Yeah! So, that's... That'll be the surprise. Paul'll come home and there'll be three of us here to see him instead of two, a bigger welcome, the more, the merrier.

ADELE. He might want some peace and quiet.

LIZ. And if he does, we'll give it to him. *After* we welcome him and he sees he's got friends. Theresa has to be told.

ADELE *exits with glass of water to the kitchen.*

(*Calling.*) Sooner the better she finds out she's being tricked.

Pause. ADELE *returns, lights another cigarette.*

ADELE. You should have met her somewhere else.

LIZ. I thought of that, but I want us to be here, the more, the merrier, three's a crowd, but four's a party.

ADELE. He might not want a party.

LIZ. Just for when he comes in. He can hang around and chat for an hour, have a brandy and do what...? Head off to bed or watch telly or...

ADELE. 'Cos he might want to.

LIZ. You give us the signal and we'll head off. Say 'Geronimo'.

ADELE. 'Geronimo'?

LIZ. That's the password. Say 'Geronimo' and I'll take that as my cue.

ADELE. See, we shouldn't... Paul's... We shouldn't...

LIZ. I know.

ADELE. ...He's...

LIZ. We'll head off. If he wants us to head off...

ADELE. ...You'll...

LIZ. ...We'll go up to the pub.

ADELE. That might be best.

LIZ. Yeah. You haven't been alone together for more than five minutes in ages. Be nice for you to get reacquainted. You can have an early night. Go to bed. Make the beast with two backs.

ADELE. Liz!

LIZ. The *beautiful* beast with two backs.

ADELE (*embarrassed*). We'll be... We won't be...

LIZ. The beautiful beast of true love...

ADELE. Stop, Liz.

Pause.

LIZ. ...With two backs.

ADELE. Liz!

Pause.

LIZ. Are you looking forward?

Pause. ADELE *looks distant.*

Adele.

ADELE. What?

LIZ. Are you looking forward? Are you all right?

ADELE. I'm anxious.

LIZ. Did I upset you, there?

ADELE. No, I'm just anxious.

LIZ. Where's his present? Bring it in, put it on the table, so he can see it when he comes in. He'll say, 'Whose is that?' And you'll say, 'It's yours.'

Pause. ADELE *looks distant.*

ADELE. Yeah.

LIZ. Go on. It's on top of the press. Go.

ADELE. Yeah.

LIZ. Go and get it.

ADELE *exits and returns with a model ship. Unmade. Still in its box.*

Put it there on the table.

She does.

No. Like this. (*Repositions box.*) So he can see the name of it and all. Lovely. (*Pause.*) Has he ever done one before?

ADELE. Not since I've known him. Wait... Lemme... Before, may...? Just thinking...

LIZ. No?

ADELE. Has he...?

LIZ. No? No?

ADELE. I don't think so.

LIZ. Good. No? Good. It's a good choice. Something to pass the time.

ADELE. Was a good idea.

LIZ. It is. (*Of model.*) Did you ever?

ADELE. Never.

LIZ. I heard that fifty per cent of those things never get finished. Fifty per cent.

ADELE. Fifty?!

LIZ. Half of them. Of every one of those things that gets bought. So, you'd better warn him.

ADELE. Paul'll finish it.

LIZ. I'm sure he will.

ADELE. He wouldn't start it if he wasn't going to finish it.

LIZ. Yeah.

ADELE. Wouldn't see the point. He'll enjoy that.

LIZ. He will. Something to pass the time. Two weeks?

ADELE. Yeah.

LIZ. Probably *take* him two weeks.

ADELE. And even if it takes longer...

LIZ. I know. He'd probably take another few days off.

ADELE. Just to finish it. Yeah.

Pause.

LIZ. Perfect present.

ADELE. Yeah.

The telephone rings. ADELE answers it. While she's on the phone, LIZ goes over to the model ship, turns it on its side, then puts it back the way it was. She looks at the door. Moves the ship forward on the table, so that it'll be in a more advantageous position.

(*Into phone.*) Hello? No, no, he's not in at the moment. Can I...? No, yes, I'm sure. (*Pause.*) I don't. If you want to try... (*Pause.*) Well, I don't know if... (*Pause. She hangs up.*)

Pause.

LIZ. What?

ADELE. I don't know.

LIZ. Who?

ADELE. Some man.

LIZ. Who was he?

ADELE. Paul. (*Pause.*) Looking for Paul.

LIZ. For what?

ADELE. Bit sinister.

LIZ. Who? The man?

ADELE. Said he was going to call around. Bit scary.

LIZ. When?

ADELE. 'Later' was all he said. He didn't sound too happy.

LIZ. How'd he sound?

ADELE. Not happy.

LIZ. How?

ADELE. Sinister.

LIZ. Sinister.

ADELE. He didn't tell me anything else. Ah, God!

LIZ. It was probably just a friend of his.

ADELE (*to herself*). Angry, maybe?

LIZ. He sounded angry?

ADELE. Sounded sinister.

LIZ. And you don't know who it was?!

ADELE. No.

LIZ. You sure? You know his friends.

ADELE. No. I don't know this one.

LIZ. Surely…

ADELE. Not this one. A scary voice, it was.

LIZ. Sinister.

ADELE. I hope he's not in trouble.

Pause. ADELE *looks distracted*.

LIZ. You all right?

ADELE. Hmm?

LIZ. What'd he say?

ADELE. Just…

Pause. ADELE *looks distracted/upset*.

LIZ. What? Adele?

ADELE. Two mi… I'm fine. I'm just… I'm kinda… (*Pause*.) I wonder.

LIZ. It'll be grand.

ADELE. That's strange.

Pause.

LIZ. Listen, why don't you…? That's a bit drab. Why don't you dress up a bit for him?

ADELE. This?

LIZ. Bit drab, Adele. What about your black trousers I borrowed on Thursday?

ADELE. Dress up?

LIZ. Impress him even more, and the sexy white cardigan. Just to give him a real welcome.

ADELE. I...

LIZ. Go on.

ADELE. Should... The woolly one?

LIZ. He'll love it, go on. Yeah. The woolly white one and the black trousers.

ADELE. I should dress up for him?

LIZ. He'll love it. A bigger welcome. We'll have the model there, Theresa'll be here to make up the numbers, the more, the merrier, a bit of style from you. Go on. It's a statement, says 'I love you'.

ADELE. Will he know that?

LIZ. Course he will.

Pause.

ADELE. Yeah.

Pause.

LIZ. Who'd have thought that, huh? 'Bout the dogs.

ADELE. Mmm.

LIZ. They can't love.

ADELE. Yeah.

LIZ. For their appearance, you'd think they'd a ton of love. Wagging their... And their actions. Wagging their little tails and snuggling, and licking your face. (*Sighs*.) Instinct.

ADELE. Yeah.

LIZ. It's a shame. I'd say it's gonna be a big disappointment to a lot of people with dogs.

The doorbell rings.

Theresa. Get some spirits out, there.

She exits to the front door. We hear it opening. ADELE *exits to the kitchen.*

THERESA (*offstage*). How are you, Liz?

LIZ (*offstage*). Theresa. Come in. Come in. Listen. I'm sorry to get you down in such a rush.

    ADELE *returns with a bottle of brandy and glasses. She stands in the centre of the room, listening.*

THERESA (*offstage*). Is it important?

LIZ (*offstage*). It is, yeah. Gimme there… (*Pause.*) Just hang it there. Grand. How are you?

THERESA (*offstage*). I'm fine. Is Adele here?

LIZ (*offstage*). She's inside. How are you?

THERESA (*offstage*). I'm fine. What's going on?

LIZ (*offstage*). I think you'll need to sit down first.

    Silence. ADELE *remains standing. Frozen in the centre of the room.*

    Blackout.

Scene Two

A typical sitting room. PAUL *sits on the sofa with a walking stick in his lap.* THERESA *enters with two cups of tea. She gives one to* PAUL.

THERESA. There you go.

    THERESA *sits down.* PAUL *drinks. Winces.*

    All right?

PAUL. Bit hot. (*Blows on it.*)

THERESA. Do you want me to put some more milk in it?

PAUL. No. (*Drinks.*)

THERESA. Good to see you. How's the leg?

PAUL. Crap. It's not my leg, it's my hip.

THERESA. How is it?

PAUL. Crap. (*Pause. Drinks.*)

THERESA. Thanks for calling in, Paul. I was getting to miss you. Getting a bit lonely. How are you?

PAUL. Where's your telly?

THERESA. I was broken into.

PAUL. When?

THERESA. Last night. The telly and the video.

PAUL. You were broken into?!

THERESA. They didn't touch anything else. Just the...

PAUL. And where were you?

THERESA. In bed, fast asleep. I didn't hear a thing. Just the telly and the video. They must've known there was somebody upstairs.

PAUL. Broken into. Jesus.

THERESA. I'm scared.

PAUL. The bastards.

THERESA. If they'd've come upstairs...

PAUL. Telly and the video.

THERESA. I didn't hear a thing.

PAUL. Did you call the cops?

THERESA. Yeah, I went down this morning.

PAUL. No help, I bet.

THERESA. Nothing. I had to fill in a few forms, but they told me...

PAUL. They told you, I bet, the fuckers. They told you there was nothing they could do.

THERESA. I never wrote down the serial number, and even if I had, they'd... The robbers would've filed it off by now, some family has a new telly and video. And the worst thing, they said...

PAUL. Useless bastards.

THERESA. ....Worst thing, and it's kind of sad...

PAUL. What's that?

THERESA. The people who have it now are probably quite poor, not well off, and they bought it, like, whatsit? Hot. A hot video because they couldn't afford a new one. But they wouldn't be, like, criminals. Just a family trying to get by.

PAUL. They should be strung up.

THERESA. But, they'd be decent otherwise.

PAUL. The coppers.

THERESA. They do their best.

PAUL. They do, all right, the fuckers!

THERESA. Since… I've been a nervous wreck all day. I feel… Do you know? If someone breaks into your home…

PAUL. We've an alarm.

THERESA. If someone breaks in…

PAUL (*interrupting, not listening*). Some of the nurses in there, Theresa.

Pause.

THERESA. They take good care of you?

PAUL. Excellent. Some nice nurses.

THERESA. Nice?

PAUL. Good-looking. Sexy nurses' gear. I don't know what it is about them.

THERESA. Mmm.

PAUL. Some gorgeous-looking things.

Pause.

THERESA. I think it's… Could be they're taking care of you, so… They're… You know, that's what's so attractive about them. Because they're there just for you and they're taking care of you. Maybe that's why they're… You know?

PAUL. They're fucking gorgeous is what it is. I asked one of them out this morning. (*Pause.*) I'm meeting her tonight.

Pause.

THERESA. Did you?

Pause. They look at each other.

PAUL. Just testing you.

THERESA. You didn't?

PAUL. Course I didn't.

THERESA. Oh.

PAUL. Testing you, I was.

THERESA. Right.

PAUL. Course I didn't.

THERESA. Why?

PAUL. Why?

THERESA. Yeah.

She moves closer and closer as they speak.

PAUL. Because… Yeah, they took care of me. Grand. But none of them were my special friend.

THERESA. Your special friend.

PAUL. Yeah.

THERESA. And who's your special friend?

She leans on him.

PAUL. Aagh. Fuck. Get away.

THERESA. Oh, God.

PAUL. Get away. Ouch!

THERESA. Sorry.

PAUL. Fucking hip!

THERESA. I'm sorry.

PAUL. Jesus!

THERESA. Are you all right? I'm sorry, I didn't mean to…

PAUL. Fucking hip!

Pause.

THERESA. I'm sorry.

PAUL. You don't take good care of me.

Pause.

THERESA. But I'm your special friend. I want to take care of you. (*Pause.*) Is it bad?

PAUL. It's bad enough. I need this fucking thing, don't I?

He shows the walking stick.

THERESA (*lovey-dovey speak*). But you have your special friend, now.

PAUL. My special pal.

THERESA. Your special pal who'll help you and who'll look after you.

PAUL. Who'll tend to me, yeah?

THERESA. Who'll tend to you specially.

PAUL. Better than the nurses?

THERESA. Much better. The way only a special... (*Kisses him.*) pal... (*Kisses him.*) can... (*Kisses him.*)

PAUL. Ah, God. Get away.

THERESA. What?

PAUL. Get away, the... Wash your face.

THERESA. What?

PAUL. Smell of dog off you.

THERESA. Oh, no.

PAUL. I told you before.

THERESA. I forgot.

PAUL. Wash your face. That's the most unhygienic thing you can do.

THERESA. I can't help it. He likes to lick my face, he likes to be cuddled.

PAUL. You stink of it. Come on. Theresa!

THERESA. I was lo... (*Pause.*) Fuck you! Fuck off if you don't like it.

Pause.

PAUL. I don't like it.

THERESA. Well fuck off, then, you're only out of hospital.

PAUL. All I'm asking you is to wash your face.

THERESA. You're not coming into my place and ordering... That's the rudest thing. My face isn't smelly. How dare you come in... How... I was playing with Toby. If you don't like it... If... Well, fuck off, then, if you don't like it.

Pause.

PAUL. Do you want me to go, then?

THERESA (*realising she's gone too far*). No, I don't wa...

PAUL. Head off on my merry way?

THERESA. No, it's just like...

PAUL. Say if I was eating garlic... I know you don't like garlic.

THERESA. No, I don't.

PAUL. So, if I was eating garlic, you'd ask me to brush my teeth and I wouldn't say no, because I know you don't like it.

THERESA. If you were...

PAUL. Garlic. Same thing here. I don't like the smell of dog, it's the exact same thing. (*Pause.*) It's just it's polite, like, it's a bit of consideration.

THERESA. Mmm.

PAUL. The smell or the taste. It's the same thing. I *want* to kiss you.

THERESA. Yeah.

PAUL. I *like* kissing you, but...

THERESA. I know.

Pause.

PAUL. Go on.

She exits. PAUL *gets up slowly.*

I'm gonna make a phone call. Is that all right?

THERESA (*offstage, calling, lovey-dovey*). Only if you're still my special pal.

PAUL. You know I am.

He makes a face, takes out a piece of paper and dials a number.

Know who this is? Is…? No. Put him on. *Him*. You know who. Put him on. (*Pause*.) Yeah, fuckface, how are you? (*Pause*.) Yeah. I just got out, so this is where it begins, do you hear me? (*Pause*.) Well, I'm sorry. I'm sorry, but, you know… (*Pause*.) That's your problem. We all have stuff to deal with. (*Pause*.) My heart bleeds. (*Pause*.) Listen. You listening? Right. Carefully, now. Fuck her and fuck you. Fuck the pair of you. I'm out and the wheel is in motion. Do you hear me? The wheel is turning.

He hangs up and limps back over to the sofa. He eases himself down painfully, takes a sip of his tea. Enter THERESA.

THERESA. All done.

PAUL. Good. Are you gonna get a new telly?

THERESA. Suppose I'll have to.

PAUL. Good.

THERESA. Who were you ringing? Adele?

PAUL. No. The bloke.

THERESA. What did you say?

PAUL. I told him the cogs are spinning. Don't say anything, Theresa. Don't open your trap, I don't give a shite.

THERESA. Don't talk to me li…

PAUL. I don't give a flying fuck, that's where the line is drawn. Anyone who has any objections… Anyone who has… They can… Look at me. (*Pause*.) Theresa.

THERESA. What are you going to say?

PAUL. In the papers, the *Echo*?

THERESA. Yeah.

PAUL. That's not for your ears. You'll find out when you read it.

THERESA. Tell me.

PAUL. It's a surprise. Tony Kelly's column. You'll see it when you read it. Look at me.

THERESA. What?

PAUL. Look at me. I want you on my side. This is just so he knows what he's let himself in for. Do you know I can't even sign on? I've another two weeks before I can go back to work.

THERESA. But you're going to get compensation.

PAUL. I don't care. I don't give a fuck. I want *him* to pay. Those fuckers think they're all-powerful. I'll show him it can be personal sometimes.

THERESA. Doesn't mean you have to harass him. You're making whatchamicallit telephone calls.

PAUL. I'll show the fucker. I'm gonna, in a few years, when I'm older, I'll be one of those poor fuckers who can't walk when it rains.

THERESA. You won't.

PAUL. Course I will. A bum hip.

THERESA. 'Bum'?

PAUL. A bum hip. A hip that 'plays up' when it rains. And it always fucking rains. Ever hear the phrase 'an old war wound'? That's what it'll be like. And it'll be 'playing up'. I'll be a, what's the word?

THERESA. Infirm?

PAUL. Fucking retard's what I'll be.

Pause.

THERESA. Your old war wound.

PAUL. Yeah.

THERESA. I think that's romantic.

PAUL. You would.

Pause.

THERESA. How long are you staying? Do you've to…?

PAUL. Adele? No. After.

THERESA. Oh.

PAUL. I'm dreading going home.

She looks at him.

But I'm not staying here. I'm going for a drink. I've a few things to sort out.

THERESA. Who are you going with?

PAUL. On my own. I need to be on my own for a few hours. Away from nurses and doctors and… I've plans to make. I'm gonna be busy for a while. Preparing and planning. Did you wash your face?

THERESA. Yep.

PAUL. C'mere.

She approaches.

Be careful, now.

They kiss.

THERESA. Let's go upstairs.

PAUL. I can't.

THERESA. A quickie.

PAUL. I can't.

THERESA. Why not?

PAUL. 'Cos of this. I can't with this.

THERESA. Try.

PAUL. What do you mean 'try'? I can't. Next few weeks, now, I'll be impotent.

THERESA. Not impotent.

PAUL. Yes, impotent. Technically, I'm impotent. I'm an impotent man. A man whose manhood doesn't work.

THERESA. For the next couple of weeks.

PAUL. Yeah. For the next couple of weeks. It still gets to me. I'm proud of my cocksmanship.

THERESA. And so you should be.

PAUL. And I like to use it. Not that it's my cock that doesn't work. It's my hip. I can't move. There's nothing wrong with my virility.

THERESA. Sure, don't I know.

PAUL. It's just my hip.

THERESA. I know. (*Pause*.) Is she expecting you?

PAUL. Who?

THERESA. Adele.

PAUL. She's got her sister over there.

THERESA. Liz?

PAUL. They can keep each other company. One of them's bad enough. Adele's hard to take these days.

THERESA. You'd think she'd be a bit more… capable nowadays.

PAUL. I'm doing the best I can.

THERESA. I'm sure you are.

PAUL. But, when you can't even talk to your wife properly…

THERESA. I know.

PAUL. And, now, since this thing… (*Holds up stick*.) I'm doing my best.

THERESA. I know you are. (*Hugs him*.)

PAUL. Watchit. Watchit.

THERESA. Sorry.

PAUL. Anyway, different things affect different people in different ways. Nah, I'm gonna go for a drink, do some thinking.

THERESA. Right.

Pause.

PAUL. We must be the unluckiest people in the world.

THERESA. You're lucky you've got me around.

Pause. He looks at her.

PAUL. What the fuck is that supposed to mean? I'm lucky…?

THERESA. No. It just means…

PAUL. I'm lucky I've got… I should be…

THERESA. …That's not…

PAUL. …I should be grateful to you?

THERESA. No.

PAUL. ...That you're around?

THERESA. That's not what I meant. Stop. I was messing. Jesus! It's good that we can...

PAUL. 'That we can' what?

THERESA. That we can have a good time together. That's all I was saying. It was a joke.

PAUL. Last thing I need's bloody jokes. (*Pause*.) Some of the nurses in that hospital, though.

Pause.

THERESA. I'm a bit, Paul.

PAUL. What?

THERESA. I'm a bit scared. Over this burglary.

PAUL. What burglary?

THERESA. The telly and the video. I feel...

PAUL. Oh, *your* burglary. Why?

THERESA. In case they come back. What's the word?

PAUL. Why would they?

THERESA. Whatsit? I feel...

PAUL. There's nothing to take.

THERESA. Very funny.

PAUL. Maybe *you* should be grateful that *I'm* around. (*Pause*.) Yeah. That's what I'll do. I'm gonna... You know Kevin? Tony Kelly's a friend of his, said he'd be interested. You know Tony Kelly?

THERESA. Is he the cri...?

PAUL. The crime correspondent, yeah. Genius way with words, he has. Kevin said he'd be interested in my version of events. Get in there now, I'm gonna talk about incompetency, I'm gonna talk about someone who doesn't do his job properly, who shouldn't *be* doing that job, who shouldn't've been doing it in the first place. Detailed description of events, and then I'll drop the bomb. (*Imitates the sound of an explosion*.) The laughing stock of the country. He won't be able to show his face for a year.

THERESA. What *is* the bomb?

PAUL. None of your business. You can read about it in the *Echo*.

He raises himself from a sitting to standing position with the aid of his walking stick and a loud grunt.

Jesus! (*Beat.*) Shite! Gimme, have you...? Pen and paper. Just a piece of paper. I'll have to make some notes.

THERESA. A piece of...

PAUL. Yeah. Pen and a piece of paper. Have you got it?

THERESA. Yeah. Hang on. (*Exits.*)

PAUL (*calling*). I'll go up and make some notes, I think it's better to write stuff down.

THERESA (*offstage*). Will a pencil do?

PAUL. Have you no pens?

Pause.

THERESA (*offstage*). No. (*Returns.*)

PAUL. Right. Just gimme the pencil.

THERESA. And there's your paper.

PAUL. Nice one. Right.

He turns towards the door.

THERESA. You going?

PAUL. Yeah.

THERESA. Have another cup of tea.

PAUL. Booze, I need.

THERESA. I've got wine and...

PAUL. ...A pint. From the pumps. Haven't had a pint in...

THERESA. Hang on here for a while.

PAUL. I can't.

THERESA. Well, can I come with you?

PAUL. No. What did...? Wasn't I just saying? I've to make notes, I've to be on my own, I've to get my head together.

THERESA. Well, I'll come up, have the one… A glass, and then I'll leave.

PAUL. Sorry, Theresa. No. Bit of solitude, gimme… (*Kisses her.*) Have to go. (*Hobbles towards the door.*) Give you a ring tomorrow, all right?

THERESA. What time?

PAUL. Some stage during the day.

She opens the door for him.

THERESA. All right.

He kisses her.

PAUL. Or the evening. See you.

The telephone rings. THERESA *jumps nervously.*

THERESA. Paul!

PAUL. What?

THERESA. Hang on a sec, will you?

PAUL (*impatiently*). Come on!

THERESA. Just till I… (*Points at phone.*)

PAUL. Think it's the fuckin' burglars or somethin'?

She answers the phone. PAUL *waits at the door.*

THERESA. Hello? Who is this? (*Pause.*) Oh. (*Pause.*) Nothing. (*Pause.*) Why? (*Beat.*) What, though? I'm a bit tired. (*Pause.*) But, what? (*Beat.*) I'm fairly tired. (*Pause.*) Is it important? (*Beat.*) All right. Yeah. Yeah. Yeah. Okay, see you.

PAUL. Who's that?

THERESA. Oh, it's just… A… Just this…

PAUL. You cheating on me, Theresa?

THERESA. No. It's a girl I know, wants me to…

PAUL. Some bloke, yeah?

THERESA. A woman. A girlfriend.

PAUL. Bit on the side?

THERESA. Paul!

PAUL. I'm testin'. Am I allowed go now?

THERESA. Yeah.

PAUL. Good.

THERESA. Thanks.

PAUL. You're welcome.

THERESA. You okay?

PAUL. Yeah.

THERESA. You sure?

PAUL. I'm crippled and I'm impotent. I'm grand. See you.

THERESA. See you.

He exits.

THERESA *stands silently.*

Blackout.

Scene Three

Another sitting room. IRENE *sits on her sofa.* WILLY *paces behind her.*

IRENE. Well?

WILLY. Mmm.

IRENE. Willy.

He sighs.

IRENE. What was he like?

WILLY. Like on telly. He listens, sits there in his chair, he says 'hmm', and 'go on', and treats you like a fucking child.

IRENE *looks at him.*

Like a... Sorry. You'd end up believing you were a six-year-old. Where's Tommo?

IRENE. He's in bed. If we decide to, Sandra said she'd come over and babysit, no problem. If we want to go out. I thought you might… If you'd like to go out.

WILLY. God!

IRENE. Yeah?

WILLY. Terrible.

IRENE. C'mon, hardshaw. You'll get used to it.

WILLY. Yeah. We can get used to anything, can't we. Doesn't mean that everything you get used to is good for you. There've been people found up the mountains in Canada've got used to eating dirty roots and smearing themselves in shite to keep warm. They've gotten used to it, but it doesn't mean it's good that they've gotten used to it.

IRENE. That's horrible.

WILLY. That's what they do, Irene.

IRENE. What did he say?

He lights a cigarette.

WILLY. They'd probably consider *us* uncivilised.

IRENE. What did he say?

WILLY. He asked me… (*Takes a pull. Exhales.*) He asked me what kind of things I was afraid of. He asked me about my history, he asked me about you, about my relationship with little Tommo, about… Listen to this. About whether I ever get angry at him.

IRENE. He's trying to cure you.

WILLY. About whether I ever get angry at my son. There's nothing wrong with me, Irene. There's nothing wrong with me. They're testing me, the bastards, and guess what? Guess what? I'm failing. Treating me like a child. Talk about humiliation. He asked me about that day…

IRENE. You weren't humiliated.

WILLY. I was humiliated. Grown-ups don't talk to each other like that. Grown-ups talk to each other like adults. We don't tell each other everything's going to be all right. We talk about adult things. We converse.

IRENE. He's your doctor.

WILLY. There's nothing wrong with me. You'd wanna hear the bloke. Talks with, you know that accent, it's Irish, but it sounds kind of English. Very... Very...

IRENE. Yeah.

WILLY. Kind of a newsreader accent, what the newsreaders have. Middle of the whatcha... session, his wife rings up, think it was his wife. All of a sudden, he's speaking like anyone else.

IRENE. His professional manner.

WILLY. Like you or me.

IRENE. Right.

WILLY. Hangs up the phone and all of a sudden, he's on the telly again, reading the news. Talking like I'm a baby, asking stupid things.

IRENE. But there's things they probably need to clear up.

WILLY. Yeah. 'To clear up.' Like how incompetent I was, how much stress I was under, like... Do... He actually asked me do I suffer from stress or nervousness? In general life, like. I'm the most relaxed man in the world. I only get worked up when... you know... (*Takes a pull. Exhales.*) something deserves getting worked up over.

IRENE. Well, he obviously doesn't know you yet.

WILLY. And the accent. Don't forget the accent, disappears when he's on the phone. Trying to determine my mental state.

IRENE. Your mental state's fine.

WILLY. My career.

IRENE. I know.

WILLY. I'll be...

IRENE. Everything'll be okay, Willy.

WILLY. And this fucker, this other fella. I don't know what I'm going to do. It was an accident.

IRENE. Well, he can't be much of a human being...

WILLY. An accident.

IRENE. ...He can't... If he can't see that.

WILLY. What to do, what to do? I'm gonna be thrown out, I know it.

IRENE. We'll see.

WILLY. I'll get the sack. Wait'll you see. The lads were all acting different in the station today.

IRENE. I'm sure they're all rooting for you, Willy.

WILLY. It's a joke. *I'm* a bloody joke. Promoted for two weeks. Two weeks and I screw up. My fifteen minutes of respect.

IRENE. Everyone respects you.

WILLY. I... This psychia... psychologist, whatever he is, I asked him, 'What about this bloke? Could he be, like, a big threat, because,' I tell him... 'because he's scaring me.' He says I have to tell him about what happened between us if he's going to be able to help me. I tell him he wouldn't understand. He says he's a psycholo... psychiatrist...

IRENE. Psychologist.

WILLY. Psychologist. It's his job to understand. See what I mean about talking like I'm a child? It's his job to understand. In his... In his fake-newsreader voice. I says, 'Not this. You won't understand this. I'll tell you whatever you want to know, but not this.' He says I have to tell him what happened between us. I can't tell him, Irene. There are some things... 'What's important at the moment,' he tells me, 'is that we... we determine your mental state and try to make you better.' Now, that's a contradiction. Why try to make me better if he doesn't know whether anything's wrong with me or not yet? Which there isn't.

IRENE. I know there isn't.

WILLY. Don't worry about that. Well, I'm sorry doctor, but this bloke's a threat that exists. Don't worry about that. You're not helping, by the way.

IRENE. I... What?

WILLY. You're agreeing with me...

IRENE. Because you're right.

WILLY. ...You're... And saying nice things, no, not because I'm right. Comforting. Thanks and all, but you're not helping.

Comforting words aren't going to help. Action will help. That's all'll do anything for me. A plan of action.

IRENE. But there's nothing you can do at the moment.

WILLY. Except smile.

IRENE. Yeah. Smile and tell the truth.

He laughs to himself. Pause.

Maybe it was the wrong thing.

WILLY. What do you mean?

IRENE. The work you're doing. I always thought you were right for what you *were* doing. When you were in uniform. Talking, you know, to people, communicating and helping people. You're more…

WILLY. I'm what?

IRENE. When you're here with me. Or even… You're more… gentle.

WILLY. Gentle?

IRENE. Or… Yeah. Or… You communicate well. You know, since… I'd been thinking. You're nice to people. I didn't think it was right in the first place, you on that squad. The DS. It's not you, you know? It's aggressive. It's not the kind of job that your character would suit.

Pause. He gives her a dirty look.

WILLY. I don't know what you're saying.

IRENE. I'm saying…

WILLY. You're saying I'm not cut out for it?

IRENE. No, I'm just…

WILLY. Well, now, thanks for that bit of loyalty there, love. You're saying I'm not man enough for the job. One minute, you're calling me 'hardshaw', the next…

IRENE. Ah, now, Willy, now.

WILLY. No, now, Irene. You think the other lads are cut out for it, but poor Willy can't hack it. How can you…? How can you tell, anyway?

IRENE. Willy, don't be silly, now. I'm not saying anything…

WILLY. Casting aspersions on my manhood, thank you very much. My own wife. I made a mistake. I'm not chicken. I'm not a fucking wimp. I made a mistake.

IRENE. I know.

WILLY. How do you know if I'm man enough for the job or not?

IRENE. Your character I'm talking about. Your character.

WILLY. I'm of a… Less-than-manly character, that it?

IRENE. I don't know why I'm…

The telephone rings. IRENE *answers it.*

(*Into phone.*) Hello? (*Long pause.*) I'd… All right. (*To* WILLY.) It's him.

WILLY *takes the phone.*

WILLY (*into phone*). Hello? (*Pause.*) I'm fine. (*Pause.*) Can you not…? I have a family. (*Pause.*) I'm trying to take care of my family. (*Pause.*) Can you not…? I may lose my job. My wife… (*Long pause. Hangs up.*) The fucking bastard!

IRENE. Willy!

WILLY. The fucker! Do you know what he just said to me? The f…

IRENE. Calm down. This is stupid.

WILLY (*raging*). The… Do you… Ffff…

IRENE. Come on!

WILLY. He… 'Fuck her and fuck you.' That's… The… He's talking about you! He's… The fffffbollox!

IRENE. Calm down, Willy.

WILLY. Fuck you, he said. To *you*. He said fuck *you*. I'll… If I could… I should've done worse. I swear to Christ, I should've done worse. If I could go back…

IRENE. Don't say that, Willy.

WILLY. Fuck him! Making… Making phone calls to our house? Insulting you? My… My wife in my own house. If I could go back, I'm telling you…

IRENE. Sit dow...

WILLY. The...

IRENE. Will you sit down? Sit down. Here.

WILLY. The ffffcccc...

He sits down. She goes to the cabinet and takes out a bottle of whiskey and a glass. She pours the whiskey and brings it over to him.

IRENE. Drink that. One go.

He does. She pours another.

Go again.

He takes it off her. Sips it.

Now. You're going to... Are you listening? You're going to calm down and think rationally. These things that are happening to us are... Are you listening to me?

WILLY. Mmm.

IRENE. Look at me, then. These things that are happening to us are bad. Yes. But what we're going to do is use our heads and not, do you hear me? Not lose our heads. Not let ourselves get worked up. We cannot let trials like this get to us. We've had fairly bad times before and we got through them, didn't we? We may not get through this easily. We may have a few losses. The job, or some money... I don't know. If you told me what the hell he was planning.

He gives her a look.

No, but we'll do it like... what you were talking about. Adults. Like civilised human beings. Willy.

Pause.

WILLY. I just... I... When I saw him coming towards me, I...

IRENE. I know.

WILLY. I reacted. In a situation like that one, like the one I was in, you see, I'm telling you, you see someone racing towards you, you can't just...

IRENE. I know.

WILLY. I was caught off-guard, but what they don't seem to understand is that I reacted the way I was taught. The way I was supposed to. They send me to a bloody psychi…

IRENE. Psychologist.

WILLY. To a bloody psychologist? Any one of the others would have done the same thing. (*Pause.*) You know?

Pause.

IRENE. Tell me what he's going to write about you.

WILLY. I can't.

IRENE. Of course you can.

WILLY. I can't. It's not… It's not me being… I physically… I actually physically can't tell you. (*Pause.*) Can you understand? (*Pause.*) Any of the other lads would've done the same thing.

IRENE. Bad luck is all it was.

WILLY. I'm not incompetent.

IRENE. I know.

WILLY. I did the right thing.

IRENE. I know you did.

WILLY. I'm trying my best to take care of you.

IRENE. I know you are.

WILLY. But I'm failing.

IRENE. No you're not.

WILLY. But I am.

IRENE. You're not. Willy. You're not. We'll be okay.

WILLY. It's him that needs the psychologist, not me.

IRENE. We'll be okay, Willy.

WILLY. Christ! When I think about what he just did.

IRENE. So what?

WILLY. And what he just said about you.

IRENE. They're only words, Willy.

Pause.

WILLY. Yeah.

Silence. WILLY *takes a drink.*

IRENE. Is that really true, what you said?

WILLY. What?

IRENE. That they, those people, up in the mountains?

WILLY. What?

IRENE. To keep warm.

WILLY. The Canadians?

IRENE. They smear... all over. Is that true?

WILLY. Their shite. Yeah.

IRENE. They don't wear clothes.

WILLY. No. They smear themselves in their own shite. Saw it in the *Echo*, some professor.

IRENE. God!

WILLY. Professor of Canadian mountain tribes or something.

IRENE. Ah, Willy!

WILLY. Something like that. Had a column, there last week.

IRENE. I couldn't do that.

WILLY. Smear shite?

IRENE. Yeah.

WILLY. If it was cold enough, Irene, you'd smear yourself in anything.

IRENE. The stink.

WILLY. They'd probably like the stink. Wouldn't be a stink to them.

IRENE. Mmm.

WILLY. Soap, now.

IRENE. Soap?

WILLY. Soap, you see. Something like soap, or something we'd see as clean...

IRENE. Ah, yeah.

WILLY. Yeah? They'd probably gag if they smelt it. This is what your man was saying. Differences in cultures. (*Pause*.) What's the story on tonight? What are we doing?

IRENE. I don't know. We could go for a drink.

WILLY. Yeah.

IRENE. Or we could stay in.

WILLY. Couple of pints'd be nice. Chat... Have a bit of a chat.

IRENE. Yeah.

WILLY. About... Not about...

IRENE. No.

WILLY. ...About normal, everyday things.

IRENE. That'd be nice. About... We could finish our...

WILLY. The Canadians, yeah.

IRENE. You could tell me a bit more.

WILLY. That'd be good.

IRENE. That's interesting.

WILLY. Was an interesting article. Yeah. Want to try and forget about this fucker for a while. (*Pause*.) Well, will we go out, then?

IRENE. Yeah. Do you want to?

WILLY. Yeah, if... We'll go out.

IRENE. Yeah.

Pause.

WILLY. I like you.

IRENE. Really? I like you. (*Beat*.) Hardshaw.

WILLY. Couple of pints.

Pause.

IRENE. What time is it? I'll run up and have a quick shower. Will you give Sandra a ring and ask her to come over? Tell her he's already asleep.

WILLY. Right. Hurry up.

IRENE. And, we're desperate.

WILLY. Right.

IRENE exits. WILLY goes to the phone, takes a piece of paper from his pocket and dials a number. He waits.

Hello. Paul Bolger, please. (*Pause.*) That's strange. (*Pause.*) Hmm. Are you sure? You're sure. All right. Have you any idea where he is? (*Pause.*) All right. That's… No, that's fine. I'll call over later. (*Pause.*) No, I'm a friend of his, I'll call over later. I'll be over anyway.

He hangs up. Picks up his glass and drains it. Goes over to door. Calls.

Irene!

IRENE (*offstage, calling*). What?

WILLY. Nothing.

He takes his coat from the chair and exits. We stay on the empty room.

IRENE (*offstage, calling*). What?

She comes into the room. Looks around.

Willy? (*Pause.*) Willy?

She stands in the centre of the room.

Blackout.

Scene Four

ADELE*'s house. Breakfast room.* THERESA *sits at the table.* LIZ *pours a couple of brandies and sits down.* THERESA *is understandably nervous.*

THERESA. Is… Paul's coming home tonight, isn't he?

LIZ. He is. Adele's looking forward to it.

THERESA. Mmm. How's his form? Is he…? How's his walking?

LIZ. I don't know. Says he'll probably have to use crutches for a while. But few weeks, he'll be back to normal. See the ship?

THERESA. Yeah.

LIZ. What d'you think?

THERESA. Yeah.

LIZ. Drink.

THERESA *drinks*.

Right. The reason I asked you down...

THERESA. Mmm-hmm.

LIZ. I didn't want to tell you over the phone, because I thought it'd be better face to face.

THERESA. All right.

LIZ. The reason...

THERESA. Yeah?

LIZ. It's too impersonal over the phone. It's something important that... To say it...

THERESA. You can't?

LIZ. It's better to be in person, face to face, one on one, having another... To have a person, because... When I tell you, you'll understand.

Pause.

THERESA. Okay.

LIZ. It's... Something like this, eye contact is needed, the presence of... And to be able to see the other person, physical and all the other.

THERESA. Right.

LIZ. All right?

THERESA. Yeah.

LIZ. Drink.

THERESA *drinks*.

THERESA. Now.

Pause.

LIZ. This is a bit... (*Pause*.) It's like... You see? This is the... In the first place, the reason I asked you to come down, because being told something like this over the phone... Anyway. I was reading the... Some... No. Nothing. It might be a shock to discover this. It's a shock, I'm sure, to find out that the love you're giving, you know? The love you're giving is one-sided and not being reciprocated and... Are you all right? Are you all right? Drink. Have a drink.

They both drink.

I was talking about this subject to Adele. I don't want to... Not that it's any of my business. I don't want to see you made a fool of. You're living a lie and I think it's about time you found out about it. (*Pause*.) He's incapable of love.

Silence.

Some... It's true. Instinct. That's all it is. By his nature, he has the incapacity to love. It's... It's in his genes, it's all instinct. Are you okay? I've been through it myself. I don't know. I'm just saying forget about love because it's an impossibility.

Pause.

THERESA (*thinking she's been rumbled*). How did you know?

LIZ. Know what?

THERESA. Know about us? How come you knew?

LIZ. I can smell him off you. Sometimes you've got hairs on you. What do you mean?

THERESA (*confused*). Hairs?

LIZ. His hairs.

THERESA. I...

Pause.

LIZ. It's all right. C'mere. Do you want a hug? Come over here.

THERESA. No, I'm all right.

LIZ. You don't look all right. Sometimes a hug...

THERESA. No. No. The... (*Pause*.) You can smell him off me?

LIZ. Not bad. It's nothing you have to be embarrassed about.

Pause.

THERESA. I feel like a gobshite.

LIZ. Theresa, you didn't know. It's all right. Sure, I only found out tonight.

THERESA. Does Adele know?

LIZ. Yeah.

THERESA. Oh, Jesus!

LIZ. I told her when I saw it, she was here with me. Don't worry, you're not a gobshite. She doesn't think so either.

Pause.

THERESA. What did you see?

LIZ. In the paper.

THERESA. The paper?

LIZ. Some professor or other.

THERESA. How does he know?

LIZ. He knows because he's a professor. C'mere. Do you want a hug?

THERESA. No. What do you mean, 'he knows because he's a professor'?

LIZ. He kn... 'Cos he's... He studies animals. A... Behaviour. He's a, a professor of animal behaviour or some such.

THERESA. How does he know about me?

LIZ. He... He doesn't know about you. Your dog. Your dog, he knows about.

THERESA. My dog?

Pause.

LIZ. Yeah.

THERESA. Oh! (*Pause.*) My dog.

LIZ. I'm sorry, Theresa. To have to... be the one to tell you.

THERESA. My dog doesn't love me is what you're...

LIZ. Sometimes if we... I'm here for you. If you want a hug, to talk about it, if you want to cry...

THERESA. Toby.

Pause.

LIZ. Toby doesn't love you. (*Pause. Drinks.*) Who the hell did you think I was talking about?

THERESA. No, I kne…

LIZ. Did…?

THERESA. Toby. I knew. Toby.

LIZ. You thought I was talking about something else?

THERESA. No, I knew you were talking about Toby. Sure the, the hairs he leaves on me, et cetera.

LIZ. Yeah!

THERESA. He's an awful shedder.

Pause.

LIZ. How do you feel?

THERESA. I feel all right. I don't know. I didn't know.

LIZ. No, well, like I said. I only found out tonight, myself. It's a horrible thing to discover.

THERESA. Hmm.

LIZ. Horrible. But, what? Would you rather have known or not have known?

Pause.

THERESA. Known.

LIZ. That's the way I'd feel. That's the way I'd feel. You don't want to go around living a lie.

Silence.

Who did you think I was talking about?

THERESA. No one. I… Toby. I knew.

LIZ. No, you didn't.

THERESA. I did.

LIZ. Do you have a secret?

THERESA. No.

LIZ. Do you have a…

THERESA. Stop, would you?

LIZ. …No?

THERESA. I wish I…

LIZ. You sure?

THERESA. I wish I did.

Pause. LIZ drinks.

LIZ. So do I. What do you think of the ship?

THERESA. Very nice.

LIZ. Paul's coming-home present. (*Calls.*) Adele! (*To* THERESA.) It's a very difficult one.

THERESA. Sure, I'm sure Paul'll be able to handle it.

LIZ. Should pass the time for weeks. The HMS *Victory*.

THERESA. It's big, isn't it.

LIZ (*calling*). Adele! (*Goes to doorway.*) Adele!

ADELE (*offstage*). Yeah?

LIZ. I was just showing Theresa the… Oh, very nice!

ADELE (*offstage*). Yeah?

THERESA. Adele!

ADELE (*offstage*). Stop.

LIZ. No. God…

THERESA. That's gorgeous.

LIZ. …Look at you.

THERESA. Adele Bolger!

LIZ. The word 'glamour' is about to be redefined. Come here.

THERESA. Come in.

ADELE *enters, wearing a sexy white top and black trousers.*

LIZ. Give us a twirl.

She does so.

THERESA. Beautiful.

LIZ. Absolutely.

ADELE. Are you sure?

LIZ. Will you...? 'Are you sure?' Get out of it.

THERESA. Adele, it's gorgeous.

ADELE. This'll be the first time...

LIZ. First time you've worn that combination.

ADELE. Yeah.

THERESA. Lovely.

ADELE. I've worn both of them before, but separately.

THERESA. Right.

ADELE. In different combinations.

LIZ. He'll love it.

Beat.

ADELE (*cheerfully*). I think I'll... (*Points at glasses.*)

LIZ. Yeah, yeah. Sit down. I'll get the glass, you vixen.

ADELE. Ah, stop.

She sits on the couch. LIZ *gets a glass from the press.*

LIZ. Here we go. You staying, Theresa?

ADELE. I'll...

LIZ. Gimme your glass. (*Pours.*) The more the merrier, am I right, Adele?

ADELE. Yes.

THERESA. I think I might just...

LIZ (*filling her own*). The more. The merrier. (*To* THERESA.) How do you feel now? (*To* ADELE.) I told her.

ADELE. Oh. How do you feel?

ADELE *begins lighting a cigarette. She offers one to* THERESA.

THERESA. I'm fine. I'm... (*Shakes head at cigarette.*)

LIZ. If you wanna talk about it...

THERESA. No. It's not that bad.

They move to the couch.

LIZ. I just thought you should know.

THERESA. No, I appreciate it.

LIZ. Good.

ADELE. Cheers!

LIZ. Cheers!

THERESA. Cheers!

They drink.

LIZ. So. Any news?

THERESA. I was...

LIZ (*interrupting, to* ADELE). What time is it?

ADELE. Twenty to.

THERESA. I... think I should be...

LIZ. Any scandal, Theresa?

LIZ *takes the model ship off the table and puts it against the wall to make more room. The girls go into chat mode.* LIZ *returns to her seat.*

THERESA. I was broken into last night.

ADELE. Ah, no.

LIZ. No way. What did they get?

THERESA. Yeah. Telly and the video.

LIZ. Ah, God.

THERESA. Yeah.

LIZ. The bastards.

ADELE. Were you upset?

THERESA. Well, I'm a bit scared since.

ADELE. Living on your own.

THERESA. This is it.

LIZ. Did your dog not bark or…?

THERESA. No.

LIZ. Didn't…

THERESA. They came in the front.

ADELE. Jesus. Must be…

THERESA. It's sort of freaky. Like, since. Say at night-time…

LIZ. …Uh-huh. Yep…

THERESA. …On my own…

LIZ. …Must be terrible.

THERESA. Yeah.

LIZ. What do you think of Paul and his injury?

THERESA. It was terrible, wasn't it.

LIZ. It was, all right. He'll come hobbling in, now. See all of us waiting, one two three, bottle of brandy, his new model ship, Adele's sexy attire…

ADELE. Ah, Liz.

LIZ. Stop. You know you look great.

ADELE. I look all right.

THERESA. You look great.

LIZ. You look great.

Pause.

THERESA. To think that they were downstairs.

ADELE (*a little distressed*). Mmm.

Pause.

THERESA. It's frightening to think that, while you're asleep, anyone can come in and wander around your house. Your things. Personal… I was trying to think of the word. Someone in my house, it made me feel…

Pause.

ADELE. You should get an alarm.

LIZ (*with bottle*). Filler-upper, Theresa?

THERESA. Eh... Well, I don't really know if I should be...

    LIZ *begins filling the glasses anyway, starting with* THERESA*'s.*

LIZ. Gets you a bit looser, warms up the blood, gives you a nice buzz.

ADELE. Makes it easier to talk.

LIZ. Loose lips sink ships, but what the hell?

    Pause. THERESA *picks up her glass.*

THERESA. What the hell? Cheers!

LIZ. Cheers!

ADELE. Cheers!

    They drink.

THERESA. Should I get an alarm?

LIZ. An alarm.

ADELE. We have one.

THERESA. I suppose...

ADELE. Make you feel safer.

THERESA. That invasion of privacy...

ADELE. Paul got one installed in March, we never had a problem. The box... You can see... You know, you can see it as you come in. Over the door. I'd say that's a...

LIZ. A deterrent.

ADELE. A... Yeah. Was reading in the *Echo*.

LIZ. Sure it is. As much as anything else.

ADELE. A deterrent. Just the sight of it. This professor, what was it?

LIZ. 'Cos, yeah. 'Cos they see it.

THERESA. Right.

ADELE. A professor of burglary prevention, it was.

THERESA. I'm gonna pop down tomorrow, see if I can get one.

ADELE (*to herself*). Home protection?

LIZ. Soon as you can, Theresa.

THERESA. Yeah.

    Pause. They drink.

    Can I use your loo?

LIZ. Sure.

ADELE. Of course.

THERESA. My bladder's just…

LIZ. Don't be embarrassed. We're all the same.

ADELE. Go ahead.

THERESA. Thanks.

LIZ. And don't forget to flush.

    THERESA *goes*.

    (*To* ADELE.) Did you get it?

ADELE. What?

LIZ. Did you smell it?

ADELE. No.

LIZ. Yes, you did.

ADELE. Liz, that's not nice.

LIZ. I'm just asking you.

ADELE. That's not nice.

    Pause.

LIZ. But, did you smell it?

ADELE. Yes.

LIZ. I told you.

ADELE. Right. Enough.

LIZ. I told you you could smell it.

ADELE. Right.

    Pause.

LIZ. Did you see the hairs?

ADELE. What? Liz! No.

LIZ. They're on her jumper. She a…

ADELE. I di…

LIZ. …She always has them.

ADELE. No.

LIZ. You didn't?

ADELE. No, I didn't. You're mean.

LIZ. Just observant, Adele. You'll see when she comes down.

ADELE. Right.

LIZ. Have a look.

ADELE. Right. (*Beat.*) No! (*Pause. Then in shocked tone.*) No! (*Pause.*) How'd she take the news?

LIZ. Ssshhh!

> THERESA *enters.*

> Did you flush?

THERESA. Of course I did. I always flush.

LIZ. I'm joking. Sit down.

> THERESA *sits.*

> I'm joking. (*To* ADELE.) Is this the last bottle?

> ADELE *shakes her head.*

> Stupid question.

They laugh. Pause. THERESA *leans confidentially towards* ADELE.

THERESA. How are you feeling these days, Adele?

Obviously she's said the wrong thing. LIZ *comes to the rescue, interrupting* THERESA.

LIZ. You should get that alarm. Now that it's happened, they might think you're easy pickings. They might come back. Might come upstairs next time.

THERESA (*alarmed*). Yeah?

LIZ. Get that alarm. Security is the best policy.

ADELE. It is.

LIZ. 'Less you *want* them to…

THERESA. What?

LIZ. That right, Adele?

ADELE. Which?

LIZ. Up the old bedroom.

THERESA. Ah, no. No.

ADELE. Liz!

LIZ. Up the old bedroom. What?!!

THERESA. No way.

LIZ. A good ravaging, now?

ADELE. Liz!

THERESA. You wouldn't!

LIZ. All depends, now, Theresa. All depends. I don't know.

They are interrupted by the sound of a key in the door. Enter PAUL. *He hobbles in slowly on his walking stick.*

PAUL. How's it going?

ADELE. Heya, Paul.

LIZ. Heya, Paul.

THERESA. Hello, Paul.

PAUL. Heya, Theresa.

He makes to take off his jacket.

LIZ. Hold it. Wait. Paul. Let me do that. (*Does so.*)

PAUL. Thanks.

LIZ (*helping him sit down*). Down. Now. All right?

PAUL. Yep. Thanks.

LIZ. No problem at all. Do you want some brandy?

PAUL. Yeah. Nice one. Dropped in for a pint on my merry way already.

LIZ *goes to get a glass.*

How are things?

ADELE. Fine. How's your hip?

PAUL (*dismissively*). Agh!

ADELE. Does it hurt much?

PAUL. No, sometimes. Not much. Something strange going on here.

LIZ *sits back down with glass and begins to pour for* PAUL.

ADELE. What?

LIZ. Something strange, Paul?

PAUL. Mmm.

LIZ. Do you notice something, Theresa?

THERESA. Me?

LIZ. Yeah.

THERESA. No.

PAUL. Adele?

ADELE. What?

PAUL. Do you notice something strange?

ADELE. I… I don't know.

Pause.

PAUL. Hmm.

Pause. He looks ADELE *up and down.*

LIZ. Ah, Paul!

PAUL (*still looking at* ADELE). What?

LIZ. Stop it.

THERESA. What?

ADELE. I…

PAUL. Sexy as hell.

ADELE *laughs.*

LIZ. Paul.

PAUL. Look at you.

ADELE. Well, you...

PAUL. Look at the sexy lady.

LIZ. Isn't she?

PAUL. Look at you.

ADELE. You were coming home.

Beat.

PAUL. For me?

LIZ. Yeah.

PAUL. Yeah?

ADELE. I thought...

PAUL. No. No...

ADELE. ...I thought...

PAUL. You thought right, Adele. No. You thought right. (*To* LIZ.) I see you didn't make any effort.

LIZ. Go to hell.

PAUL (*to* ADELE). Stand up.

She stands.

That's beautiful.

ADELE. The combination.

PAUL. That's what it is. Can I have a kiss?

She kisses him, then sits down.

This is nice. (*Drinks.*) How are things, Theresa?

THERESA. Fine.

PAUL. Long time no see.

THERESA. Yeah.

LIZ. Theresa was broken into the other night.

PAUL. Yeah?

LIZ. Robbed her telly and her video.

PAUL (*to* THERESA). Yeah?

THERESA. Just my telly and my video.

PAUL. You were lucky. (*To* ADELE.) Look at you.

ADELE. Stop.

LIZ. I told her she should get an alarm.

PAUL. You should. You should.

THERESA. I'm going to have a look tomorrow.

PAUL. You should. (*Drinks*.) Agh!

Pause.

ADELE. Are you glad to be out?

PAUL. Too right. The nurses in there.

THERESA. Nice?

PAUL. Rough. You must be joking. Big… Awfully rough they are. Picking you up and putting you down. Big matrons treating me like a sack of potatoes. (*To* ADELE.) I was telling you.

LIZ. You poor thing.

PAUL (*to* ADELE). You'll be gentle with me, won't you. Course you will. I need a gentle hand at the moment. You look gorgeous.

ADELE. Thanks.

PAUL. My special pal.

ADELE. *My* special pal.

   THERESA *almost does a double take at this.*

LIZ. Adele.

   LIZ *makes a signalling motion with her head.* ADELE *gets the model ship.*

PAUL. What's… For me?

ADELE. Yeah.

PAUL (*taking it*). Oh, brilliant.

ADELE (*sitting down*). That's to pass the time.

PAUL. Brilliant.

ADELE. Liz picked it out.

LIZ. I did not.

PAUL *is opening the box.*

ADELE. You did so.

LIZ. Well, you paid for it.

ADELE. *We* paid for it.

PAUL (*taking out pieces and looking at them*). Well, thanks, the pair of you. What do you think, Theresa?

THERESA. It's lovely.

PAUL. Look at the size of those pieces.

LIZ. What's that? A gun?

PAUL. A cannon. Jesus. That'll take a while.

ADELE. Well, it's to pass the time.

Pause.

PAUL. Thank you. (*Kisses her.*) Thanks.

THERESA. Maybe I should get something like that, now that I've no telly.

PAUL *has broken the little cannon off its frame. He shoots* THERESA *with it, making the sound with his mouth.*

PAUL. Size of them.

LIZ. It's got every little detail.

THERESA. Have you ever done one of those before, Paul?

PAUL. Not... When I was a little boy, I used to. But not in years.

ADELE. Who were you in the pub with?

PAUL. On my lonesome.

LIZ. There's no stopping him, he's only out of the hospital.

ADELE. Why were you on your own?

PAUL. Ah, I just had to have a think about things. It's a big deal getting out and coming home. Make a few plans, I wanted to get my head together a bit. Just to...'Cos whether I like it or not, life's gonna be a bit different from now on. Things changed the minute that fu... Soon as it happened. Isn't it amazing? Little event like that. An occurrence... Still... (*To* ADELE.) We can talk about stuff later if you want.

ADELE. Yeah. If you want.

PAUL *takes a drink*.

PAUL. So, how come you're here, Theresa?

THERESA. We...

LIZ. Paul!

PAUL. I'm only asking. I'm not being rude. (*To* THERESA.) Was I being rude?

THERESA. No.

PAUL. I wasn't. I was just asking. I didn't expect.

LIZ. I asked her down.

PAUL. You rang her, did you?

LIZ. Yeah.

PAUL. Right.

THERESA. Liz read something in the paper and she felt she should...

LIZ. About dogs, Paul. Do you know that dogs are incapable of love?

PAUL. What?

LIZ. This professor in tonight's paper says so.

PAUL (*kissing* ADELE). Thanks for the model.

ADELE. You're welcome.

LIZ. Dogs, Paul. It's not in their gene structure to be capable of love.

PAUL. Dogs.

LIZ. Here, it's... (*Hands him the newspaper.*) There.

PAUL (*taking a quick glance*). That's rubbish.

LIZ. He says so.

PAUL. Doesn't make it true. What do you think, Theresa?

THERESA. Yeah, I...

PAUL. Doesn't make it true.

LIZ. Well, that's why... I wanted to tell Theresa.

Pause.

PAUL (*to* THERESA). That your dog doesn't love you.

THERESA. Yeah.

PAUL (*to* LIZ). You're fucked.

LIZ. It says so there, Paul.

PAUL (*to* THERESA). She got you all the way down here. (*Pause. Reads.*) A professor of canine psychology. That should tell you. The only bloke worth reading in that rag is Tony Kelly. Do you ever read him, Theresa? Crime correspondent?

THERESA. Em... I don't...

PAUL. Good bloody writer.

THERESA. Is he?

PAUL. Genius, he is. Very good.

ADELE. I have to go to the weewee. (*Rises and exits.*)

LIZ. Don't forget to flush.

PAUL. Look at her strut.

LIZ (*to* THERESA). I'm only messing. (*To herself.*) Where's the...? (*Calling.*) Where's the other bottle, Adele?

ADELE (*offstage*). What?

LIZ. The other bottle.

ADELE (*offstage*). What about it?

LIZ. Where is it?

ADELE (*offstage*). It's in the cabinet inside.

LIZ. Right. (*To others.*) You on for some more?

PAUL. Pour away.

She pours.

LIZ. The more, the merrier, huh?

PAUL. Yep.

THERESA. That's enough. Thanks.

LIZ. I'll just get another one.

> LIZ *exits. While she is gone,* PAUL *and* THERESA *look very uncomfortable. Each looks down at the table as if the other isn't there.* LIZ *returns with another bottle of brandy and sits down.*

PAUL (*drinks. Confidentially to* LIZ). How is she?

LIZ. She's fine.

PAUL. Everything's...

LIZ. Yeah. She's grand.

PAUL. Who bought the ship?

> *Beat.*

LIZ. I did. (*Beat.*) She's grand.

> *Pause.*

PAUL. This fucking adventure's all she needs.

THERESA. Will I head on?

PAUL. No.

LIZ. No. No. Theresa.

PAUL. Sure, you're here.

LIZ. Have a drink. You've started.

> *They drink.*

PAUL. What do you think of this dog business, Theresa?

THERESA. The... What Liz said?

PAUL. Yeah.

THERESA. I don't know. It wouldn't really affect me much. If... I mean, it's true. Then that's... I don't know if it'd make any difference to me. I like my dog.

PAUL. Do you belie...?

THERESA. It's not a person, though. It's only a dog.

LIZ. But you like it.

THERESA. Yeah.

LIZ. You like it a lot.

THERESA. It's a dog. I like it as…

PAUL. But do you believe about…?

THERESA. I like it…

LIZ. A lot.

PAUL. But do you believe what Liz said?

LIZ. I didn't say it, I…

PAUL. Well, in the paper.

LIZ. The professor.

PAUL. Do you?

THERESA. Do… I don't know. But, even if it's true…

PAUL. It's not.

LIZ. It could be.

THERESA. It wouldn't affect me, I don't think. It's only a dog, so I don't really mind. Lovewise. Long as it's there, especially now after the… the burglary, I'm glad there's somebody around. What's the word I'm trying to think of? Anyway, love me or not, he can still provide me with some company.

Enter ADELE, *looking upset again.*

PAUL. Okay?

ADELE (*sitting down*). Yeah.

He kisses her.

PAUL. Do you believe it?

ADELE (*distant*). What?

PAUL. About the dog. Are you all right?

ADELE (*upset*). I'm… Yeah. Just a… Gimme…

LIZ. Adele?

ADELE. I'm a bit…

PAUL. D'you need…?

ADELE. There's… Gimme two minutes.

LIZ. You all right, Adele?

ADELE. Gimme… Yeah. Leave… (*Pause. Upset. To* PAUL.) Someone rang.

LIZ. Oh, that's right!

PAUL (*to* ADELE). Who rang?

ADELE (*starting to cry*). Someone.

ADELE gets up and leaves the room, distressed. PAUL *gets up and follows.*

PAUL. Adele!

THERESA. Should I go?

LIZ. No, no, she's all right. (*Calling.*) She all right, Paul?

PAUL (*offstage. Calling*). Yeah, she's grand.

THERESA. I think I should go. I shouldn't really…

LIZ. Stay where you are. She… It'll pass in a minute. (*Very serious.*) Theresa. Adele's a bit ill.

THERESA. Well, should I not go, then?

LIZ. No, no, no, you're grand. She sometimes gets a bit confused or addled or frustrated, something. She's all right. Paul knows. Bit sick. Kind of a nervous… Stressful situations, you know? She has these fits. Falls down, so she needs to be, you know. Nothing major, now, it doesn't damage her or anything, but they take a while to pass. Kinda… (*Demonstrates a fit.*) You know? But not dangerous.

THERESA. I…

LIZ. She's fine, she's pills, she's not having one now. Stay put, we're having a few drinks.

There is a knock on the door.

Who's this, now?

LIZ *goes out to answer it.*

We hear the door opening.

(*Offstage*.) Yes?

VOICE (*offstage*). Is eh... Paul Bolger home, please?

LIZ (*offstage*). Yyeees. Who shall I say it is?

VOICE (*offstage*). I'm the man who shot him.

Blackout.

ACT TWO

Scene One

The same. A few minutes later. PAUL *sits on the sofa.* WILLY *stands. They are alone.*

PAUL *and* WILLY.

WILLY. You were running. You were running, you were coming towards me.

PAUL. Trying to stay out of trouble.

WILLY. But, yeah, but when it happened, all I could think about was...

PAUL. How powerful you were.

WILLY. No. What?

PAUL. We talked about this at the hospital. Think you've got the power and the right.

WILLY. Right to what?

PAUL. Right to do things.

WILLY. Do what?

PAUL. Do stuff and all, going around shooting guns.

WILLY. Shooting?

PAUL. Shooting guns and all, going around in your cars, flying around, skidding. I know youse.

WILLY. I'd never shot my gun before, shot it at a person.

PAUL. Going around, then.

WILLY. What?

PAUL. Going around in your cars, flying around.

WILLY. Well...

PAUL. Deny that, you fucker.

WILLY. ...Sometimes we...

PAUL. A-ha. Think youse are it. Can you deny it?

WILLY. ...Sometimes we drive fast.

PAUL. Right.

WILLY. But we don't think we're it. Least I don't.

PAUL. 'Cos you're not.

WILLY. What?

PAUL. You're not it.

WILLY. I don't think I am.

PAUL. Think you're Don Johnson or something?

WILLY. It wasn't my fault.

PAUL. Whose fault was it?

WILLY. It was an accident.

PAUL. Well, maybe if you'd've been a bit more careful, now. Don Johnson doesn't shoot without thinking.

WILLY. It was...

PAUL. Don Johnson takes aim.

WILLY. Too much was going on. I didn't have time to think.

PAUL. You'd more time than me. I didn't have any time.

WILLY. I know.

PAUL. Time enough to feel pain.

WILLY. I'm sorry.

PAUL. On my merry way round the corner, BANG! Time enough to go into shock, know what I'm saying? On my merry way home to my wife. You could've killed me. You could've easily hit me somewhere else.

WILLY. I know, I...

PAUL. In the head or something, got me. In the heart. Could've blown my head off, Jaysus! In my eye or something.

WILLY. If I...

PAUL. Jaysus!

WILLY. If I could…

PAUL. In my… Shut up, will you? Shut your mouth. You're in my house, have the common decency not to start interrupting me. As soon as…

WILLY. I'm sorry, I…

PAUL. …Will you? You're doing it again.

WILLY. I'm sorry.

PAUL. This isn't some gangster's… hideout you're doing a… thing on, this is my house. (*Pause*.) What was I…? My belly. Shot in the belly can kill you. Shot in the chest, doesn't even have to be your heart. Where else? The eye, now'd be the worst. See what I'm saying? See how serious what you did is?

WILLY. I know how serious it is.

PAUL. What d'you want?

WILLY. I came for… To ask you…

PAUL. Ask me what?

WILLY. To stop.

PAUL. Never.

WILLY. Please.

PAUL. I will never, I will never.

WILLY. But…

PAUL. I will never.

WILLY. Tell me why, then.

PAUL. You know why. Look at the state of me. I'm in flitters. My hip's in flits, I can't walk without my stick. In tatters, I am. See that? That's all I'll be doing for the next few weeks, now, 'cos of you. Sitting on my arse, trying to build the, whatsit?

WILLY. HMS *Victory*.

PAUL. The HMS *Victory*. Recovering. There's a few weeks of my life wasted, now. On that fucking thing.

WILLY. That's a beautiful ship.

PAUL. That's not what I'm on about.

WILLY. I know it's not.

PAUL. I know it's a beautiful ship.

LIZ (*entering from upstairs*). Sorry, Paul.

PAUL. What are you…?

LIZ (*indicating brandy bottle*). Can I…?

PAUL. Yeah. Go on. Hang on. (*Pours himself a glass.*)

LIZ (*to* WILLY). Nice, isn't it?

WILLY. Lovely.

LIZ. Should keep him occupied for weeks, now.

PAUL. How is she?

LIZ. Ah, she's fine. You know.

PAUL. Good. How's Theresa?

   Beat.

LIZ. She's fine, too.

PAUL. Good.

LIZ (*taking bottle*). Jaysus, she's gas, isn't she?

PAUL. Who?

LIZ. Theresa. C'mere. Did you notice…? (*Looks at* WILLY.) I'll ask you after. (*Exits.*)

WILLY. Do you have a family?

PAUL. None of your… No. I have a wife.

WILLY. Her?

PAUL. You must be joking.

WILLY. Your wife…

PAUL. Don't talk about her.

WILLY. My wife.

PAUL. Yours.

WILLY. My son. It's not just me you're hurting. My family had nothing to do with anything. When they read it... They're going to be hurt and they did nothing.

PAUL. That's life, man. It's like me being shot, you know? Kind of stuff happens.

WILLY. What the hell were you doing there?

PAUL. I told you before, a mate of mine lives there. The whole block isn't criminal. See, it's this kind of attitude, now...

WILLY. I wasn't saying...

PAUL. ....This attitude, just because someone lives in a place...

WILLY. I wasn't...

PAUL. You think you can judge these innocent people who don't have the money to live anywhere else?

WILLY. I don't.

PAUL. And this kind of fucking attitude, now. This kind of attitude, going around firing your gun, could take someone's eye out.

WILLY. Yeah.

PAUL. Could you imagine?

Pause.

WILLY. When you phoned my house tonight and what you said to me. To my wife. About my wife.

PAUL. What did I say?

WILLY. You said 'Fuck her'. You said fuck me and...

PAUL. Fuck you.

WILLY. What did she do to you?

PAUL. Look. I said it. I meant I don't care. I don't know your wife, if she happens to get hurt, then... You know.

WILLY. Let me tell you this. Let me tell you this, waiting to go out and get someone, it's not exciting, it's far from exciting. Maybe for the other lads. I'm telling you this, now...

PAUL. I'm not particularly interested.

WILLY. Let me tell you this. This is just now, to, if I could make you understand the, the... pressures... inherent.

PAUL. Go on. Fucksake!

WILLY. That day, the day it happened was a Friday, we were sitting in the office, I was only on the squad two weeks, we were sitting in the office waiting for a phone call, could get a phone call from any number of snitches...

PAUL. 'Snitches'?

WILLY. Yeah.

PAUL. Like in...

WILLY. In... On telly, yeah. That's what we call them as well.

PAUL. Right.

WILLY. We've warrants there for three or four dealers and we're waiting to see which one we'll get a snitch on. Sitting there filling in the warrants.

PAUL. You fill them in first?

WILLY. Just so we won't have to worry about it later. Still have to get the district judge's signature. So, the phone call comes.

PAUL. Snitch.

WILLY. One of the snitches. This fella, Maurice Joyce.

PAUL. The snitch.

WILLY. No, the fella.

PAUL. Oh, right. Who youse're...

WILLY. Who we're, yeah, who we're...

PAUL. Uh-huh.

WILLY. Snitch gives us the address and the squad goes mad, 'cos Maurice Joyce's wanted for murder on top of being a dealer. That couple shot up at Whiteoaks. Did you...?

PAUL. I did, I read it.

WILLY. Two of them shot in the head.

PAUL. In the *Echo*. Tony Kelly column.

WILLY. I don't want to go up against a murderer. I don't want to put myself in that situation. I'm telling you this, now. I'm telling you this so maybe you'll...

PAUL. Right.

WILLY. So you'll maybe…

PAUL. So youse get the info. The tip.

WILLY. The squad goes mad, we're gonna catch a killer, we'll get a curry after to celebrate. Off we go, straight to the detective commissioner's house, he's out in the garden trimming his hedges. We skid up…

PAUL. 'Skid up', yeah? See what I'm saying?

WILLY. I wasn't driving.

PAUL. Strange, though, isn't it? Youse 'skid up'.

WILLY. We're in a hurry to get there, case he leaves.

PAUL. Go on.

WILLY. This is my first time, now. Judge signs the warrant, 'Good luck, lads,' off we go.

PAUL. Pull a handbreaker off, yeah?

WILLY. I don't remember. We go to the flat. Maurice Joyce is the third floor. The lads are still discussing curries.

PAUL. What's this about curries?

WILLY. Whenever they do a successful job, they have a curry.

PAUL. Very good. Pint's not good enough for them, no?

WILLY. It's just a thing they do.

PAUL. More elitist behaviour, you see? Handbreakers, curry, go on. Fuckers thinking they're it, go on.

WILLY. We get out the battering ram.

PAUL. Youse have a battering ram?

WILLY. To knock the door down.

PAUL. Right.

WILLY. Knock on the door…

PAUL. What are youse knocking on the door for if youse have a battering ram?

WILLY. Have to knock on the door and identify youself.

PAUL. I'd just plough my way in, surprise them.

WILLY. That's the rules.

PAUL. That's a bit stupid now. Giving them a chance? I'd knock the fucking door down, catch them in the act, don't give them the fucking chance, the bastards.

WILLY. I know.

PAUL. Go on, go on. Youse knock on the door...

WILLY. We knock on the door, tell them it's the DS, we've a warrant.

PAUL. 'DS'?

WILLY. Drug Squad.

PAUL. Course.

WILLY. Then we knock down the door. Have to do it as quick as possible before they flush the stuff down the jacks or swallow it.

PAUL. Right. After...

WILLY. Run inside...

PAUL. ...After giving them a warning.

WILLY. It's the rules.

PAUL. It's stupid. Go on.

WILLY. Get inside and there's no one there.

PAUL. But your...

WILLY. The snitch. I know.

PAUL. He told youse a lie.

WILLY. Well, they could've been there when he said, but...

PAUL. Right. Right. In the meantime...

WILLY. ...Time we get the warrant signed and all.

PAUL. Which is why youse fill them out at the station.

WILLY. Save time.

PAUL. Right. That's smart, now.

WILLY. So, in we go.

PAUL. Smart thinking. How many of youse is there?

WILLY. Three men and one woman.

PAUL. You're the woman, yeah?

WILLY. No, I'm not the woman.

PAUL. Does the woman have a gun as well?

WILLY. No. She's there to…

PAUL. Good. Go on. This is interesting.

WILLY. I'm telling you this, now, so you'll know what I was… what I was thinking. My…

PAUL. Yeah. Yeah. It's interesting.

WILLY. …Kind of pressure I was under.

PAUL. Youse get into the flat and there's no one there.

WILLY. And there's no one there. Hear someone calling outside. Youngfella at the front door about sixteen, strung out to fuck, says, 'Is Maurice there?' Door's on the ground and he doesn't even notice.

PAUL. No way.

WILLY. Strung out to fuck.

PAUL. Doesn't even notice the door!

WILLY. He just wants a fix, so I tell him Joey's not here. So, he's, 'Ah, I'm dying for a fix, man,' giving it all that, and then, 'Ah, sure here he is.' Maurice Joyce and four or five other blokes come around the corner, the walkway, McDonald's bags in their arms. They spot us, we spot them, out with the guns, us and them. McDonald's up in the air, they scatter, everybody scatters, running downstairs into other flats, disappearing, firing their guns behind them. Guess what Maurice Joyce shouts?

PAUL. What?

WILLY. 'Youse'll never take me alive.'

PAUL. Jaysus!

WILLY. Thing is, he meant it.

PAUL. Murder rap on him.

WILLY. Exactly. Rest of the squad flies after them and I was left standing there like a fool. All happened so fast, I'm left thinking, where the fuck did everyone go? Wondering what to do and then you come along. Flying around the corner, running towards me, running at me.

PAUL. On my merry way home, that's all.

WILLY. I panicked. Do I shoot, do I run?

PAUL. Innocent me on my merry fucking way.

WILLY. All in a split second. Do I fight? Am I gonna die? I pointed my gun and... I overreacted, I panicked, it was all so fast, I pointed my gun and I fired. (*Pause*.) Now.

Pause.

PAUL. Now what?

WILLY. I told you what happened. I told you how scared I was. D'you see the, the confusion, the pressure I was under? I was scared. I've admitted it to you. D'you see what kind of...?

PAUL. Admitted what?

WILLY. I was scared, I was confused, I...

PAUL. Admitted what? I'm sitting here... I'm sitting here listening to you telling me how cool the fucking Drug Squad is.

WILLY. What?

PAUL. Your guns and your cars, skidding up to the Judge's gaff, with your battering rams, you're boasting. Poor little junkie, too strung out to notice a broken door and youse use it as a source of mockery?

WILLY. It's what happened.

PAUL. Tony Kelly's got a way with fucking words, hasn't he.

Pause.

WILLY. I've given you this. I've told you stuff I wouldn't even tell my wife.

PAUL. What have you given me?

WILLY. Something... I'm trying to... Something of myself.

PAUL. Of your...

WILLY. Yes, of…

PAUL. You didn't tell me everything.

WILLY. What?

PAUL. What happened when you shot me, you know? What's this all about?

WILLY. Well, you saw that.

PAUL. I'd my mind on the bullets in me.

WILLY. I told you, the pressure… The, the… I told you how I was…

PAUL. I wasn't really concentrating.

WILLY. The pressure…

Pause. PAUL *stands up.*

PAUL. You pissed yourself. The man from the Drug Squad pissed himself.

WILLY. I don't want people to know.

PAUL. I was lying on the ground with two bullets in me, did I cry? I took what happened like a man. I didn't lose control of my bladder like a woman.

WILLY. Stop.

PAUL. How can you live with yourself, no I won't stop. I have to let people know there's a woman in the Drug Squad, you sad bastard. Down on your knees, whingeing like a three-year-old, going weewee like a baby. 'Awww. I'm sorry. I didn't mean it. Awww…!' Me down there filled with hot lead, I didn't wet myself. Oh, no. And I saw you tying your jacket around your waist, you sneaky fucker. Least I know how to bite the bullet. Least I can take it. Youse all think you're such fucking men.

WILLY. Stop it. Stop that fucking…

PAUL. What'll you do? Cry?

WILLY. Just don't…

PAUL. Weewee in your drawers? You baby, you woman. Don Johnson wouldn't've pissed himself no matter who he shot. Don's like me. Don can bite the bullet.

WILLY. Don't print this. Please. My wife…

PAUL. Ah, now.

WILLY. I'm being punished. I'm seeing a psychologist.

PAUL. Why?

WILLY. Because...

PAUL. Because you go around shooting people?

WILLY. No, because...

PAUL. Because you've a bed-wetting problem?

WILLY. He tells me I could be suffering from whatsit? Post-stress...
Post-shooting something or other. They're trying to see if...
They're trying to see if I'm incompetent.

PAUL. Incontinent?

WILLY. Incompetent. Do you not understand?

PAUL. Tony Kelly's good at the old wordplay, isn't he? I wonder
how he'll write this up, now. See if he'll make up a bit of
wordplay using them words. Incompetent and...

WILLY. What can I do?!!!

PAUL. Listen to me. You're wasting your time.

WILLY. If you could...

PAUL. You're wasting your time, Mister Incontinent. Read all about
it. Think you can come in here, showing off with your Drug
Squad stories, thinking you're Don, with your guns and your cars
and your fucking curries, thinking you're Don, thinking you're
fucking great.

WILLY. You're...

PAUL. Telling me stories?

Long pause.

WILLY. You're jealous, you cunt.

PAUL. What?

WILLY. You're fucking jealous of me?

PAUL. Of piss in the bed? Calling me a cunt in my own gaff?

WILLY. What the fuck have you got to be jealous about?

PAUL. Go and ask my…

WILLY. You were well in there. Right up to the end.

PAUL. I was interested.

WILLY. You're jealous. You cunt.

PAUL. Calling me a… Calling me a… (*Impersonating him.*)
'Awwww!'

WILLY. You're… You're…

PAUL. 'Awwww!'

WILLY. I don't belie…

PAUL. 'Pssss. Pssss. I didn't mean it. Awwww!'

LIZ (*offstage*). You fucking bastard! (*Enters from upstairs.*)

PAUL. 'Awwww!'

LIZ. I said, you bastard.

PAUL. What?

LIZ (*calling upstairs*). Get your fucking arse down here!!

PAUL (*to* WILLY). You've to go. Talk's over. Finished.

LIZ. Theresa!

PAUL (*to* WILLY). Get out! (*To* LIZ.) What's up?

WILLY. If I could… Another time…

PAUL. What?

WILLY. If I could…

PAUL. Read all about it. Tony Kelly. Crime correspondent. The
Echo.

LIZ (*calling upstairs*). Theresa! Get your hole down here!

PAUL (*to* WILLY). Now! Out!

    WILLY *leaves*.

LIZ. How dare you?

    THERESA *enters from upstairs*.

THERESA. Em… She's em…

PAUL. What's going on?

LIZ. Guess, you thick.

THERESA. You're wrong, Liz.

LIZ. I'm...

THERESA. You're wrong.

PAUL. What the fuck is...?

LIZ. I'm wrong?

PAUL. Making a show of us in front of...

LIZ (*to* PAUL). You fuckhead. (*To* THERESA.) You certainly made a... (*To* PAUL.) You fuckhead. All she wanted... (*To* THERESA.) You should've kept your big mouth shut.

THERESA. Liz. This is all... There's a...

ADELE (*offstage*). Get her out, get her out!!

PAUL. What happened? What are you...? (*Calling*.) Adele!!

THERESA. You're thinking stupid, the wrong things.

LIZ. Don't you...

THERESA. How can you...?

LIZ. Don't do that.

PAUL (*calling*). Adele!!

LIZ. You're no man, Paul Bolger.

THERESA. What's she talking about?

PAUL. Liz. What are you...?

LIZ. You know fucking well. The dark trick. (*To* THERESA.) The dark fucking trick. Get out.

THERESA. Paul.

PAUL. You'd better head on.

LIZ. Get out.

ADELE (*offstage*). Get her out!!

Pause.

THERESA *exits the house. Pause.*

PAUL. What's going on?

LIZ. What kind of a husband are you?

PAUL. You're in my house, Liz.

LIZ. What kind of a man...? I don't give a good fuck whose house I'm in. That poor girl up... That poor girl...

PAUL. Liz.

LIZ. Shame on you, you mouse.

PAUL. What were you drinking?

LIZ. Same as you. Shame on you. She's up there. She's up there. I'm trying to take care...

PAUL (*calling*). Adele!! Adele!!

LIZ *goes upstairs*.

Adele!!

Blackout.

Scene Two

Morning. PAUL *is sitting on the edge of the sofa in his underwear. A blanket thrown off him.* LIZ *is making breakfast throughout the scene.*

LIZ. We all feel the same.

PAUL. We don't all feel the same. I should have something flat to sleep on for my hip. I've to keep my back straight. (*Pause.*) Look at the dip in that.

LIZ. You should have slept on the floor, then.

PAUL. Look at that.

LIZ. I see it.

PAUL. I'm not sleeping on the floor. (*Pause.*) My bed's straight, now. Big pit in the middle of it. (*Pause.*) Tough night, Liz.

LIZ. Yeah.

PAUL. Where's my stick?

LIZ. Where'd you leave it?

PAUL. Well, if I knew that... Ah, fuck it. What happened, Liz?

LIZ. She opened her big mouth, how could you?

PAUL. I'm only human.

LIZ. Bit of self-control, Paul.

PAUL. What happened?

LIZ. We were upstairs talking about Theresa's burglary and she was telling us how scared she was when she's on her own. She was scared about this and she needed someone to listen to her, to understand, and she said... Bit of attention, you know? And she said, 'When Paul's there...' That's what she said. 'When Paul's there...' Then she shut her mouth and you could see she knew she fucked up. Course we copped it.

PAUL. That could mean...

LIZ. Copped it goodo.

PAUL. That could mean anything.

LIZ. But it doesn't mean anything, does it?

PAUL. Going through a difficult patch, Liz.

LIZ. So am I.

PAUL. Difficult time in my life.

LIZ. So am I, so's Adele.

PAUL. With this bloke, this copper. I've to see things through.

LIZ. See what through?

PAUL. Ah, now.

LIZ. See what?

PAUL. Ah, now... You know?

LIZ. See? D'you see, Paul?

PAUL. What? (*Pause*.) Can I've a...?

LIZ. Get it yourself.

She goes upstairs. PAUL *looks for his stick, then goes to his model ship. Sits down at table. Opens box. A knock on the door. He goes out and opens it.*

IRENE (*offstage*). Hello.

PAUL (*offstage*). Yes?

IRENE (*offstage*). I'm... Willy's wife.

PAUL (*offstage*). Who's Willy?

IRENE (*offstage*). Willy's the... the man who shot you.

PAUL (*offstage*). Sent you around, did he?

IRENE (*offstage*). No, he didn't. Can I come in?

PAUL (*offstage*). I'm only up.

IRENE (*offstage*). Just for a minute.

PAUL (*offstage*). I don't know. Wife of the enemy. Haven't got my wits about me yet.

IRENE (*offstage*). I won't keep you.

PAUL (*offstage*). Did he send you around?

IRENE (*offstage*). No, he didn't.

PAUL (*offstage*). I'm only up.

IRENE (*offstage*). Just for a...

PAUL (*offstage*). Jaysus! (*Pause.*) For a minute.

They enter.

IRENE. I just wondered if you'd seen him.

PAUL. I saw...

IRENE. You saw him.

PAUL. I saw... Last night.

IRENE. He didn't come home.

PAUL. To your gaff?

IRENE. Yes. No.

PAUL. Oh.

IRENE. He didn't come home, I waited up all night for him, you see, you see, we were going to go for a drink and I went up for a shower and...

PAUL. Look at that couch.

IRENE. What?

PAUL. Lie down on that couch.

IRENE. I will not.

PAUL. See how it dips in the middle?

IRENE. I see it.

PAUL. Good.

IRENE. You saw him?

PAUL. He was here last night, causing hassle.

IRENE. How are you?

PAUL. I'm crip...

IRENE. Is he here?

PAUL. No.

IRENE. No?

PAUL. He left.

IRENE. How are you?

PAUL. I'm crippled and I'm imp...

IRENE (*interrupting*). No. No. I don't care. Did he say where he was going?

PAUL. No.

Pause.

IRENE. What are you going to write about him?

PAUL. You'll see it.

IRENE. Is it bad?

PAUL. I don't know. You mightn't think so.

IRENE. Why not?

PAUL. You mightn't think so. That's you…

IRENE. How bad?

PAUL.…But him, now…

IRENE. How bad is it?

PAUL. It's bad enough…

LIZ *enters with a jumper in her hand. She throws it to* PAUL.

LIZ. Here.

PAUL.…For him.

LIZ. Who's this?

PAUL (*putting on jumper*). The copper's wife.

LIZ. You're his wife.

PAUL. He didn't come home last night and she's worried.

LIZ. Oh, God.

PAUL. We don't know where he went. (*Turns back to his model ship, begins examining pieces, etc.*)

LIZ. Sit down. Go on. Sit down. He didn't come home?

IRENE. I'm getting worried.

LIZ. He's… Your husband…

IRENE. Yes.

LIZ. Sit down.

IRENE *sits*.

He's a policeman. Why should you be worried about him if he's a policeman?

IRENE. He might…

LIZ. That's it. I mean, if he's a policeman…

IRENE. He might do something.

LIZ. What might he do? Don't be afraid.

IRENE. I'm afraid for him.

LIZ. You're… Okay. I'm listening, you're afraid.

IRENE. Yes.

LIZ. You're afraid, you're alone. All right. You're alone, you've got a problem, your husband's missing, you need someone to talk to.

IRENE. No. I nee...

LIZ. I'm here, you can talk to me, a cup of tea?

IRENE. No thanks. I'm not really...

LIZ. Okay. Tell us where he usually goes. We can sort this out.

IRENE. Em...

LIZ. Where does he usually go?

IRENE. He usually... I don't...

LIZ. If you tell us that, then. If we know where he goes usually...

IRENE. Yes, he...

  Pause.

LIZ. Well?

IRENE. When?

LIZ. What?

IRENE. When? He usually comes home to me.

LIZ. When he's upset?

IRENE. He usually comes home to me.

LIZ. I'm going to make us a cup of tea. (*Exits to kitchen. Returns.*) You've someone to talk to, now. You've a problem, you've someone to talk to, a confidante, a cup of tea. Nice?

IRENE. Em...

LIZ. Nice?

  Pause.

IRENE. Yeah.

LIZ. Nice. What are you afraid of? I'm Liz.

IRENE. Irene.

LIZ. Nice to meet you. (*Of* PAUL.) Don't mind him. Tell me what you're afraid of. He won't come back?

IRENE. I don't know.

LIZ. He'll come back.

PAUL (*of ship*). Ah…! Jaysus!

LIZ. Don't mind him.

IRENE. Are you sure…? He didn't…?

LIZ. I don't think so. Paul?

PAUL (*of ship*). Fucking hell.

LIZ. Paul!

PAUL. What!

LIZ. He didn't say where he was going?!

PAUL. Are you making tea?

LIZ. I'm making a pot. If you want some you can get it yourself. (*To* IRENE.) Did he say where he was going?

Pause.

PAUL. I'll make myself some coffee.

LIZ. Bit of domestic strife, Irene. Paul!

PAUL. Who!

LIZ. Irene's husband. The Gard.

PAUL. I don't know. No. Have we coffee?

LIZ. A fair bit of drink was consumed here last night, Irene.

IRENE. Really?

LIZ. A fair bit. We're all a bit…

PAUL. This thing's impossible.

LIZ. You can have a cup of tea and afterwards you can ring home, see if he's come back.

IRENE. Okay.

LIZ. That sound all right?

IRENE. Yeah.

LIZ. Good. (*Exits to kitchen.*)

Pause.

IRENE (*to* PAUL). Are…?

PAUL. Mmm?

IRENE. My husband.

PAUL. Don't talk to me.

LIZ (*offstage*). Don't talk to him. He's in the bad books.

PAUL. My bum hip's at me.

LIZ (*offstage*). Your what?

PAUL. This thing's impossible, Liz.

LIZ (*entering with tea*). A child.

IRENE. Is he your husband?

LIZ. You must be joking.

IRENE. Whose…?

LIZ. Upstairs. She'd a harder night than the rest of us, God bless her. That right, Paul? (*To* IRENE.) A hard old night. (*To* PAUL.) Paul!

PAUL. Did you see the dip in that couch?

There is a knock on the door. LIZ *goes to answer it.*

WILLY. Hello.

LIZ. Ah! Your wife's here. Come in.

WILLY. My wife?!

IRENE. Willy?

LIZ and WILLY *enter.*

PAUL. The man who shot Liberty Valance.

IRENE. Willy. I'm worried stiff, where were you?

WILLY. Thinking.

LIZ. Would you like a cup of tea, Willy?

WILLY. No thanks.

LIZ. Have a cup of tea.

IRENE. Thinking where?

WILLY. I spent the night at the station.

LIZ. Told you there was nothing to worry about.

IRENE. Ah, Willy.

WILLY. I needed to be on my own.

LIZ. You might as well…

IRENE. You should have rang.

LIZ. Cup of…?

WILLY. I didn't want to talk to anyone. I went up to the station, had a few cups of coffee… It was quiet up there. I sat at my desk and just… just had a long, hard think.

Pause.

LIZ (*pouring tea*). You might as well have a cup of tea.

IRENE. And where did you sleep?

WILLY. On my desk.

IRENE. Ah, Willy.

WILLY. It's good for the back.

PAUL. It is.

WILLY. Flat surface.

PAUL. Flat. Yep.

WILLY. I've slept worse places.

LIZ. Well, he's back now, anyway. Sit down, Willy.

WILLY. Sorry to be back again.

LIZ. It's all right. Sit.

He sits.

WILLY. Sorry for disturbing you.

LIZ. No bother. Sugar?

WILLY. No thanks.

LIZ. There's the milk.

IRENE. Doctor Kielty called, Willy.

WILLY. That's nice of him, now, Irene.

IRENE. He wanted to know why you weren't at home.

WILLY. That's nice of him. And was he using his RTÉ newsreader accent?

IRENE. He wa...

WILLY. On the phone, it was probably his normal one, was it?

IRENE. I don't remember.

WILLY. Then again, he was talking in a professional capacity, so...

IRENE. He said you were suffering from post... Something related to shooting. Post-shooting something.

WILLY. I have to do something.

IRENE. Post, related to...

WILLY. I thought we could have a chat.

IRENE. Related to trauma.

WILLY (*to* PAUL). I thought we could have a chat.

LIZ. I don't think he's in the humour.

IRENE. I think you shou... Willy!

WILLY. What?

IRENE. I think you should come with me.

LIZ. Paul?

PAUL. I'm not in the humour. (*Goes out to make coffee*.)

IRENE. He said you're suffering from... Let's go home. He said he needs you to call in today.

WILLY. Don't know if I'll be able to, Irene. May not be able to.

IRENE. Why not?

WILLY. May not be able to.

IRENE. What's up with you, Willy?

WILLY. Nothing's up with me, Irene. I'm just saying I may not be able to.

IRENE. Why not?

PAUL *enters*.

WILLY (*to* PAUL). I've a proposition for you.

PAUL. I'm busy. (*Sits at ship.*)

IRENE. Why won't you be able to, Willy?

LIZ. Drink your tea, Willy.

PAUL (*of ship*). Where'd you get this bloody thing, Liz?

LIZ. Tell us your proposition, Willy.

WILLY. I can only tell it to Paul. Paul.

PAUL. What?

WILLY. Can I just…?

PAUL. Fucking hell!

WILLY. It'll take me just, that's all, two minutes.

PAUL. All right. Tell me it.

WILLY. Ah, now, we ca… The women'll have to step outside.

IRENE. Why?

WILLY. It has to be private between him and myself.

LIZ. Ah, well, if that's the case…

IRENE. Why can't we hear?

WILLY. Irene!

LIZ. All right, Irene, they want to go *mano a mano*, head to head, let's go inside. C'mon, two's company.

IRENE. What happened to sharing?

WILLY. I'll share with you after.

LIZ. Irene? They need privacy.

IRENE. I'm going home.

LIZ. Sure you can stay here. We'll go inside, have a yap.

IRENE. I'm going home to our son, Willy.

WILLY. Go on home to Tommo.

IRENE. What the hell are you up to? And sleeping on your desk? What are you up to? I need you to… I need you… What are you doing here with these people?

WILLY. I'll see you after.

IRENE. Why won't you be able to call in to Doctor Kielty?

WILLY. Not 'won't'. Just may not be.

IRENE. Why not?

WILLY. Not not. May not.

IRENE. Tell me what's going on, Willy.

WILLY. I'll see you after, Irene.

IRENE. Do you not trust me?

Pause.

WILLY. No.

Pause. IRENE *heads for the front door.*

IRENE. I'll be at home if you want me. Willy?

WILLY. Right. You'll be at home.

IRENE *leaves.*

LIZ. There's no need for that, now.

PAUL. You right, Liz? Come on.

LIZ. No need at all. That's no way to talk. (*Exits upstairs.*)

PAUL. I hope you're not gonna start your boasting, now.

WILLY. No. I was in the station last night, there was a copy of last night's *Echo*. Did you read it?

PAUL. No.

WILLY. There was an article, this woman, professor of…

PAUL. I don't read that shite. I read Genius…

WILLY. Professor of…

PAUL. …Tony Kelly. That's it. I don't know how you can read those fucking eejits.

WILLY. The emotion professor. You know her?

PAUL. I know her. I don't read her.

WILLY. Solves problems.

PAUL. Seen her picture, she's a dog.

WILLY. A woman wrote in, her boyfriend had cheated on her, they were fighting all the time because of it, so the emotion professor told her, this was her advice, get out and sleep with someone else.

PAUL. Do the same thing.

WILLY. Balances things, makes her feel equal. Got me thinking…

PAUL. That was her advice?

WILLY. Yeah.

PAUL. Jesus!

WILLY. So…

Pause.

PAUL. So…?

WILLY *takes out a pistol and puts it on the table.*

Jesus! Is that real?

WILLY. I need it for my proposition.

PAUL. Jesus!

WILLY. All right?

PAUL. Is it real?

WILLY. Yes. Now. You ready?

PAUL. That's a…

WILLY. Yes. It's a gun. This article got me thinking. I want you to shoot me.

PAUL. What?

WILLY. Do the same thing to me as I did to you.

PAUL. Shoot you.

WILLY. What I did to you. Then we're quits. Like the emotion professor says. Balance things out so it won't be between us any more. Do the same thing to me.

PAUL. Twice.

WILLY. Twi... (*Pause.*) If you, yeah, if you want. I don't want you to kill me, now. Shoot me. You can shoot me in the leg, the hip, like yourself, the arm...

PAUL. Is it loaded?

WILLY. It will be when you do it. Bit of balancing out.

PAUL. Some action.

WILLY. Bit of action to settle things. You shoot me instead of printing about the... You know, what I...

PAUL. You pissing yourself like a baby.

Beat.

WILLY. Yeah.

PAUL. Can I hold it?

WILLY. Get the feel of it.

PAUL (*picking it up*). Heavy.

WILLY. Yep.

PAUL *aims the gun at various objects in the room.*

Well?

PAUL. It's tempting, I can tell you.

WILLY. Then do it and solve all our problems. I'm sick of this inaction.

PAUL (*putting gun down*). And get arrested.

WILLY. Sure how will you get arrested if we keep our mouths shut? All we've to do is get rid of the evidence, clean up the blood, get rid of the gun. You drive me close to the hospital, my car, we'll dump the gun in the river on the way. I don't know who shot me, I didn't get a look, someone I arrested. Long as we keep out mouths shut, who's gonna know?

PAUL. It's tempting.

WILLY (*taking out silencer*). Got this so it's quiet, who's gonna know? I saw enough of the bloke to know he wasn't limping, so how could it be you? Put something under me to collect any blood, we fuck that in the river as well.

PAUL. It's fucking tempting.

WILLY. Did you tell anyone yet?

PAUL. About…

WILLY. Yeah.

PAUL. No.

WILLY. Your wife?

PAUL. No.

WILLY. 'Cos if we do this, we're quits. You shooting me cancels out you telling on me.

PAUL. Yeah. No. Nobody knows yet.

WILLY. So, come on. (*Pause*.) I made you a cripple.

PAUL. Yeah.

WILLY. I shot you.

PAUL. If I…

WILLY. Twice. I know you want to. Do this and promise me that's the end of it. Revenge.

PAUL. There's… You're tempting me, Pal.

WILLY. An eye for an eye.

PAUL. You're tempting me.

WILLY. Let's see if you've got what it takes to put a bullet in someone.

PAUL. Oh, I could do it.

WILLY. See if you're man enough.

PAUL. I'm man enough to take it.

WILLY. But are you man enough to dish it out?

PAUL. More man than you.

WILLY. Well, I'm man enough to take it.

PAUL. Well, then I'm man enough to dish it out.

WILLY. Well, then, show me, then. Show me and we're quits. Even things up, do the deed, do this. (*Pause*.) Do it.

PAUL *picks up the gun, aims it at the audience*.

PAUL. All right. Yeah.

WILLY. Yeah?

PAUL. Yeah.

WILLY. All right. (*Begins loading the gun*.) Okay if we do it here?

PAUL. Course.

WILLY. Kid's at home.

PAUL. How old's the kid?

WILLY. Kid's six.

PAUL. Nice. (*Pause*.) Young one?

WILLY. Youngfella. (*Pause*.) Get this fucking thing over with, yeah?

PAUL. Settle it.

WILLY. Exactly.

PAUL. Done?

WILLY. You'll have to get rid of them.

PAUL. Oh, that's right, yeah. (*Calling*.) Liz?!! (*To* WILLY.) Hang on a sec. (*Calling*.) Liz!!

LIZ *enters with* PAUL*'s stick*. WILLY *puts gun in pocket*.

LIZ. How's it going?

PAUL. We're having a good chat.

LIZ. So our peace talks are coming to fruition?

PAUL. Yeah.

LIZ. Brilliant. Here. (*Throws him stick*.)

PAUL. Where'd you find it?

LIZ (*to* WILLY). And you're mean. Don't think I'm talking to you yet, speaking to your wife like that.

PAUL. Where'd you find it?

LIZ. Upstairs.

PAUL. How's Adele?

LIZ. Not good, Paul.

PAUL (*to* WILLY). My trusty stick.

LIZ. Bit upset.

PAUL. I wasn't upstairs last night.

LIZ. Well, that's where I found it.

PAUL. Do youse want to go out to the pub?

LIZ. Well, do youse? A drink, the right atmosphere, a serious discussion…

PAUL. No, we'd prefer to…

LIZ. Drink and an old chinwag?

PAUL. We'd actually prefer to stay here, Liz.

LIZ. We're fine here.

PAUL. Well, we'd actually…

LIZ. Youse go down. The right atmosphere, neutral ground, pints instead of shorts…

PAUL. The atmosphere's grand here, Liz.

LIZ. I don't know if Adele's in the right shape.

PAUL. Nice hot whiskey, get her, huh? Do the trick. Adele likes the old hot whiskeys with the clove things. Willy and myself need to… Don't we?

WILLY. Need to…

PAUL. But why not you two…?

WILLY. …To… Here's the right…

PAUL. It is. D'you know what I mean, Liz?

LIZ. I don't, Paul.

PAUL. 'Cos, like, if youse go down to the pub…

There is a pounding on the door.

Who the fff…?

LIZ exits to answer it.

THERESA (*offstage*). Liz! I'm sorry it happened, but I'm scared.

THERESA enters, LIZ behind her.

Paul! I've no one else to turn to. They came, they came back last night, I'm on my own.

LIZ. They came back?

THERESA. Last night. I heard noises. I can't stay there on my own again.

PAUL. I'm a bit tied up, Theresa.

LIZ. You're hearing things.

THERESA. No, Liz.

LIZ. Are you sure?

THERESA. Paul. I'm sorry. They were...

WILLY. Who's this?

THERESA. Who...? You're here again. You're a Gard, aren't you?

PAUL. Theresa, we're a bit busy.

THERESA. You're that same bloke who...?

WILLY. Yes.

THERESA. Why can't you do anything? You shot him so why can't you protect me? Why can't you catch these people?

LIZ. Sit down there, Theresa.

THERESA. I'm scared, Paul. I'm sorry.

PAUL. What about your dog?

THERESA. Toby's... Against thieves?

LIZ. Theresa.

THERESA. Against bandits and murderers? (*To* WILLY.) You bastard, you're all alike. (*To others*.) And rapists? Toby doesn't give a fuck about me anyway. You said so yourself, Liz, the professor said. He'll leave me to these, these villains. (*To* WILLY.) Do you know what it's like to have someone break into your own domain? To have them prowling around while you're helpless asleep? They could've cut my throat. They could've had their wicked... I feel violated, I feel...

LIZ. Theresa. Relax. Talk rationally, if you sit down...

THERESA (*to* PAUL). I was violated and you don't care. Do you know how that feels?

WILLY. I do.

THERESA. What? You...? No, you don't.

WILLY. I'm being violated the same way. Of course I know how it feels. Privacy. I'm going through...

THERESA. But you don't know.

PAUL. 'Violated'?!

WILLY. Yes, I do know. Privacy?

THERESA. You're a Gard. How can you?

PAUL. Fucking 'violated'?!!

WILLY. But I do.

THERESA. How can you?

PAUL. Fucking violation, you're talking about?!!! I'll tell you a few, one or two facts about violation. Violation's a bullet entering your body, piercing your skin and pushing its way inside you. Inside where it shouldn't be. Tearing through your flesh and shattering your bone and pushing its way right inside you. That's violation. Youse haven't a clue what you're talking about.

ADELE enters, stands in the doorway.

What kind of a bullet was it?

WILLY. Thirty-eight calibre.

PAUL. Through my hip, missed the socket by millimetres, came out my arse. Another one through my pelvis, lodged inside me, had to be taken out. Someone broke into your fucking house? Try taking a bullet some time, youse wimps! Youse're all so fucking sorry for yourselves, well what about *me*?

ADELE. What about me?

Pause.

PAUL. What about you? You don't know what it is either.

LIZ. Paul!

PAUL. Get over it. I got over this.

LIZ. Paul! There's no need for that!

PAUL. Should try taking a bullet some time.

Pause.

ADELE. Get out of here, Theresa.

THERESA. Someone broke into my house again, Adele.

ADELE. Did you not invite them into your bed, you tramp?

THERESA. I'm... I'm... You're the ones who... who've always...

ADELE. Get out, you fucking tart, you. I won't let you get away with this, I'm not taking this. Go home to your fucking dog...

THERESA. Adele!

LIZ. Adele, calm it.

ADELE. The smell off her, Liz. Do you know you stink of dog? Do you know you've the smell of a dog in fucking heat off you? No wonder you've no friends.

LIZ. Ah, Adele, now.

ADELE. Get out of my house, the stink of you. The stink. Go to your dirty mutt, fucking, your moulting fucking... mongrel, dirty hairs all over you. He's the only one who'll love you.

THERESA. Paul!

ADELE. He's the only one who'll love you, my husband has nothing to say to you. Go to your doggie.

LIZ. Go on, Theresa. I'll drop over later to check up on you.

ADELE. What?

LIZ. Go on, now.

THERESA. I'm afraid, Liz.

LIZ. This is a bad time.

THERESA. I'm alone.

ADELE. She's her dog.

LIZ. I'll drop over to you.

THERESA. I'm scared.

LIZ. I'll knock six times and shout 'Geronimo' in the letterbox.

THERESA. Will you?

LIZ. I will.

THERESA. Geronimo?

LIZ. Six knocks and 'Geronimo'.

ADELE (*screaming*). GET OUT!

THERESA. Paul?

ADELE. Come on.

> ADELE *walks* THERESA *to front door and puts her out.*

Out!

She comes back in.

PAUL. Jaysus! (*Beat.*) You all right? (*Pause.*) Listen, do you and Liz want to go down to the… pub, have a bit of a…

ADELE. I hate you.

PAUL. …Hot whiskey with the…

LIZ. Ah, now, Adele.

ADELE. No, Liz. No. And you dropping over to her?

LIZ. Well, she's…

ADELE. She's bad.

LIZ. …She's scared, she's alone. I thought…

ADELE. I'm fucking alone. (*To* PAUL.) You're not the only person lives in this house. You're not the only person has it hard. We're supposed to help each other. We're husband and wife, we're… I'm not taking it any more, we're supposed to help each other.

PAUL. And we are.

ADELE. You're helping yourself. You're helping yourself to the fucking… What's her…?

LIZ. Theresa.

ADELE. …The smelly woman. The doggie woman.

PAUL. You know it's hard for me, Adele.

ADELE. You big baby. (*Pause.*) You're such a baby.

PAUL. What did you have to wear that gear for?

ADELE. What gear?

PAUL. The top, the sexy stuff, was that a joke?

ADELE. What?

PAUL. Parading yourself in front of me.

ADELE. What's that got to do with her?

PAUL. Theresa?

ADELE. Why were you seeing her?

PAUL. I was horny. (*Pause.*) You know?

Pause.

ADELE. But you know I'm not able to.

LIZ. Able to what?

PAUL. Of course you're able to. I'm your husband.

ADELE. You spoke to the doctor.

LIZ. Able to what? What's this now?

ADELE. You know I'm sick.

LIZ. Do I know this?

ADELE. You told me you understood. You told me it was okay.

PAUL. Well, I don't.

ADELE. You promised me.

PAUL. I know I did.

ADELE. You said you understood.

PAUL (*shouting*). Well, I don't understand. All you've to do is spread your legs!!! All you've to do is spread your fucking legs for your husband!!! For your man!!! That's all you've to fucking do!!!

ADELE. I… I… If I…

PAUL. Buying me a ship to pass the time?

ADELE. …Paul…

PAUL. You open your legs, that's all there is fuckin' to it. Is that so fucking hard?!!! I've to go off with the dog lady.

LIZ. Adele.

ADELE. Need… I need…

PAUL. Is that so fucking hard to do?

LIZ. What do you need?

PAUL. With the fucking dog lady.

ADELE. Need to… Just, if you gimme… I need…

LIZ. Adele.

> ADELE *runs upstairs.*

> Adele!

> LIZ *runs upstairs.*

PAUL (*to* WILLY). Are we right?

WILLY. What?

PAUL. We right? Let's go. You got the gun?

WILLY. But your wife…

PAUL. We right?

WILLY. Right for what?

PAUL. For this. Are we right? The gun. Come on. Gimme the gun.

WILLY. But they're still…

PAUL. Fuck them. You want to do it, we're doing it now, come on, give it to me.

LIZ (*offstage*). Adele!

WILLY. You sure? Is there something…?

PAUL. Do you want to do this? Come on, we've to do it now. If we don't do it now, we're not fucking doing it.

WILLY (*attaching silencer to gun*). Just wait till I…

PAUL. Hurry up. Gimme.

> PAUL *takes the gun.* LIZ *comes downstairs and runs into kitchen. Hurried. Distressed.*

> She all right?

> LIZ *comes out with* ADELE's *pills and runs up the stairs.*

> Liz! (*To* WILLY.) Right. What do I do?

WILLY. Cock it.

PAUL. Right. I know that. There bullets in it?

WILLY. Is your wife okay?

PAUL. She's fine. What next, is it loaded?

WILLY. Where do you want me to stand?

PAUL. Stand there.

PAUL *goes to the kitchen, comes back with a towel.*

WILLY. Are you sure she's okay?

PAUL. Happens all the time. Stand there. (*Throws* WILLY *the towel.*)

WILLY. What's going on?

PAUL. Are we doing it or what?

WILLY. We are.

PAUL. Well, come on, well.

WILLY. I'd prefer if you did it quickly.

Pause.

PAUL. Hold your horses.

PAUL *begins spreading newspapers on the floor.* WILLY *helps him.*

LIZ (*offstage*). Paul!

WILLY. Aim it, by the way, when you're aiming it, aim it a couple of inches below your target because there's a kick and it can throw you off, okay? Don't want you hitting me in the wrong place.

PAUL (*pointing at newspaper*). Know who that is?

WILLY. Yeah.

PAUL. Who?

WILLY. Tony Kelly.

PAUL. Genius.

WILLY. You'll get me to the hospital?

PAUL. I'll drive you straight after. Just let me get my... (*Deep breath.*) Okay.

LIZ (*offstage*). Paul?!

PAUL. Okay.

WILLY's looking upstairs.

Willy? Willy, are we doing this?

WILLY. Yeah.

PAUL. Where do you want it?

WILLY. The leg, the hip, just not the middle.

PAUL. Right.

WILLY. Or the head.

PAUL. The leg or the hip.

WILLY. The leg or the hip.

PAUL. Well, pick. Which?

WILLY. What?

PAUL. The hip or the leg?

WILLY. Oh. The leg.

PAUL. The leg.

WILLY. Is it properly cocked?

PAUL (*cocking it*). Yep.

WILLY. All right, go. The leg, is it?

PAUL. Yeah.

WILLY. All right, go.

PAUL aims.

LIZ (*offstage*). Adele? (*Pause. Louder.*) Adele?! (*Pause. Hysterical.*) Adele!! Adele!!

PAUL (*lowering gun*). Just gimme a second.

WILLY. Aim carefully.

LIZ (*offstage*). Adele! Paul!

PAUL. Just give me a second or two. Have to… work myself up.

WILLY. Take your time.

PAUL. Just give me a minute.

LIZ (*offstage*). Paul!

PAUL. You've never been shot before.

WILLY. I'm about to.

PAUL. It hurts.

WILLY. Well, come on, then.

PAUL. Hold your horses. (*Pause. Aims gun.*) You all tensed up?

WILLY. Yeah.

PAUL. The right leg, right?

WILLY. The right one.

PAUL. You right?

WILLY. Thanks for not telling them. About the...

PAUL. Forget about it. I'm not your friend.

WILLY. I know you're not.

LIZ (*offstage*). Paul!!

PAUL. Good. Are you right?

   Pause.

WILLY. Okay. Two inches lower.

PAUL. Two inches. Right.

   Pause.

WILLY. Ready?

   Pause.

PAUL. Yeah.

   Long pause.

LIZ (*offstage*). PAUL!!!

WILLY (*almost simultaneously*). GO!!!

   Blackout.

   The End.

HOWIE THE ROOKIE

For my parents
Hugh and Patricia O'Rowe

Howie the Rookie was first performed at the Bush Theatre, London, on 12 February 1999 (previews from 10 February). The cast was as follows:

THE HOWIE LEE   Aidan Kelly
THE ROOKIE LEE   Karl Shiels

Director   Mike Bradwell
Designer   Es Devlin
Lighting Designer   Simon Bennison

Characters

THE HOWIE LEE

THE ROOKIE LEE

PART ONE

The Howie Lee

Smoke.

Black smoke ahead there, north end of the field.

Thick, billowin', curlin' up.

Somethin' burnin'.

Me, The Howie, south end, amblin'.

Approachin'.

A figure.

A man ahead, some fuck standin' there, stick in his hand, proddin' whatever's burnin'. Makin' sure it all goes up.

Me, The Howie Lee, gettin' closer now.

Passin' through the field, me way home.

Field, the back of the flats there, back of Ollie's flat, me mate Ollie's an', Jesus, it *is* Ollie, little fire built, he's standin' there, watchin' it, one hand in his pocket, now an' again, stick prods the burnin'... whatsit?

What *is* it?

Come close. All right, Ollie?
All right, The Howie?
Stop, stand, cock me tush.
The fuck're you burnin'?
Me mat, he says.

Ollie's flat befits a messy cunt like him.
Kip the night, you kip on the guest mat under an oul' slumberdown.
You're a bloke and you're game, you can kip in the bed *with* him.
Game meaning gay, neither of which I am, furthest thing from, so I go the mat. Or did.
On the mat, I kip.

Did! Kipped!

It's gone, now. That's it he's burnin'.

Burnin' the quilt as well, so if you want to kip over, the future, only place is the single bed, now, you spoonin' him or him spoonin' you, neither of which, like, fuck both of which, 'cos I don't like either.

Me mat's gone, he says. Me mat's burnin'.
'Cos it's got a disease and it can't be slept on.
'Cos it's got scabies.
Scabies?
Mat's got scabies, *I've* got scabies, he says. I've this cream on me, I've all over me body. Have to leave it for twenty-four hours, have to burn me mat.

Itchy? I asks him.
Itchy all over, he says. Are you itchy, a-tall?
Haven't slept on your mat in while, now.
Lucky you, he says. Wouldn't wish it upon you.

Adios, Ollie, says I. Adios, The Howie, then home.
Keys out, front door, open an' in, ignorin' everyone, The Howie this, that, The Howie, fuck youse.

Up to me bedroom, slide the bolt of privacy an' peace.

Peace and quiet, nice.

Dirty rags, polish me tool, nice one.

Lie back, catnap an' repose.

Bangin' on me door, the oul'one, wake up, she's fuckin' *poundin'* on me door.
Get off the bed, over, slide the bolt an' out the landin', swayin' left an' right, the sudden rush of blood to me head. The oul'one standin' there, bad breath, ugly, dresses nineteen-fifties popsock teeny-bopper, very few grey cells, the oul'fella's even less, he does as she says, not because she's powerful, no, not because he's scared of her…

Tom?! The oul'fella. Tom?!
What?
You comin' up The Fort?

Yeah.
… But because he's nothin' better to do.
Nothin' better, 'cos he *knows* no better.

You're wanted on the phone, she tells me.

Pick up, it's Ollie.
Ollie with the mat, who I met.

C'mere, he says. Me an' The Peaches is after someone. Would you
like to be after someone with us?
Who're youse after? I says. I asks.
Someone you'll like bein' after, but someone who I can't tell you,
'cos of The Peaches, he says. 'Cos it's The Peaches' fuckin' skit.

Ah, now, this is all a bit fuckin' skulduggerous, I says.

But, it's The Peaches' *skit*, he says. Call up to me after.
After me dinner?
Yeah.
Right. But, what's up?
After your dinner.

Hang up, smell of carrots an' parsnips. Lovely.

Bit of bad, now, bit of hassle, the oul'one.
Tryin' to eat me dinner, sittin', she's at me.
At me goodo, she's in me face; popsocks an' cardigan.

Mind your brother. Mind Mousey.
I'm busy.
Me an' your oul'fella's goin' The Fort.
I'm busy, get out of me face.

Wears this spangly glitter shit on her cheeks, 'cross her nose, her
glasses magnify, make it flash at me, gimme a tense nervous.

I won't get out of your face.
Leave me alone.
No, I *won't*. You *mind* The Mousey Lee.
No, I won't.

So forth, enter the oul'fella.

Cycles fifteen miles to work and back every day.
Got a bad ticker, was told take it easy or die, so he saved for a car.
Saved, went without, like, sacrificed.
Walkin' by Harry Moore's one day, saw a handicam.
Now, has the handicam, fuck the car.
Fuck the ticker, fuck his life, full fuckin' stop.

She's standin' over me, naggin', *he's* standin' over the two of us,
handicam perched, red light flashin', the record light, tense nervous
becomes migraine.

Carrots an' parsnips in the bin.
No, no, no I won't. No, I *won't* mind The Mouse.

Up the jacks.
Up, shower, freezin', cold enough to stop me heart – I love it –
dressed an' down.

Mousey.

There's The Mousey Lee, kitchen now, sittin' on an armchair,
watchin' me.
I say, I'm sorry, I'm busy (feel a bit guilty), I can't, man.

Mousey's five, he just started school.

Do you understand, The Mouse? I've business.
He does, he under… *Course* he understands, he's the brother, you
know?

He's the fuckin' brud, he is.

Out the front door, oul'one behind me, oul'fella behind her.
Trip on the step, I go on me snot.
Side of the road, I'm out on me snot, oul'fella's gigglin' like a
youngfella, he got me goodo, got me on video.
I'm down, change rollin' round, silver an' copper, fuck it, he's
comin' towards me, now, red light flashin'.
Up, go.
Come back, he says.
Fuck that.
Come back for your money.
He's laughin' hyena-style, she's not, she's mad. Mad in both, mad in
all senses.

Fuck the money.

Call up to Ollie's.

Ollie comes out, call up to Peaches'.

Not in the best of moods, Peaches, have to say. Big dirty puss on
him.
I wanna know why we're here, his oul'one's kitchen, but it's his skit
an' he wants to go out first.

Bein' teased righteous, I am, 'cos they know I'm a curious fucker.

Delayin' me, they are.
Delayin' me earlier, delayin' me now.

Tell me somethin' first.
We go out first.
A *morsel*, man. Tell me who the fuck we're after.

After someone, you're lookin' for them. Gonna give them a hidin',
hurt them, you're chasin' them.
Someone's after you, you're hunted.

Tells me we're after The Rookie Lee.

Nice one, says I. Thank you. I enjoy bein' after people. Thanks for
tellin' me. Specially… (*At last.*) Specially cunts like The Rookie Lee.
Handsome cunts. Specially cunts with the same last name as me.

Lee as in The Bruce.

So, we're after The Rookie righteous.
Why, Peaches?
After.
Goes for a piss before departure.

Don't flush, I says.

Out he goes, in comes Avalanche. A monster. Peaches' sister. Sixteen
stone, size forties on her chest, few tats.
She's askin' can she come with us.
Not tonight, sister.
She belches in Ollie's face, mid-sentence, Jaysus, doesn't even
know she does it. She's talkin' 'bout gettin' a *new* tat – A tat on me
gat, she says – Ollie's tryin' to keep his head averted, breathe
through his mouth, he doesn't get the bile stink off her breath.

Jacks flushes, in comes Peaches. Nice one, Peaches.
Bollox! he says.
Nice one for flushin' the jacks, now I've to flush it *again*…
Bollox! he says.
…waste *more* fuckin' water.
Aahhhh!

Flood from me cock. Piss. A nice one.
Footsteps on the stairs, someone behind me.
I know who.
A hand on me business, Jaysus, holdin' it.
I know who.
Aimin' it for me, shakin' the last drops.

Avalanche.

Had her once, have to say.

Starts pullin' me off bandy, wringin' me flute.

Fuck it, tell the truth, I had her three times and dug it to fuck. Far as she's concerned, sexual prowess, you know, fuckin' tech*nique* is measured in poundage an' far as… or stoneage… fuckin' *ton*nage, an' far as I'm concerned, she's right 'cos I've been there and I've measured and had that good time and *been*, you know, that fuckin' scales, 'cos I let *her* go on top.

Oh, yeah.

One of these days, she'll kill me an' I won't mind a fuckin' bit.

Whisperin' in me ear, now, askin' me to come into her bedroom.
No, I says. Shut up or your brud'll hear.
Slip into me room an' slip into me womb, she says.
Shut the fuck up, I says, take her hand off me flute.

Tells me she's gonna be in Flaherty's in town till late if I wanna hook up. Say I'll see. Say if I manage to slip away. Good enough for her. Off she goes, down the sittin' room, her grotesque arse bet into a pair of ski pants – not the white ones, thank Jaysus, see her piss-flaps an' everything – the *black* ones, down the stairs and out of me sight.

Back the kitchen go I.
Me an' Ollie, no Peaches, where's Peaches?

Have patience, The Howie. Peaches is ill, says Ollie. He's a bit weak.
Oh. What?!
He's not in the best, you'll find out why. Just let him go at his own pace.

More skulduggery.

Enter The Peaches, Youse right?
Enter The Peaches, *Vámonos*, he says, exit the boys, passin' the sittin' room on the way, Avalanche lettin' rip a nice one – a belch, like, not a fart – loud enough we hear it through the door.

Into the streets, Rookie Lee's gaff bound, *after* him, you see, not too far.
Knock, not in, no lights, where?
Knock, no answer, where?

Up the new shops.

Call them the new shops the last ten years, 'cos ten years ago, when they were built, that's what we called them *then*. Built in a circle, their backs face out to keep bandits at bay.

Rookie Lee sometimes hangs round Video Vendetta video rentals. He's not there, so we sit on the wall an' we smoke.

Might still turn up.

Two smokes. Three. Four for Ollie – God bless his lungs – still no sign.

Sittin' there, spot an oul'one goin' in the Vendetta, Stall it, boys, follow her in, this oul'one, arm in a cast, stitches in her face, name's Susan.

My oul'one knows her, calls her *Skip* Susan.

All right, Susan?
All right, she says.

Crashed her car into a wall, few weeks ago.

Gards an' firemen pulled up, car was wrecked, but she wasn't in it.

Men were sent to look around the area, see if she was wanderin' round, delirious or somethin'.

Was an hour 'fore someone thought about lookin' in the big yellow skip was behind the wall an' there she was all wrecked to bits, unconscious. Must've wandered off an' climbed in.

Shock, you know?

Poor woman had no insurance, nothin'. Damaged herself a bit financially too. She's off work, single, not too mobile.

D'you wanna babysit for me brud? I says. For The Mousey Lee?
Bit of charity, you see?
The oul'one an' oul'fella's goin' down The Fort, need someone to mind him.
Em… she says.
Your decision, man, I says, you want a penny or two.
Ring the gaff 'fore half eight, I says, writes the number on her cast.
You can watch your video there. Winks at her stylish.
Few bob in it for you.

Back the wall.
Peaches, Ollie an' me perched.

Peaches, Ollie says. Peaches. D'you wanna…? Bein' gentle with him, now, talkin' softly.

… D'you wanna tell The Howie your story, now?

Peaches tells us a story.

This is what I've been… Yep. At last. Story they were holdin' back from me.

At fuckin' last.

A funny story, but sad. Feel sorry for him, I do.

'Cos, see, he slept on Ollie's mat too. Only he went to his doctor, 'stead of just going to a chemist, gettin' the scabie cream. Went to the doctor, this Paki dirtbird, Coovadia and Coovadia gave him this *other* stuff, this black-and-white days cruel muck, burned the poor fucker up.

Gave him torments, it did.

Peaches Senior, the old man, found him lyin' on the jacks floor in his nip, bollox shaved to bits – Doctor Dirtbird told him to shave it – he's screamin' his head off, rolling around asking to be put down like a dog.

Like a fuckin' mungrel!

Shaved bollox is the funny bit. Torments of Hell's, I think's the sad bit. Askin' to be put down like a dog's just pathetic. His oul'fella filled the bath with freezin' water, put him in and left him there for an hour till his skin stopped burnin'.

The whole process left poor Peaches a bit fuckin' drained to say the least. Even to look at him now…

An' his oul'fella saw his shaved bollox.

This is the bit that depresses The Peaches the most.

It depresses me as well. Someone has to pay for The Peaches' sufferin' an' shame an' The Rookie, me namesake in Lee-ness, was the last person before him, he tells us, to sleep on that mat. One night after a party, he asked Ollie could he kip in his place, the neck, the dirty *neck* on him. Ollie couldn't say no, 'cos Ollie's bent an' The Rookie's sexy, thought he'd get him into the sack, give him a ridin', but straight Rookie, *hetero* Rookie, chose the mat.

An' if he was the last person to sleep on it, then he either caught the scabies *off* it or gave the scabies *to* it.

If he caught it, he would've said something, he would've warned us and he didn't.

He kept his fuckin' mouth shut.

Which means he infected it.

Which means he infected the boys.

Which means we're after him, the handsome cunt.

A green Hi-ace van pulls in the car park, Flann Dingle and Ginger Boy jump out.
Flann Dingle's fat and sweaty, Ginger Boy's short, ginger hair, red enough it could stop traffic.

All right, lads? We know them.
In they go, the Vendetta, new release/action adventure.

Out they come – John Woo, *Last Hurrah for Chivalry* – ask us we wanna come down the Mercy loop, mile an' a half, snakin' road, watch Ginger Boy surf on the roof.
Peaches doesn't, he's not in the best, wants to conserve his strength for batterin' The Rookie.
Well, d'you mind waitin', The Peaches? Course he doesn't.
You spot The Rookie, keep him talkin'.
Be back in a quick.

Ginger Boy gets on the roof an' shouts, Punch it, Flann Dingle! an' *vámonos!* down the Mercy.

We hang out the side door, lookin' up at Ginger Boy.

What d'youse think? asks Flann, all perspiry behind the wheel.
Very good, we say; our heads all windswept. *Very* good.

Funny thing's we're probably in a more dangerous position than Ginger Boy, two of us hangin' out the side door, swerve to avoid the one-two-three bus, tryin' to get an eyeful of the little fuck dicin' with a flattenin'.

Bottom of the loop, hang a U, Ginger Boy grabbin' the roof rack for dear life an' back up we go, this time sittin' in*side* the van, 'stead of hangin' out the side door, two thick monkeys. But we're thick monkeys for *gettin'* in the van in the *first* place, we're tryin' not to retch, 'cos sweaty Flann Dingle's the essence of stench. Stinkball like him.

Fuckin' dung beetle.

Deposit us, Flann Dingle. Deposit us up the new shops 'fore I'm sick. (Not to his face, now.) No wonder Ginger Boy travels on the roof. (To ourselves.) No wonder Peaches didn't come.

That a…? That a…? What's that? That The Rookie Lee? Where? Stop, stop the van. Stop the van, that's The Rookie at the bus stop, stop.

Flann Dingle stops. Doesn't stop, Ginger Boy's on top. Doesn't stop, slows down. Out the back window, sketch! whatsit, aaagh fuck! a bus, a bus, the one-two-three, he's gettin' on, he gets on, he's goin' to town. Into town, all the way, fuck! Peaches, standin' there beside the bus stop, watchin' him get on, doin' a dance, a shimmy-shuffle of indecision, left to right an' back, doesn't know whether to follow or wait, so waits.

Let us out, Flann Dingle, give us some fresh air (in our minds, now), let's away from your stench. (Not to his face.)

Deposited.

Alone. Green Hi-ace pissed off.

Waitin'.

Waitin', sayin' *Typical*. You leave a place for five fuckin' minutes, fuckin' *typical*.
Rookie on the bus, town bound.
But…
Typical.
But…
What?
Asked him where he was goin', didn't I? says The Peaches, pleased as punch.
Asked him his destination an' he told me Chopper's. Chopper Al's of Lime Street. Amen't I good? Amen't I clever?

He's *very* fuckin' clever.

Pass the time, Ollie starts goin' on about how a strong body odour can be attractive in a man. Not in Flann *Dingle*, say, but in *some* men. I don't wanna hear. Peaches is interested, asks lots of questions. Clarifies. In a better mood, now, 'cos he's a bead on The Rookie, we've a bearin'.

Wonderin' if Skip Susan rang the gaff.

One-two-three, nice one.

Boardin', boardin', down the back, seats facin', feet up.

Bus driver's fast, he wants his tea. Twenty K, twenty minutes flat. Nice.
Alightin', alightin', Dame Street deposited.

People meetin', standin' round, yappin', strollin', chinwaggin'. Out of the way, we've no time, we're on business. We're forgin' ahead, excuse us. But enjoy yourselves all the same. Don't mind us.

Shortest distance between two points is a straight line, but since we can't walk through walls an' buildin's, it's up Rowney Street – All right, Peaches? I am – right at the green, left an' right down Lime Street, Chopper Al's, What's the plan?

Ah, the plan.

Pretend we're his mates.

Pretend we're not after him. Sup a couple, nab him outside after so's not to rumble front of The Chopper.

Enjoy ourselves.

Yeah, Peaches?
Fine, he says.

And then we make our move.

In we go, so, spot The Rookie an' two birds, dolly birds, blackie and blondie – their *hair*, like – sit down, no invite, fuck that.

All right, The Rookie Lee? says I, All right, me namesake?

A good move, that. A social move.
You me an' The Bruce Lee.

Peaches orders. Up the bar, probably wants to steel himself a bit, his emotions before he sits down, faces the man caused all his pain an' shame.

Blackie an' blondie. Dolly, they are, think The Rookie Lee's the bee's knees, little does the bee's knees realise, he's not gettin' his hole tonight.

Neither blackie *nor* blondie he's gettin'.

A *hidin'*, he's gettin' for what he done to The Peaches.

Peaches returns. Pints for the boys, we socialise.

Startin' to feel a bit embarrassed, though.
Bit uptight in meself. Not talkin' much, leave it to Ollie.
Bein' a faggot, he doesn't get overwhelmed by the dollyness.

Chattin' away there, charmin' fucker *like* him.

Lack of success with birds, I have.
Have to say…
Hence, fuckin' whatser… Avalanche.

An' I keep catchin' the blondie one's eye, for fuck's sake.
Every time I look at her – shite! – she looks at me the exact same time.

Probably thinks I'm after her.
(The romantic sense, like, not the other… the batterin'.)

Look at her again, she catches me eye again.

Look at her again an'… Fuckin' *hell!*

Look to me left an' The Rookie's doin' somethin' similar, 'cept he's wired, observant, head cocked, cuttin' his eyes me direction. Look and his eyes twitch away.

D'youse want another pint? he asks us.
Are you buyin'?
No, he says, but I'm goin' up.
We give him money, he goes up.

Ollie goes the jacks.

Me, Peaches, blondie and darkie, all a-circle.

I'm quiet, feel shy without Ollie's gab.

Dollies start talkin' among themselves. Good.

Go to say somethin' to Peaches, but he's lookin' towards the bar.
Lookin' up at The Rookie.

Not lookin', no.

Starin'.

Rememberin' the shame, his oul'fella, I can see it, the scabies' pain.

Dollies stop talkin', go quiet.
Dollies can see it too, can sense it.

Rookie at the bar.

Peaches watchin', sneerin', givin' him the evil eye.

Rookie with the fidgets, itchy, tryin' not to scratch front of the dollies.

All a-quick, Peaches can't hold it in any more, explodes, lunges, blindsides The Rookie. I stand up. Rookie lands against the bar, Peaches lunges again, tries to sandbag him; fast an' hard, but sloppy. Rookie dodges, picks a pint off the bar, fucks it at us, dives over a table, but it's only a ha'penny dive an' he lands on top. Booze pell-mell, scrambles off, beelines for the door, he's out. But we're already runnin' across the table he dove across, then out the door, spot him, up the street, after him like The Christie; like The fuckin' Linford, flutes bouncin' around heavy an' all, sprintin' righteous, sprintin' like the Dickens, gainin'. We're gainin' goodo, gainin' ground, gettin' closer, movin', movin'. Down a lane he goes, best place to get him – quiet, solitary – I make a final burst, power forward, me lungs burn, me muscles boil, I pound ahead like a thoroughbred, snortin' an' whinnyin'.

I dive.

Very smoothly. Nothin' ha'penny about *my* dive.
I'm like Tarzan.

I dive.

Like the fuckin' *Weissmuller*, I am.

I dive, I sail, I take him down.
I take down my prey like a feral hunter and hold him tight as Peaches runs up, huffy and puffy, three men standin', three hearts poundin' loud, three lungs, pairs of lungs, suckin' louder, suckin' hard.

Then softer, then calmer, then quieter.

Then quiet.

Peaches lays in.

Body shots, head shots, not too hard, have to say, gently bruisin' the handsome cunt's ribs. Split lip, good one, swollen eye swellin' up. The Rookie tries to defend himself. He's feeble. I hold his arms anyway.
I hold his arms, but I'm a bit put off. Not really into it. Must be all that runnin', me stomach's queasy.

Peaches finishes off with a right-left combo to the mush, right hook to the darby.

Weak Rookie, battered Rookie drops, exhausted, Peaches breathin'
hard again.
Rookie's not too hurt, drops from the run, not the hidin'. Peaches is
weak, not much weight, but he's satisfied.
We got him.

Satisfied?
Yeah.
Back to Chopper's?
Let's go.

Ollie's standin' outside, forlorn, smokin'. Chopper Al fucked him
out after the hassle, after the fucked pints an' the Weissmullers
'cross tables. Pissed off he missed all the action, pissed we went
when he was havin' a shite, but what can we do?

Peaches is on a high, but. Vengeance exacted, look at him, bouncin'
up the street like a baby. Wants to go home, drop down The Fort,
drink there so's he can just *roll* home, 'stead of havin' to taxi or bus it.
Ollie concurs, tells Peaches it's a good deduction.

I concur with that deduction, he says.

But *I* don't concur. Don't concur a-tall.
For one, the oul'one an' oul'fella's in The Fort.
For two, I'm feelin' horny. Me mickey's a bit sensitive and I'm
thinkin' 'bout Peaches' sister, Avalanche down Flaherty's.

Course I don't say this, I say See youse tomorrow, boys, a job well
done an' off they go an' off *I* go.

Strollin' nice, lookin' forward, hopin' she's still down Flaherty's,
Flann Dingle an' Ginger Boy swing past, green Hi-ace with the
slidin' door open.
Shout over, Are you goin' home? Would you like a jaunt?
I wouldn't, says I. I'll stall it here, many thanks.

Off they go.
Mellow. No toolin'. Cruisin'.
It's that kind of night.

Continue me stroll.

Stop at a phone box, ring home.
Two rings, three, fou... almost four, pick up, Hello?
It's Susan, Skip Susan, she took me up, went over, good one.
Chat with her a minute, everything all right?
He's a dote, she says, your brud, The Mousey Lee.

He is, I say. Happy, now.
Duty done, oul'one appeased.

Hang up, I continue me stroll, there's footsteps behind me, runnin',
tryin' to catch up, fuck's that? Spin round quicko, Jaysus, it's
blondie. Blondie from Chopper Al's. Catches up, says her mate's
gone home, am I goin' on? she says. I say I am.

Are you comin'?

Her nostril opens a bit.
I am, she says.

Jesus Christ!

This kinda thing doesn't happen very often, now.
Neither the invitation, *nor* the nostril.

Name's Bernie, she tells me. Sexier than Av, she gives me a horn.
Name's The Howie Lee, I say.
I've a horn 'cos I've a chance, an invitation for you know what.
Unsaid at the time, but said. Implied. I can see it.

Implied with a flared nostril.

An' I know it's me machoness she's attracted to.
Me dangerousness.

Didn't find her sexy in the pub, 'cos I'd no chance. Find her sexy
now.

Stroll on lustful, me mickey followin' the beck of a nostril that
widens an' says Let's.

Let's.

Did youse get The Rookie Lee? she asks me.
I say, We did. But got him gentle.
Says she'd like to've watched, 'cos she likes watchin' blokes
scrappin'.

A-ha!

Were youse after him over the fishes? she says.
The fishes?
He said someone was after him over fishes.
Wasn't fuckin' *us*, I say. Is that why he was so nervous?
I don't know, she says, an' that's that.

That's all the interest she shows.

Must be one of them cold-blooded dollies.

She links me arm an' we stroll on romantic.

Are you goin' to Dave McGee's bash tomorrow night? she says.

Fuckin' Dave McGee.

Rich Dave McGee went away, made his fortune, in the nuts-an'-
bolts-makin' business, came back, built a huge gaff down Canal
Way, just at the edge of the mountain, there.
Eleven months of the year, he travels, one, comes home, throws a
big, big bash for the whole town.
One an' all's invited.
One an' all goes.

I says, Are *you* goin'?
She says she is.
Well, then, I says, maybe *I* will, too.

An' I get the feelin' she wants me to.

We go to Reagan's.
Good. Once it's not Flaherty's.
Pint, a white-wine spritzer, an' Bernie – have to remember her name
– she's lookin' a bit shitfaced, now, shitfaced but sexy, a bit touchy,
bit loosey-goosey.
Touchin' me leg, hand, thigh.
Talkin' close, sweet breath, bit boozy.

Jesus, hand on me leg, she's talkin' 'bout her brother she lives with,
just the two of them, brother she takes care of 'cos he's sick. Askin'
me do I understand? Brother she's looked after for years, works in
her local Spar to provide for him.

Tell her that's respectable.

'Cos there's no one else, she's responsible.

Tell her that's admirable.

An' she starts to go on...

Tells me she's savin' to put him in a special school for special
people that he'll only get out of twice a month so she can live her
own life and it's expensive and she works hard to save and she
deserves a night out.

Bit resentful, now, must say. Resentful of her brud.

I says, Of *course* you deserve it.

She's on the tear tonight an' she's *goin'* to Dave McGee's party tomorrow an' that's all there is *to* it.

Bit fuckin' bitter.

You're right, I says.
That's all there is to it, she says.
You're fuckin' right.

An' on she goes…

There's a film John Wayne was in…

Was a Western…

No.

An' on she goes anyway, an' who gives a fuck?
An' I'm gettin' a pain in me hole.
Less loosey, now, have to say, feelin' a bit less goosey, 'cos I can't get a word in edgeways.

Another pint, another spritzer.
An' on she goes.

An' two more.

An' on she goes.

Into the jacks, *Jesus*!
Respite an' a heavy dribble.

Someone behind me, *fuck*…in' hell, a soft warm belch, a hand on me flute. I dry up, spin round, it's not a bloke, thank Christ.

Not a bloke, but The Av.
Av in the gents, doin' that trick again, grabbin' me business, The fuck did *you* come out of?

We ridin' tonight?
I'm with someone.
I saw her, she says, she's a pig.

I turn back, resume me interrupted stream of yellow.
Finish, shake, Av takes me aside.
If I don't fuck her tonight, she'll tell Peaches I fucked her before.
She's horny for me, she's jealous of Bernie; Bernie's locks, looks, Bernie's figure, fuck.

I'll be in Flaherty's, she says an' she's gone.

So fuckin' disappointed!

Go out, tell Blondie, tell Bernie, Sorry, man, have to go. Have
business. Have to meet me mates, I says.
But, c'mere, I says, can I have your number? Give you a shout?
You're not that good lookin', she says. Crushes me.
But I'm a good goer, I says.
You're not the *only* man, you know.
Look at her eyes. Bloodshot, unfocused, she's pissed.
… I'm scopin' this fuckin' bar while you're in the jacks, she says,
got the attention of *many* a horny fellow. *Many* a hunk I've the
attention of, now go away so's I can click, thank you very much.
So, I go, hangin' me head, an' 'fore I reach the door, I hear a thunk.
A loud thunk. Loud enough I turn an' her head's on the bar, her eyes
closed, bit of blood, there, small trickle.

Looks like she cut herself.

Barman lifts his eyebrows at me as if to say, She with you?
Shrug me shoulders as if to say, You must be fuckin' jokin'.

Fuck her. She should be at home anyway.

Flaherty's.

A dirty dive. Av's type of place.
Place you can fuck in the jacks easy an' there she is at the bar, arse
enough for three stools, she's wearin' – good Jesus – the white ski
pants, the see-through ones. I wanna do it now, get it over with, 'cos
I'm not in the mood any more. Could've had somethin' good, 'stead
of *this*.

Avalanche wants to have a pint first.

Fine, fine, we'll *have* a fuckin' pint.
But not said like that, now, said nice.

Drink our pints, I buy a snack bar an' munch it.

Smoochy music's playin', small dance floor, you can dance.
Av pulls me up, we dance, we waddle, only ones up.
Lots of wind in the Av tonight, rumblin's inside, belches over me
shoulder.
A dance, a shift. Open-mouth splashers, I hold her close. Close so's I
can feel the belch in her chest risin', can stop kissin' before it
reaches her mouth.

Dancin' drunk, fuck, *too* drunk, trip over each other's feet, we go down.
Ninnies over diddies, we're all a-crumple, people lookin', laughin', a sight we must be.

I'm gone off, tell her I'm goin' home.
Get up, help her up, tell her I'm tired. I've a migraine, forgive me, tell her I don't feel too well. *Something.*

People still lookin', few still laughin'.

Don't know what's wrong with me tonight.
Feel strange in meself.
Feel like I'm goin' through some kind of change.

Want to go home.

She's upset, fuck her.
She feels unwanted, unloved, sorry *'bout* you. Sorry *'bout* you, man, I've to go.
Goin' home, don't *want* a ride.
Couldn't get it up if I did.

When it suits you, she says, she shouts, when it suits you, that it?
Shoutin' at me, hysterical, I'm embarrassed doublo now, we're like a real-live couple havin' a tiff.

As if.

Wanna turn to everyone in the bar an' say, Me an' her. As fuckin' if, huh?

Dirty fat cunt like her.

An' on she goes, variations on when it suits you and storms out, waddles up the street – Jesus, those ski pants – lurchin' one side of the path to the other.

I get the one-two-three. Another driver wants his tea baddo, fifteen minutes home.

Get home, I get in the door.
Get in the door, the oul'one's there, cryin'.

What's wrong with you, the oul'one?
Takes a while to answer, looks at me, snivels, says I'm a bastard 'cos I wouldn't babysit. All I fucking need, I want peace.
Bastard 'cos I wouldn't babysit, 'cos Skip Susan had to babysit.

Susan babysat, Susan fell asleep.

Mousey went out, let himself out, saw money at the edge of the road.

Oh, no.

Saw money, wanted it. Coins.

Oh, no… Somethin's…

Silver an' copper.

Somethin's fuckin' comin'.

Night-shift Sam 'cross the road, backin' his truck out, felt a bump. D'you understand?

You little hump, she calls me.

Felt a bump, stopped, came round, saw Mousey there, The little Mousey Lee, lyin' there, parts… parts of him crushed, you could see it. Dyin'.

You humpy cunt, she calls me.

Mousey, money still in his hand, she says. Know what he said?

Spangly glitter shit's runnin' down her face.

How much is that? he said. Held the money out, his little body broken to fuckin' bits, asked, How much is that?

Then he dropped the money 'cos he was crushed.

Crushed an' dead.

Your brother's dead, 'cos you wouldn't babysit, because you wouldn't do what you were told.

That can't be… Hang on…

'Cos you wouldn't do what you were told, she says.

That can't be right.

It's your fuckin' fault.

Shoutin' brings the oul'fella down, handicam at the ready. I dodge by him, push him aside, back out the front door, goin' on me snot the exact same spot I did earlier, expect laughs an' get fuck-all.

Up straight away, get up an' move.

Oul'one an' oul'fella at the front door, but not laughin'.
Not laughin' this time.

Cryin'.

Don't look back.

It's your fuckin' fault.

It's your fuckin' fault.

Keep movin'. Get away. Get away from that house, that street.

It's your fuckin' fault.

The fuck can it be my fault?

PART TWO

The Rookie Lee

Oul'fella left us for this tramp, this ten-years younger hooer could slicken up better than the oul'one.

Moved in with her treated her as his ever-lovin', neglected me – the fuck – me sisters. The oul'one hit it hard then, whiskey an' vodka.

Thought it made him virile, he did, such a stud, but I showed him what a *real* stud is.

Down The Fort one night, met the tramp, bought her a drink. Chatted, flattered, flirted, lured, seduced, *fucked* this dirty Jezebel, stole the oul'fella from us.

Handsome bastard, I am. Bit attractive to the dollies, they're into me. Find them easy to pick up, easy to get. Break hearts an' hymens, I do.

Took her home the flat that night, ploughed her rapid, sent her away without her ninnies.

Followin' day, called up the oul'fella.

All right, son? he says. These are your bird's, da, says I, holds out the dirty ninnies. Left them in the flat last night when we were doin' it. Doin' what? says he. Doin' lodgy-bodgy, says I. Take a sniff. She was wet.

Haven't seen him in about twenty months, now.

I call up early.

Desperate.

Tramp answers. The oul'fella there? I say. Go away, she says. Da! I shouts.

Out he comes, lookin' haggard. What do you want? Money.

Do I look like I've money? he says, an' he doesn't. He looks like a knacker.
How much are you lookin' for?
Five hundred quid, says I.
(*Snorts*.) Goes like that. (*Snorts*.) Now fuck off, he says, shuts the door on me.

Walkin' away, the door opens again.

How's your oul'one?
She's good, I say. She's still doin' the courses.
Good, he says.
Better than you, you cocksucker.

Door slams, opens a*gain*.

The Rookie.
What?!!
Have you started seein' them pitbulls yet? he says.

Slams the door a final time.

When I was young, the oul'fella told me 'bout the ancient Mayan Indians.
Mayans believed God of Death shows himself to a man many times before takin' him, like, before he dies.

One man might keep seein' a black panther if he lives in the jungle, the same black panther.

Desert it might be a vulture or a particular camel or somethin'.

Vision here might be a… say a crow or a pitbull terrier.

So, see, when he said Have you started seein' them pitbulls yet, it meant, May you be dead soon, which is what I think of him too, 'cept I desperately need some fuckin' money.

Down The Fort for fortification, I'm in the jacks, checkin' me wounds.

Black eye, split lip, scrapes, not too bad, that Peaches is a bit weak.

Him an' The Howie Lee, me namesake, givin' me the bates over who knows what?
Sort of thing can go on, *does* go on.
One minute, people's your buds, next, they're after you, some reason you don't know. Can happen, happens, goes on.

Probably think they got me baddo, the dirtbirds.

Didn't get me baddo a-tall, but.
Got me all right.
Got me such a way I've still me faculties.

Scared, but.

Last night was nothin' to what tonight might be.

Fuckin' itchin's gettin' bad. Might have to go to Coovadia soon, tell
me I've some kind of STD or somethin', laugh in me face.

It travels, it does. Was in me belly, now it's down between me leg
an' me sack. Me bollox, itches the good thing.

Wash me hands an' go back in the pub.

Bushmills an' ice, please, John. Good bloke. Sit in the corner, I'll
bring it over. I do and he does, double for a single, pricewise, 'cos of
me injuries, see, 'cos he feels for me, gives me empathy.

I sit.
I sit and I sip.

I think.
I scratch a bit.

A woman comes in the pub, arm in a cast, all writin' on it, Jaysus,
stitches in her face, carryin' messages. Plonks at the bar, orders a gin
an' tonic.

Think about Ladyboy.

Some people say when he was born, his oul' dear threw away the
body an' raised the afterbirth.

Some say he's called Ladyboy 'cos of an ingrown flute.

Was a Frenchman, Pierre, Ladyboy taught him one sentence, Kick
me in the nuts, told him it meant Where's the toilet? an' people bein'
what they are...

Pierre confronted Ladyboy over it, pointed at him like that.

Pointed. Jabbed.

As Ladyboy opened wide, just before he took these two fingers off at
the knuckles, Pierre swore he saw three sets of teeth instead of one.

Like a shark.

People fear The Ladyboy.

Rich Dave McGee an' Ladyboy're close enough, they buy each
other gifts. Last year, Dave's visit home, he got Ladyboy bettas.
A red betta an' a blue betta.

Last week, I bumped into Ladyboy in the street, few lads crouched
round a clear bucket of bettas, these little fish that's supposed to
fight, supposed to knock each other's blocks off.

Ladyboy tells us the fishes're from Siam, which is Thailand an' they
fight them like cockfightin'.

He's tryin' to get them to fight stylish, so's he can put on a show for
McGee at his annual bash down Canal Way, the edge of the
mountain, way of respect, a show of thanks.

Bettas, they're called, says Ladyboy. Chink fightin' fish.
Chink meanin' Oriental.

But Ladyboy's gettin' pissed off, the fish won't fight.
Prods them with a wooden spoon, tryin' to agitate them, but they're
lazy little fucks, one of them's a big stringy poo hangin' out its hole,
wants to be left in peace.

Watchin' Ladyboy an' his wooden spoon.
Got this itch, don't know where it came from.
Down in me shoe, under me foot, got me finger stuck in there,
Ladyboy prods the red fish, down the side, there, I'm standin' on one
foot, hoppin' a bit, balancin', prods it again, I scratch hardo, itchin's
intense, I get bumped.

Slightly.

Softly.

But hard enough I topple over fuckways, hit the bucket and the
bettas bolt. Fishes flop in the grass, Ladyboy's livid, everyone
panics, Fuck're the fishes? stompin' around, the fishes're fucked,
man, crushed underfoot.

Flat.

Dead.

Ladyboy looks at me.

Tells me if I don't want me kneecaps gone, seven hundred quid, I'm
to pay him for his bettas. For new ones. 'Cos that's how much they
cot. Bring it to Dave McGee's, to his party, so Dave can meet the
fuckhead who crushed his gift to his good friend, The Ladyboy.

Scared, 'cos tonight's the night, sip of me double, burney down, nerve-tampin' taste, tonight's the night, this party.

Be there.

Be there or I will shoot you in the kneecaps an' they will be gone. An' you will not be able to walk properly for all the days.

Be there with the money.

I've gone to everyone I know. I've borrowed and wheedled all I can, everyone tells me to fuck off. Oul'fella was me last chance.

I've no mates.
No mates, I've only birds I shagged.
Went to all the birds I shagged, birds think I'm it. Got two hundred quid.

Need five hundred more.

Think.
Think.
Take a sip.
Think.

I don't know what to do.

Maybe I deserve what I get for... No, for nothin', I didn't, I never did anything that bad. I never hurt anyone.
Maybe a couple of dollies.
Emotionally.
Unintentionally.

Sup of whiskey, big sup, brainstorm.
Brainstorm, brainstorm, think.

Woman at the bar orders another gee an' tee, it's only two minutes after the first, perched there hunky, her plastic Spar bags around the stool.

She turns to me, says, 'cos I'm the only one else in the bar, says, Me painkillers...
Eh... Sorry?
Me painkillers, she says. They make me drowsy.
Do they? I says.
Make me sleepy, she says, the fuckin'nutcase, all broken up. Betcha her husband battered her or somethin', told her, Get out there. Get the fuckin' shoppin'. Get me some grub to put in me...

Idea.
A-ha.
Idea.

Up an' out. Up an' out of there.
Off.
Off to Ashbrook.

I'm off to Ashbrook, see this dolly I met last night, dolly who's into me. She's money, she's savin', if I can charm the ninnies off her, then borrow the *money* off her. In between, maybe knock the *arse* off her...

I know she lives in Ashbrook but I don't know where.
Know she works checkout in a Spar, see that woman's shoppin' bag reminded me.
Know she goes home for her lunch, know she's no car.
Deduce she walks.
Deduce she works where she lives.
Gonna investigate. Find a Spar in Ashbrook, find her there.

Headin' through The Close, spot The Howie Lee, Peaches' mate 'cross the green, sittin' on a bench, smokin'.

Howie that held me for a batterin'.

He spots me, stands up, he shouts.
I turn.
He calls me name.
I'm gone.
I'm gone up The Limekiln Lane.

Go the long way, take me twice as long, now, balls! Get there before one anyway.
Slow down, now, I'm safe.

Relax.

Left him for dust, I did.

Look for, can't find, *find* it. Find the Spar, hope me deduction's right, inside, blonde-haired dolly bird – Next please – *is* right.

Fuck she get the big plaster on her head?

Sidle up, say Hello. D'you wanna meet?
Lunch, she says.
Your place?

Yes, she says. 'Cos she's *into* me, see.

Fifteen minutes' wait, compare Baxters soup to Campbell's,
pricewise, healthwise, kills time.
Baxters's best, it's not condensed.

Let's go, we go, her gaff.
Hop on her. Me brother, she says, he's in school.
So?
He comes home for lunch.
Oh. Kiss her mouth, we'll tell him we're wrestlin' or somethin'.
Kiss her tongue, we'll tell him we're playin' the *Gladiators*.

Ninnies off, get her nippy.
She keeps kissin' me wounds. They turn her on to bits.

Lodgy-bodgy hard. Come quick, a post-coital caress, she deserves it,
we dress.

Microwave lasagne, tasty, come to the point.

Lend me money.

Why?
I owe it.
What makes you think I have it?

Best of banter, back an' forth, finish grub, nam, nam, lully, liked it.

That money you said you were savin' for your brother's school. His
special school. Whatsit, a month's?
Six, she says.
Six months' tuition. Lend me the money an' I will tutor him meself.
I will teach him, not only Peter an' Jane an' Spot the Dog, but I will
teach him the facts of life. I will teach him the manly things of how
to survive in a world of pain, made doubly worse 'cos he's slow.

You know nothing of manly things, she says, you know nothin' 'cos
you run away from people in pubs.

Sore point, me lack of manliness, so it slips out.
Cunt.
Get out, she says.
Thanks for the lodgy.
… An' fuck you, she says.
Not too well handled, that. Bit rubbish.
See, I shouldn't've rode her yet. The ride should've been the carrot I
dangled.

But I'm not leavin' yet. Stand me ground, I'm gonna persuade.

Call her a cunt again.
Get out!
Cunt! (Can't help it.)
Out! she says.

Key in the door, bollox, the brother.

Calm it, quiet, don't wanna scare the fucker, might give him the idea I'm dangerous.

Steps into the room, he's six foot tall, built like a human white puddin', looks inbred.

I wanna tousle his hair, some reason.

Opens his mouth, he can't talk too well. Figures, 'cos of his face, his moon face, he's a, whatchacall, which?
Down syndrome, she says.
The poor fucker, I say. Not tryin' to... Well. Yeah. *Tryin'* to be a funny cunt.

Get him, she says.

Out of the blue, he roundhouses me in the face, rings me ears baddo, knocks me into the wall. Stagger round, tryin' to get me sea legs, another roundhouse, awkward as fuck, like a dolly's dig, but powerful, much more powerful than The Peaches' was, knocks me down, it does. I hear her through the din in me ears, the ringin'.

That's one thing I do not stand for, she says. I do not stand people givin' my brother the mock.

I can't believe this. Second time I've got the bates in two days an' what've I to look forward to tonight?
Another one.
Another, probably the worst.
Probably the worst batin' ever.

Me stereo! she squeaks, I'm tumblin' over it, landin' in a hape.

Have to do somethin', now, I'm thinkin', get out the door, *somethin'*. C'mon, now, The Rookie. Shake me head like in the funnies, the ringin' lessens, head clears a bit.
But, he's blockin' the door.
He's blockin' the door an' he's purple.
Only one way out, has to be done. One way, the only way.

Better than facin' the white-puddin' boy, now gone purple.

Look round, spot the stereo.

Nobody gives my brother the mock, she says.

Pick up the stereo, *Me stereo!!!!* fuck it through the window.

Follow it through, dive. Dive. Dive.
Then tuck.
Tuck, roll, I hit the deck, glass in me back and follow through to me feet. Nicely judged, that, now run.

Front of me, bollox.

Front of me, The Howie. The Howie Lee, blockin' me escape.

Turn back, run into the puddin' boy, he gets me in a neck-grab, squeezes. Air's trapped, brain's cut off from oxygen an' blood, feel meself gettin' dizzy. See your one lookin' at me through the window, cryin', me stereo! Over an' over. Me stereo! Feel me consciousness, slippin'… slippin'… slippin'…

Bam! Then, I'm dropped.
All a sudden, dropped, coughin' up gook, me throatpipe's all throttled.

Bam! Bam! I look up, The Howie's layin' into the puddin' boy, plantin' punch after punch on his stomach an' ribs, poundin' double-quick, flurrious furious combos, weakens the middle area, starts throwin' head shots, snappin' it back like that. Bam! Bam! Snap back. Bam! Down to the ribs, I hear a crack, *Jaysus*, he's a goer. White-puddin' boy may as well be on Mars, he's grabbin', graspin' at the air, while The Howie bobs an' ducks, hooks, jabs an' chops, chops, chops the jolly giant down.

No problem to him a-tall.

Easy as pie.

Puddin' boy sits in the grass all stunned, The Howie bends over him, gives his hair a little tousle, he starts whingein', callin' his ma, the sis comes out – only he's callin' the *sis* ma – and hugs him, holds him.

The *sis* is ma.

Ah, here, now.

Too ashamed of her son to call him son, calls him brud, did you ever hear the fuckin' like?!

You all right? he asks me, The Howie.

I can't answer, 'cos now *he's* tears tumblin' down his face as well, makin' hic-hic noises, sobbin'.

The fuck's everyone cryin' for?

You all right? he says.
Are *you?* I say.
Asks me what the fuck I'm talkin' about.

Headin' off a short-cut back road, wee-wah, wee-wah, coppers?
Coppers for us? Coppers for the scrap? The smashed window?
Comin' to nab us?
Wee-wah, closer.

In a bush, this bush, down. Crouch an' observe. The Howie's still sobbin'.
Corner in eyeshot, wee-wah's closer.

Any second.

Any second.

Over the bushes linin' the road, down at the turn, I see somethin' movin', somethin' red, hoverin' along the tops, comin' towards the bend.

Whatsit? Whatsit? Reveal yourself.

An' it's Flann Dingle's van, Ginger Boy on top, doin' sixty, tools past fasto, kicks up dust in our faces, followed by Gardamobile, wee-wah, hot, hot, hot pursuit, copper intent on capture.

Stop at the primary school, we perch on the steps, he stops sobbin', starts talkin', he's sorry. Wants to help me. Won't tell me why. Just does.

Feel sorry for the bloke.
Says he wants to make up to me what he done to me.
Say he already has.
Says he hears I'm in trouble.
Who told you?
A birdie.
A birdie?
A dirty birdie, that cunt set the puddin' boy on you told me last night.

Don't be angry, he says. I didn't actually *do* anything with her.

All contrite, like, as if I could do anything 'bout it anyway.

Tell me your woes, he says. Tell me your woes 'bout the fishes an' I will help you.
You know about the fishes? I says.
I believe there's fishes involved, he says.

So, I tell him me woes an' he helps me.

He helps me a way I don't understand.

Me itchin's bad, man, me ribs hurt, I can feel me eye, me bruised eye throbbin' from where I was battered, but feel me itchin' worse, it's another sort of pain.

Asks me why I'm itchin'. Tell him I don't know why, but I'm dyin' scratchin'. Asks me what do I know about the scabies?

Who're they? I says.

Come with me, he says.

Takes me to the chemist's, buys me a gift, some ointment. Tells me to put it all over me body, bollox, hole an' all , leave it for a day. Don't wash an' it won't itch any more.

How do you know? I say.
'Cos I do, he says.

It's all a bit fuckin' mysterious.

Saves me bacon, cures me ills, astounds me.

I go all introspective an' pond'rous for a minute.

I will help you with The Ladyboy, he says. Out of the blue.
I will help you with The dirtbird Ladyboy.

Like he read me fuckin' mind.

Like a fuckin'… a fortune-teller.

Then he reaches out an' touches me bruised eye. Gently. Gently. Not gay, like, just… And then he puts his hand once through me hair, like that, starin' at me like he's thinkin' 'bout somethin' else.

Home, shower, ointment, all over, even crevices. It stinks. I won't smell too attractive at the party tonight. Doesn't matter. I'll be there on business.
Comb me hair carefully, all the same. Dress neat, dress nice, look in the mirror long.

Habits die hard, I'm stylish.

Me wounds.
Startin' to stop hurtin'. Stop hurtin' baddo, start lookin' goodo. Look
like a warrior, I do.
All right, there, love? I say, practisin'. Habits die hard.
All right there, love?

Me voice trembles like a pansy's.

Meet down The Fort. Whiskeys, high stools, The Howie leans
forward, gives me a good sniff, nods, says, Good man.

I tells him I'm still itchy. He says, Patience, man, it doesn't happen
straight away.

I ask him how we're gonna deal with The Ladyboy? Doesn't tell me.

Won't.

Tells me a story instead.

Huddle.
Huddle in.
Huddle an' hark.

Had to collect his little brud, name's Mousey from playschool one
day. Homeward, had to take him by the primary school. Stopped for
a gander, kids on their breaks, horsin' in the yard.

Next year, you'll be in there, he tells the brud.
Will I? says the brud.
You will, says The Howie.

Youngfella strolls over the gate, youngfella, seven or eight. Hello,
says The Howie. Youngfella spits a gozzy on the brud, no reason,
greener in his face, runs away back into the yard.

Three o'clock, hometime, The Howie stalks the school, follows the
youngfella home. Youngfella goes in, has his dinner, comes out to
play. Meantime, The Howie's after collectin' the brud, The Mouse,
bringin' him back up. Goes over the youngfella, throws him on the
ground an' gives him a clatter, holds him there by the ears. Tells The
Mouse to get the biggest, biliest, snottiest fuckin' gozzy he can an'
drop it into the youngfella's face.

The Mouse does.

Sticky green thing.

Youngfella doesn't like it a-tall.

Why tell me this? I says.
Cos… Puts his fingers up, two pints, like that, two pints, two
whiskeys, 'cos I wanted to tell you about me an' The Mouse.
Nice one, says I. Nice one.
Pints an' shorts on the bar.
To The Mouse, says The Howie, pint in the air.
Nice one, says I. Hoist mine high.

Road to rich McGee's.

Sun's goin' down, a warm night comin' on, see Flann Dingle an'
Ginger Boy pass by perpendicular, slowly now, not followed, Ginger
Boy sittin' on the roof.

Somethin' sparks in me head.
Somethin' to do with Flann Dingle an' Ginger Boy.
Sparks but doesn't ignite.

It'll come to me, some stage.

Gettin' the butterflies, now. Startin' to taste pennies an' twopences,
the unknown, The Howie Lee versus Ladyboy, me in the middle.
Have to trust him things'll be okay.

Hard to trust when I'm brickin', but then, he saved me today, saved
me bacon.
An' he knew things, knew how to stop me itchin'.
Even now it's less.

So I kind of believe in him.

Hear the music 'fore we see the gaff. Two gaffs made into one,
detached, people millin' outside, lights, coloured lights out the
window, laughin', happy.

Taste of copper in me mouth gets stronger, the adrenaline.

Halitosis in the air. Feel it more than smell it.
Howie wrinkles his nose.
He feels it too.

An' it dawns on me.
Flann Dingle. Flann Dingle, the Hi-ace an' The Ginger Boy.
The Mayans.
Been seein' them all day, too much, too many times.
Thinkin' 'bout death comin', form of a green Hi-ace.

Comin' to get me.

Approach.

Approach an' in, party business, masses of cunts lookin' dandy.

Who's that? That's not… I think it is. I think it's Matt. Matt Dillon, the actor. Dave McGee must be mates with the stars an' all, now, Matt in his long black coat, smokin' a fat cigar like the superstar he isn't, hasn't hacked it decent in years, fuckin' dollies millin' round him.

Bump into The Chopper Al.

Hi, Chopper Al, says The Howie, sounds like he's sayin' the High Chapperal.

Last I saw of *you*, you were after *him*, Chopper says to The Howie. Points at me.
We're the buds now, says The Howie. Did you see The Ladyboy? Why? says the Chopper.

'Cos now I'm after *him*.

Chopper Al says nothin'.

Chopper Al goes white, backs off, disappears.

An' like that, so does me fear.

In, around, no sign of The Ladyboy, one room, another, no sign, stairs, up them.

Spot Matt down in the hallway, Matt, I shouts. Matt.
He looks up an' I have to say it.
You've lost it, man.
What's that, buddy? Big grin on his puss.
Give it up, man, I says. It's no use.
Brown-sauce face, he knows *exactly* what I'm talkin' 'bout.

Matt Dillon, the brown-sauce man.

Up the stairs, check three rooms, into a fourth, bare, wooden floorboards, spacious.
An' who's there only The Ladyboy. Ladyboy an' Dave McGee, best of mates, heads close, whisperin', couple of conspirin' cunts.

A-hem.

That's The Howie.

A-hem.

Clearin' his throat loud, Ladyboy looks at me an' me fear comes back quadruplo.
All right, bud? he says. Have you got me money for me dearly departed, for me fightin' bettas?

Don't know what to say.

… Or do I have to wreck your knees, turn you into a gammy boy?

Fuck do I say?

Well…?

I fart.
A hot one.
Deep an' loooud.
Just comes out with the fear, me hole's instinct to void itself.

Everyone goes quiet. The smell wafts across the room. It's like we're waitin' till it reaches The Ladyboy's nostrils.

They quiver.
Once. Twice.

So it's like that? he says.

Mustn't've liked it.

I'm sorry to hear you take that attitude.

All right, Ladyboy?

The Howie.

All right, Ladyboy?

An' The Ladyboy's lookin' at The Howie now an his eyes're squintin' 'cos The Howie's here an' The Howie has a bit of a rep himself.

Howie's rep is, an' everyone knows this, he's a goer goes all the way.

Key in the door, The Howie turns, locks it, puts it in his pocket, turns back to The Ladyboy.

An' then his fists clench.
An' his veins knot.
An' he rocks on his heels.

Back… an' forth. Back… an' forth. Back… an' forth.

An' Ladyboy takes off his coat, folds it on the windowsill.

An' no one says anything 'cos nothin' *needs* to be said.

An' back... an' forth The Howie rocks.

Dave McGee backs to the wall.

I back to the other wall.

An' The Ladyboy bends his knees, his body goes all springy.

There's ladies an' gents, I can hear them, arriving outside the door.
The Chopper Al's been talkin', spreadin' the ska.

The Howie Lee versus The Ladyboy an' no one'll see it.
No one 'cept me an' Dave McGee.

Me bowels an' bladder feel all open inside me.

An' all becomes quiet as they look at each other intense an' hungry,
their jaws all knotted up; patient like boxers waitin' on the bell.

I fart again.

An' they go for each other.

An' there's boxin' an' punchin' an' it's excitin' stuff.

Circle, a skirmish an' part, circle, a skirmish an' part.

Good technique an' strategy.

But then, stances are dropped, just like that, closed hands open an'
the snarlin' starts.

Jabs an' uppercuts, feints an' parries are abandoned as useless,
traded for tearin' an' pumellin' an' cuts an' eye flaps hangin' an'
groin shots over an' over.

I nearly go.

I nearly piss meself.

'Cos it's not normal fisticuffs any more, not Marquess of
Queensberry.
It's blood an' bone.

An' no more nearly, I *do* piss meself, hardly notice.

A vision of blood an' teeth, right there, of skin an' hair an' they're
flyin' so fast round the room, I'm afraid if they touch off me, I'll
scald, I'll burn.

A bangin' on the door outside.

Fuck off.

Shoutin' an' poundin'.

They wanna come in, see the berserkers brainin' each other, hear bones poppin' an' crackin'.

Well, they can't. Fuck them.

Ladyboy bites The Howie right through his face, snaps again for a better grip an' shakes him round on a rubbery neck, tearin'.

Comes away with a piece of red an' white in his mouth, spits it all juicy.

Red freckles spot Dave McGee's face an' rich as he is, he vomits an' faints.

Time passes real slow.

Me piss is cold on me legs.

Pummellin' gets louder from outside.

An' on they go.

An' on they go.

Stop.

An' then they stop.

They pause an' circle, two of them are breathin' hard, but it doesn't sound right, 'cos noses've been snapped, the air's goin' in an' out fuckways.

An' I can see the white, the horrible white of The Howie's snaggle tooth through his cheek, a dirty gobbet hangin'.

Ladyboy's left leg's exposed, his trousers ripped from crotch to foot. White foam seethes out between his teeth an' bubbles.

Somethin' heavy's bangin' against the door outside.

They're both a shambles, but their eyes're black an' smokin'.

They go again an' so do I, a warm flood.

Howie smacks Ladyboy's head off the wall, leavin' a blood an' hair stain.

Ladyboy's head snaps forward, teeth poppin', poppin' at Howie's neck, walks into a poleaxin' right.

An' on like this.
They're still goin', still tradin' damage back an' forth, I'm gettin' used to skin on skin sounds.

But gettin' a bit slower now.

Slower an' slower.

Both cryin', I think, a weird kinda keenin' sound.

They're windin' down.

Exhausted.

The odd bandy punch, or mis-aimed kick, an accidental clash of heads.

An' slower still.

Till Ladyboy, knackered, his bein' the weaker flesh; spent, spent like seed, like spunk, sinks to the floor, sits, then lies down.

An' the door comes crashin' in, crushed by a beer-keg batterin' ram.

Too late.

The Howie walks by me an' out, doesn't even look at me.

Huge crowd, there, reaches all the way down the stairs out the street, quiet, now. Watchin' him. Howie limps buckled to the end of the landin' away from the stairs.
Crowd scuttles sideways like a clutch of crabs to let him through.
He sits down against the jacks door.

His head's down. I can't see his face.

We watch.

We listen to his strange, fucked-up breathin'.

Ruination.

An' way, way in the distance, I'm sure I hear a siren.

Knocked sideways, fuck is that?
Three bods march along the landin', knockin' people aside, three bods I know.
Ollie Murphy, The Peaches an' The Peaches' monstrous sister, Avalanche.

Down the end of the hall, Peaches picks poor Howie, tired Howie up. Him an' Ollie hold him there.

Hold him, tell him, how dare he? How dare he presume to fuck The Peaches' sister? How dare he fuck her an' dump her like a dirty toerag? Behind The Peaches' back? Makin' her think someone loved her when she was unloveable? Givin' her hope?

See his face, now, his expression, a man come to the end of somethin'.

Are youse after me, lads? he says.

An' they pull him sideways an' run him into the jacks an' towards the window, an' out he goes, screams an' shouts, but doesn't fly.

Doesn't fly, drops.

Music stops an' I run downstairs, me an' everyone else an' out the front door an' a crowd, push me way, get in there, see me mate, see The Howie, The *good* Howie on the railin's, spike through his back an' out his shoulder, teeth showin' through his cheek, wretched.

Wretched.

An' we stand an' we watch an' he smiles an' I know why, it's 'cos he looks so ridiculous an' all's still an'quiet.

All right? I says to him.
All right, he says. Are you itchin'?
An' I'm not. Didn't notice, but haven't itched all night.
No, I say.
That's the cream, he says. It's beginnin' to work.

An' listen.

Listen, the distance.

A siren.

Faint. Then closer.

Ambulance an' fire brigade comin' to cut The Howie off the railin's, make him better.
An' everyone, same idea, backs up to make room, leaves a gap for the emergency boys to drive on in.

An' louder gets the siren an' here comes the emergency boys, only it's not the firemen an' it's not the ambulance, it's Flann Dingle an' Ginger Boy, powerin' the Hi-ace round the corner, doin' ninety, siren's the Gards in hot pursuit, Ginger Boy's on his hunkers, clingin' to the roof rack.

An' Flann should turn off here, but he doesn't, maybe can't an' he powers ahead, straight forward, straight for The Howie an' two hundred people turn their heads away, all together, all at once an' squeeze their eyes shut.

An' as I close mine, that last moment, I'm sure I see – I'm positive – the Howie's body come apart by itself, just before the two tons of metal slams into him, me mate, me new, me impaled mate, me namesake the name of Lee, me saviour, an', eyes closed, I can hear the sound of metal grindin', metal of the Hi-ace, metal of the railin's an' I can't open me eyes, till the Gardamobile does a movie skid an' a fellacopper an' a slappercopper get out an' go round the front of the mangled Hi-ace where no one else'll go.

An' the slappercopper comes back white, starin', shakin'.

An' the fellacopper comes back cryin'.

There's another body there, he tells the slappercopper. There's two bodies. The impaled boy and the boy with the ginger hair, went off the roof.

Look in the van, the slappercopper says.
You.
No, you. I'm not goin' near it.

An' they argue on about who's gonna look in on Flann an' I skeddadle 'cos I can't take it.

Walk along thinkin' 'bout how maybe the Mayan God of Death appeared to The Howie, not me. Appeared to The Howie in the form of the Ginger Boy...
and Flann Dingle...
and the green Hi-ace van.

End up outside The Howie's, somehow, Howie's oul'one's an' oul'fella's gaff, got an urge, an urge to yak, to knock in an' give them the ska. Tell them the story of The Howie's death.

Let them know he was good at the end.

Stand there, watchin'.
Watch there, thinkin'.
Knowin' I won't go home, go anywhere till I do this.

So up I go, a rap on the door, a man answers.

Can I come in? They don't know.
What's it about?
The Howie. They don't know yet.
Come in, he says, you're very photogenic, he says.

I've somethin' of importance to tell you, I says.
Well, in that case, I'll go fetch Mrs Lee, he says.
That might be best, I says, puts me in the sittin' room to wait.

Sit down, telly's on, some kind of video, home video.

Young boy in a suit.
Little boy, five or six years old.
Sittin' where I'm sittin' on the sofa.

Hand comes into the frame, steadies his shoulder, stays there.

The boy's face is grey.

His eyes are on mine.

His expression doesn't change.

MADE IN CHINA

Made in China was first performed at the Peacock Theatre, Dublin, on 10 April 2001 (previews from 5 April). The cast was as follows:

PADDY	Luke Griffin
HUGHIE	Anthony Brophy
KILBY	Andrew Connolly

Director	Gerard Stembridge
Designer	Bláithín Sheerin
Lighting Designer	Ben Ormerod
Sound Designer	Cormac Carroll

Characters

PADDY

HUGHIE

KILBY

ACT ONE

Lights down. Buzzing. Lights up to reveal an apartment, front door right, door to kitchen, left, window at back. Buzzing. HUGHIE *enters from kitchen, goes to window, looks out/down. Goes over to front door, pushes button on intercom.*

HUGHIE (*into speaker*). Yeah?

PADDY (*through speaker*). You right, man?!

> HUGHIE *buzzes him in, puts the front door on the latch, exits to kitchen. Pause.* PADDY *enters, soaking wet, wearing a snorkel jacket, zipped right up, hiding his face. Looks around him, tries to zip down his hood.*

HUGHIE (*popping his head into the room*). What's the jack, man?

PADDY. Fuckin' hell!

HUGHIE. Bit of bad, yeah?

> HUGHIE *disappears again.* PADDY *continues at the hood.* HUGHIE *returns with a towel.*

> Out the other day, I was, an'... Give us a shot. (*Attempting to open* PADDY*'s zip.*) Was out the other day, man... (*Hurting his finger.*) Ouch! (*Attempting again.*) Right? an'... (*Of finger.*) Agh! (*Giving up.*) You're gonna have to lift it over your head.

> PADDY *lifts the snorkel over his head.*

> What was I...?

> PADDY *hands the snorkel to him.*

> Hunky. Fuck was I sayin'?

PADDY. You were out.

HUGHIE. That's right... Heavens opened an' I nearly wept. Faggot an' 'all, I know, but it just set me off. Frustration, disappointment...

PADDY. ...Wet...

HUGHIE. ...Wet, man. Oppression... (*Hanging up snorkel.*) The fuck happened this?

There is a huge rip down the side.

PADDY. Wait an' I tell you...

HUGHIE. Nasty!

PADDY. ...Yeah, moseyin' up Pike Avenue, I was an'...

HUGHIE. This tonight?

PADDY. ...Me way over. An' your man, that fat-fuck copper. Dolan, is it? Beset me, the fuck, fucked me in a puddle...

HUGHIE. *Beset* you?!

PADDY. Came out of nowhere. Yep. Riefed me bod sneaky an' sent me fuckin' flyin'.

HUGHIE. An' what'd he say?

PADDY. Said nothin', man. Swaggered off, left me all prostrate in the gutter. (*Beat.*) Guffawed.

HUGHIE *does CopperDolan's laugh.*

Hmm.

HUGHIE. No?

PADDY *does CopperDolan's laugh.*

Not bad. Not bad...

PADDY. Cheers.

HUGHIE. ...Not *great*, now.

PADDY. Me fuckin' snorkel.

Pause.

HUGHIE. Say he saw you with meself, man.

PADDY. Say so?

HUGHIE. ...Thought you were an echelon. Say he confused you.

PADDY. But I thought with the treaty an' all, he couldn't go near youse.

HUGHIE. Well, where'd it happen? What'd you say, Pike Avenue? You see? That's outside...

PADDY. I see. Puppacat's…

HUGHIE (*simultaneous with 'Puppacat's'*)….Puppacat's boundaries, yeah. Echelons go outside those, man, it's watch your fuckin' hoop. Treaty doesn't exist past the Bannerman Flush, so for future reference, occurs again, man, don't speak, don't look at him. Not that you *did*, but…

PADDY. No, but don't give him a reason.

HUGHIE. This is it, man. 'Cos that's all he wants.

PADDY. Right. Reason to smack you.

HUGHIE. Smack or arrest you, the fuck!

Pause.

PADDY. Might be time to put it out to pasture.

HUGHIE. Mmm. Which?

PADDY. Snorkel.

HUGHIE. Might *be*. You gonna get a new one?

PADDY. Might *do*. Or somethin' else, maybe.

HUGHIE. Get somethin' looks well. Not that your snorkel didn't.

PADDY. No.

HUGHIE….But it didn't. Have to say, now. You want, I'll come with you.

PADDY. Will you?

HUGHIE. Give you a hand, sure. We pop down to Poppin' Mossey's an' peruse relaxed, yeah? Take our time an' see what we can… (*Jumps suddenly.*) *Fuck*… in' hell!

PADDY. What…?

HUGHIE (*fiddling at his hip*). *Fuck*… in' beeper. (*Gets it turned off.*) Have it on the hummin' thing, I do. You know the hummin' thing?

PADDY. The *vibratin'* thing.

HUGHIE (*looking at pager*). Frightened the muck out of me. (*Of number.*) Kilby.

PADDY. Show?

HUGHIE (*handing it to him*). Fuck does *he* want? Got it down the Windsor Market.

PADDY. No mobiles, no?

HUGHIE. I wouldn't *get* a mobile, Paddy. Give meself skull cancer, all that? *Fuck* that. Fuckin' brain carbuncles?

PADDY. Brain what?

HUGHIE. Carbuncles, man. That's what you get. Dirty warts on the fucker. Anyway, the bloke told us Pacino uses the same one in that film *Heat*. You know it?

PADDY. Plays the copper.

HUGHIE. Same as Pacino's, he says. I tells Kilby, you know what Kilby says?

PADDY. What?

HUGHIE. 'Is that a karate film?'

PADDY. You're jokin'!

HUGHIE. Karate film with fuckin' Al Pacino!

PADDY. You're gonna ring him back?

HUGHIE. Fuckim, he thinks I'm goin' out in that, he can suck me... (*Bends forward suddenly, holds stomach, in pain.*)

PADDY. You all right, man?

HUGHIE. Fuckin' belly's seizin' up. (*Continues to wince, bent forward, then relaxes a little, sits back.*) Fuckin' hell.

PADDY. What's it? D'you want somethin'?

HUGHIE. Fuckin' pissed-off-ness, man. No thanks. Feels like, you know your grill gets dirty? Every so often a lump of grease... You know that?

PADDY. Yeah.

HUGHIE. ....Explodes? Pops up?

PADDY. I know it.

HUGHIE. Like that. Scalds the fuckin' belly off me.

Short pause.

PADDY. What d'you mean 'pissed-off-ness'?

HUGHIE. With it all, Paddy; with *them* all, fuckin'...

PADDY. People, is it?

HUGHIE. *Cunts*, man. Not people. Dirty rotten... Excludin' yourself. Yourself an' meself.

PADDY. Right.

HUGHIE. ...*Cunts*, they are!

Pause.

PADDY. Is it your oul'one? Don't wanna...

HUGHIE. No. What *happened* me oul'one?

PADDY. Yeah. Don't wanna be...

HUGHIE. *No*, man. She'd be exempt as well, by the way.

PADDY. Right. Well, *course* she would. Course, an' how is she?

HUGHIE (*looks at him*). 'Fer not to...

PADDY. Fine.

HUGHIE. You mind? Bit fuckin' distressin'.

PADDY. I understand, man. (*Standing up, picking at his trousers.*) You all right now?

HUGHIE. What're you doin'? Yeah, I'm grand.

PADDY. Pants're stickin' to me.

HUGHIE. Pants?

PADDY. Yeah.

HUGHIE. Your *trou*sers.

PADDY (*going over to the radiator, feeling it*). The scaldy stomach of stress, you have. That it?

HUGHIE. That's fuckin' it, man.

HUGHIE *exits*. PADDY *begins taking his trousers off*. HUGHIE *re-enters*.

Fuck're you doin'?

PADDY. Don't wanna be sittin' in wet all night. D'you mind? (*Hanging trousers over the radiator.*) Me upper body's dry, like, protection of me snorkel an' all. It's just me bottom half.

HUGHIE. What about a new pair? Kettle's on, by the way. Go with the jacket, like. No? Or a shirt somethin' like this, product of John Rocha. You know John? Looks like your man out of *One Flew Over the Cuckoo's Nest*, the Chief.

PADDY. He an Indian?

HUGHIE. Course he is. (*Short pause.*) The Chief?

PADDY. No, your man. The bloke you're...

HUGHIE. *Ah*, no. Irish, man. Far's I know. So, what d'you think?

PADDY (*going over to snorkel*). Think a new jacket's about as far's I'm willin' to go, man. For the moment, anyway. Say the kettle's on?

HUGHIE. I did, yeah.

PADDY. Sage, man. So... (*Taking a videotape from snorkel pocket.*) *Big Boss*? (*Sitting back down.*) Or *Eight Diagram Pole Fighters*? Which one d'you wanna go? Good double.

HUGHIE. It is, but...

PADDY. *Excellent* double. Distract you from your woes, man.

HUGHIE. ...Bit of bad news, Paddy. Don't think we're gonna be able to go either. Have to split after.

PADDY. Out?

HUGHIE. Have to do some stuff. (*Beat.*) Regrets, man.

PADDY. Ah, now, you could've *told* me, Hughie. Jaysus.

HUGHIE. I know.

PADDY. Went down the phone box, an'...

HUGHIE. ...The rain, but...

PADDY. ...an' gave me a ring at least. *I* came down in the rain.

HUGHIE. But you'd your snorkel, Paddy.

PADDY. Ah, now, lay off the fuckin' snorkel, will you? Come on.

HUGHIE. All right. Regrets.

PADDY. So, d'you want me to head? Or...

HUGHIE. Ah no, sure we've an hour or so. What about that? D'you wanna hang around for...?

PADDY. Sure, fuck it. Have to wait till me pants dry a bit, anyway. So, c'mere…

HUGHIE. There's… '*Pants*'?!

PADDY. *Trousers*, fucksake! Whatever!

HUGHIE. There's the kettle, now.

They stare at each other. Long pause. PADDY *exits to the kitchen. Pause.*

Got this killer headache yesterday mornin'. Thought it was a tumour I developed or somethin', come from all the bile I've been buildin' up.

Over following, PADDY *in and out of kitchen doing tea business.*

PADDY. 'Count of what?

HUGHIE. Huh…?

PADDY. Why were you buildin' up bile?

HUGHIE. 'Count of cunts, man.

PADDY. I *know* cunts. Who?

HUGHIE. Puppacat. (*Pause.*) Fuck askin' me to do some business tonight. 'Bit of business, Hughie.' Like that. On'y not askin'…

PADDY. Right. Tellin'.

HUGHIE (*simultaneous with 'tellin''*). Fuckin' tellin'. Which is why we can't watch the flick, man. (*Pause, sips tea.*)

PADDY *turns his trousers over.*

Still. This is what comes of bein' an echelon.

PADDY. Downsides?

HUGHIE. *An'* up, man. Like an'thin'. You don't deserve the rewards you reap if you're not prepared to toil.

PADDY (*looking out window*). An' you do reap, man. You can't deny. Your threads, this pad…

HUGHIE. I'm not denyin'.

PADDY. You're just complainin', that it?

HUGHIE. Zactly, man. Just havin' an oul' moan, I am. (*Pause.*) Eh, Paddy.

PADDY. What? Oh. (*Puts his flute away. Sitting down*.) So, what's he want you to do, man?

HUGHIE. You know Bernie Denk? (*Pause*.) You *do*, man. Green boots, got the little moustache, there…

PADDY. *Oh*, yeah. Yeah…

HUGHIE. …The duffel…

PADDY. …I know him. What d'you think of that duffel?

HUGHIE. *Muck*, man. You thinkin' of gettin' one?!

PADDY. Well…

HUGHIE. Fuck *that*, Paddy. There's more style in your snorkel. Fuck was I?

PADDY. Is he the one got up on his oul'one?

HUGHIE. They *say*.

PADDY. …They say got up on his oul'one?

HUGHIE. That's him. Fuckin' Puppa wants me to break his pins.

PADDY. Hmm. (*Pause*.) See the problem there's…

HUGHIE. It's not fuckin' appropriate.

PADDY. Well, it's not the 'propriate *time*, man.

HUGHIE. That's, yeah.

PADDY. …You know? For *you*.

HUGHIE. Well, that's what I *mean*, man.

   Pause.

PADDY. Do *you* think he got up on her?

HUGHIE (*jumps in fright*). Bollox! (*Checks his pager*.) Fuckhead again, for fuck's sake. I don't see why he can't be the one goes up, does it 'stead of annoyin' me all fuckin' night, permy cocksucker *like* him. I'm puttin' that on beep. (*Pushes buttons and the pager beeps*.) Hear that?

PADDY. Is he?

HUGHIE. What?

PADDY. A cocksucker. I *did* hear it.

HUGHIE. Fuckin' right he is. (*Pause*.) You mean in the… What d'you mean?

PADDY. In the faggot sense.

HUGHIE. *Ah*, no. I'm talkin' 'bout the insultin' sense, sense he's one of the fucks makes…

PADDY. The cunts.

HUGHIE. …makes me bile sizzle. The cunts, I should say.

Beat.

PADDY. Should ring him back.

HUGHIE. I'm not goin' down the phone box that weather.

PADDY. You can wear me snorkel.

HUGHIE. I'm on'y goin' out if it's me oul'one.

Pause.

PADDY. You know I called up, man?

HUGHIE. The hospital?

PADDY. Yeah. Family only, but.

HUGHIE. That's right. So you know it's serious. Every time this thing goes off I think it's the hospital. They're the only ones supposed to have me number in the *first* place. Course *Puppacat* has to ask for it. An' not askin' but tellin'.

PADDY (*simultaneous with 'tellin''*). …Tellin'. Yeah.

HUGHIE. …Has to give it to Kilby then, so every time the fuckin' thing beeps…

PADDY. Hums.

HUGHIE. …Whatever. Vib*rates*… I suspect the fuckin' worst. You know?

PADDY. She's not *that* bad, is she? (*Pause*.) I mean, I know she's *bad*, but I thought…

HUGHIE. You know what I'm sayin'? Me look, man?

PADDY. What?

HUGHIE. *Leave* it.

PADDY. Your look is sayin' 'leave it'.

HUGHIE. I don't wanna talk about it. Although, thanks for callin' up an' all. 'Preciate it. As I'm sure she would've, mad as she is about you.

PADDY (*going over to trousers, turning them over*). An' me about her, man. Big time. So what did Bernie...?

HUGHIE. Paddy.

PADDY. What?

HUGHIE. Your flute, man.

PADDY (*putting his flute back in*). Fucksake! So what did Bernie Denk do you've to break his pins? No, first... *Did* he get up on his oul'one?

HUGHIE. You're obsessed with this.

PADDY. I wanna know what you heard.

HUGHIE. I heard, yeah. I heard maybe they had a, what would you...? A relationship. A love affair. But there's no evidence, so...

PADDY. It's hearsay.

HUGHIE. Gossip. Yeah. It's inadmissible, so...

PADDY. Right. Go on.

HUGHIE. So, you know your woman reads the palms? Nancy.

PADDY. The cripple?

HUGHIE. She's not a cripple, man, she's minus a leg. She's a fuckin'...

PADDY. Peg.

HUGHIE. ...Nancy with the peg leg. Okay, well...

PADDY. I know her. She's a little tent down the West Yard.

HUGHIE. Right, well that's Puppacat's set-up.

PADDY. Is it?!

HUGHIE. She goes up to his gaff, private consultations, star charts, the lot, right? He's into it an' 'parently she's accurate. Anyway. Last few weeks, seems Bernie Denk's hangin' round Nancy.

Puppacat says he's been broachin' her in the street, accostin' her ominous. An' it's hard for her to 'scape the fuck…

PADDY. What with the…

HUGHIE. Zactly. How fast can you hoof it hoppin'? Hangin' round her tent an' all, but she doesn't wanna say an'thin' for the time *bein'*, 'cos…

PADDY. She hasn't gone to Puppacat?!

HUGHIE. This, no. This stage, he's just bein' a nuisance.

PADDY. What was he sayin' to her?

HUGHIE. The Puppa didn't say.

PADDY. An' why was he after her?

HUGHIE. Well, the Puppa didn't say, just…

PADDY. All right. Right…

HUGHIE. So, *last* week, all right? Middle of the night, she hears noises out her back garden, she's in the sack, like, ganders out her window, who does she click only Bernie Denk. Bernie standin' there, ganderin' up…

PADDY. Scary stuff.

HUGHIE. Well. For a woman.

PADDY. That's what I mean.

HUGHIE. …Just ganderin' back at her. So she starts gettin' fretful. This is startin' to go *beyond* nuisance. Maybe he wants to commit rapeage or somethin'. *An'*, course, coupled with the *other* thing. Him gettin' up on his oul'one.

PADDY. The rumours.

HUGHIE. *Yeah*, the rumours. But if you're scared enough, rumours become fact, don't they? Bloke's out your back in the middle of the night, starin' up at your bedroom window, fuckin'… *madness* in his eyes… Far as you're gonna know or *want* to know, he's a pervert…

PADDY. The nightmare becomes reality.

HUGHIE. The nightmare, *zactly*… Becomes, *zactly*. An' it *did*, 'cos two nights later, the fucker breaks in, all right? Breaks in, *wrecks* the place. He smashes a hole in her telly, tears the curtains to flits, the fridge, all the grub in her fridge, he fucks on the floor, tramples it. She's in the sack listenin' to all this an' what does she do...?

PADDY. You're jokin'!

HUGHIE. ...Comes downstairs an' confronts him. What does *he* do but gives her a good hard kick in the peg leg, kicks it so hard, he knocks it out from under her. She's standin' there, hoppin', should say, shoutin' at him, thinkin' righteous fuckin' indignation's gonna, you know...

PADDY. Women!

HUGHIE. ...do the job...

PADDY. ...Fucksake! *Bang!!!*

HUGHIE. Down she goes, whacks her knee off the ground. Smashes it. I says to Puppacat, 'Why've I to break *both* of Bernie's pins? Is one not enough?' His reasonin's if *she* was incapacitated, which she is...

PADDY. She's *no* pins now.

HUGHIE. Well, she *has*, she's *one*.

PADDY. None that *work*, though.

HUGHIE. Then, no. Then he wants Bernie Denk put in the same situation an' may he be grateful we don't cut one of them *off* 'cos they don't grow back.

PADDY. They don't.

HUGHIE. It's gone, it's gone an' get used to fuckin' hoppin'.

Pause.

PADDY. Would you get up on her?

HUGHIE. Nancy?

PADDY. Yeah.

HUGHIE. No, I wouldn't. But I wouldn't smash her knee either.

PADDY. Suppose, you do the deed, man, yeah?

HUGHIE. What's that?

PADDY.…You pay the fiddler. I don't see why *you* should be the one, but…

HUGHIE. Zactly.

PADDY.…has to…

HUGHIE. Zactly. *Be* the fuckin' fiddler. Just think they'd have a bit more sensitivity, the night that's in it.

PADDY. Zactly, man. Bit more tact an' all.

Pause.

HUGHIE. D'you want another cuppa?

PADDY. Yeah.

HUGHIE (*picking up cups*). Think your trousers need a turnin'.

HUGHIE *exits.* PADDY *goes over to radiator, begins turning his trousers.* HUGHIE *re-enters, stands in the doorway.*

They dryin'?

PADDY. They're hot. (*Turning them.*) Don't know if they're dryin'.

HUGHIE. They're heatin', they're dryin'.

Pause.

PADDY. What would you wear if you were me an' you were lookin' for a pair of trousers?

HUGHIE. Thought you weren't gettin' any.

PADDY. I'm just askin'.

HUGHIE. Well, d'you know what you like?

PADDY *thinks.*

All right, look… All right? I'm free Thursday…

PADDY. 'Head of you, man.

HUGHIE.…Poppin' Mossey's…

PADDY. An' I'm free too.

HUGHIE. A browsal… Good… A perusal. You know, bit of a…

PADDY. 'Preciate it, man. An' I *do* know. Just, you know… I'm not lookin' for an entire wardrobe makeover.

HUGHIE. That's fine, Paddy. (*Exiting to kitchen*.) You're makin' a start, though.

PADDY (*to himself*). Just tryin' on some things, man.

Intercom buzzes.

Eh… Hughie?

Intercom buzzes.

Hughie!

HUGHIE *enters, goes over to the intercom.*

HUGHIE (*into speaker*). Yeah?

KILBY (*through speaker*). Don't 'Yeah' *me*, you cunt.

HUGHIE (*buzzing him in. To* PADDY). Kilby.

HUGHIE *goes over to the front door, opens it, puts it on the latch, heads back into the kitchen. Pause. Enter* KILBY. *Short, black leather jacket, umbrella, blond perm.*

KILBY. Hughie? (*To* PADDY.) Where is he? (*Calling*.) Hughie! (*To* PADDY.) Fuckin' hack of this place!

HUGHIE *enters with two cups of tea, stops in the doorway.*

(*To* HUGHIE.) The fuck are you doin'? (*To* PADDY.) Story, fuckhead?

PADDY. What's the jack?

KILBY. Give that a shakin', will you? (*Hands umbrella to* PADDY. *To* HUGHIE.) The fuck're you doin'?

HUGHIE (*putting tea on table*). What?

KILBY. I'm after comin' all the way down here in a blazin' fuckin'… in a monsoon, man. Hadn't got me brolly, I'd be fuckin' *drenched*, I would. (*To* PADDY.) That right, Paddy? *Shake* the fuckin' thing. Drowned, I'd'a been. (*Looks at* PADDY*'s boxers*.) The fuck were youse faggots up to? (*To* HUGHIE.) What am I after walkin' in on? Is this a fuckin'… Is this one of them rendezvous or somethin'?

PADDY. Me pants are wet.

KILBY. Your fuckin' *pants*?!!

HUGHIE. His trousers.

KILBY. I... (*To* HUGHIE.) Right. (*Beat. To* PADDY.) They're wet?!

PADDY. The *rain*, man.

KILBY. Oh. Had you no brolly? Will you *shake* the fuckin' thing? I thought youse were suckin' each other's cocks or somethin'. (*To* HUGHIE.) Here, fuckhead. The fuck's wrong with you, you can't answer your beeper, huh? Have me out there bravin' the hurricane.

HUGHIE. Was waitin' till it relented, man.

KILBY. Have you no sense of manhood about yourself a-tall, no? No sense of the machiz, you couldn't go round the corner? It's only a shower, the name of fuck. (*To* PADDY.) Should be dry, man.

PADDY *continues to shake umbrella*.

Paddy?

PADDY *stops*.

Should be dry.

PADDY *leans the umbrella against the wall, sits back down*.

(*To* HUGHIE.) It's only a fuckin' drizzle. D'you know what I mean? Tell him, Paddy.

PADDY. Ah, well... Have to disagree now, Kilby. I've been there, you know? Experienced a bit more than a drizzle.

KILBY. What did you experience?

PADDY. *I* don't know, but...

KILBY. *Well*, then. (*Short pause. To* HUGHIE.) Hughie...

PADDY. ...A deluge or somethin'.

Pause.

KILBY. You wouldn't know a deluge if it hit you on the fuckin' head, you prick. (*To* HUGHIE.) An' that's why you didn't answer?! That's bad. (*To* PADDY.) You smart prick, you, Paddy. (*To* HUGHIE.) That's bad, now. If that winchy measure of respect's all Kilby commands, then maybe he'll have to... (*Mimes the action of taking a badge from his chest and throwing it down*.) throw down the tin badge, give up his deputyhood, you know what I'm sayin', Paddy? Step outside the law prevents the dispensin' of swift justice. (*Miming*.) Just below the ribcage. Fuckin' rupture you. Would you like that? Don't think you would. (*Short pause. To* HUGHIE.) Would *you*?

HUGHIE. No.

KILBY. Didn't think you would. Think you'd like gettin' wet better, wouldn't you? Think you'd face the deluge as your man says, quicker than a… (*Miming*.) Phoenix Eye Fist below the ribcage from Kilby. All right, Paddy? What's your cock doin' on your lap?

PADDY (*looking down*). Fuckin'… Agh !! (*Puts his cock away*.)

KILBY. You notice *he* wouldn't tell you? Could've been restin' there all night, he wouldn't open his mouth. But you'd notice his *eyes* lingerin' all right. Be lickin' his chops, he would. (*To* HUGHIE.) Wouldn't you, man?

HUGHIE. I would.

KILBY. I *know* you would. Don't need to fuckin' tell me. (*To* PADDY.) Moistenin' his lips, he'd be, an' fidgetin'. Adjustin' his crotch an' all.

HUGHIE. D'you wanna cuppa, Kilby?

KILBY. Fuck that tea shit.

HUGHIE. Coffee?

KILBY. Maybe it's fuckin' coffee I want. Are you not supposed to be pin-breakin'?

HUGHIE. I am.

KILBY. You can no more pin-break than I can fuckin'… stroke me twat, man. When are you doin' it?

HUGHIE. In a while.

KILBY. Don't give me this obscure shit, man.

HUGHIE. 'Bout an hour.

KILBY. …Don't Mister Miyagi me. An hour?! You've to do it sooner.

HUGHIE. Well, I'll…

KILBY. No. No. You've to do it sooner. He's at home, now. What happens you call up, he's gone out?

HUGHIE. I don't know.

KILBY. ...Huh?

HUGHIE. I do it tomorrow?

KILBY. But Puppacat's payin' you to do it today. May not pay you a-tall, may get rancorous instead, man, have to *be* a puppy, you know? Send Kilby down to… (*Miming*.) break your kneecap with a foot-stomp. Now, I'm after ringin' the cunt, all right? That's one of the 'vantages of havin' a phone.

HUGHIE. Kilby, you're the one wrecked it.

KILBY. Axe-kick, Paddy.

PADDY. Yeah?

KILBY. Booze an' karate, man. (*To* HUGHIE.) Rang the cunt, he's in, Hughie. (*To* PADDY.) Destructive combo. (*To* HUGHIE.) He's in, he's the prime of health. Get up there an' break his pins 'fore he splits out an' you can't. Okay?

HUGHIE. Right. I'll just…

KILBY. Just finish your tea, get your fuckin' arse up there. (*Picks up* PADDY*'s videotape*.) This yours, Paddy?

PADDY. Yeah.

KILBY. This the one with the bit…? Which *is* it?

PADDY. Which?

KILBY. Fights the fat fucker?

PADDY. Yeah.

KILBY. ...Batters him. Some good fuckin' bits in that. Youse watchin' it after?

PADDY. Yeah.

KILBY. Wouldn't mind seein' that, now. Could I watch it with youse?

HUGHIE. I've to do this, Kilby.

KILBY. How long d'you think it takes? You're not fixin' the fuck, you're breakin' him. Paddy'll still be here when you get back. (*To* PADDY.) Won't you? (*To* HUGHIE.) With his cock hangin' out all steamy. So go, come back, we'll watch Bruce do it proper. Yeah? Watch him break *more* than pins. (*To* PADDY.) Bit in this where he breaks your man's neck?

PADDY. Whose?

KILBY. Some fuck's.

PADDY. He breaks a couple.

KILBY. Yeah?

PADDY. Breaks a few.

KILBY. Lookin' forward, then. (*To* HUGHIE.) Oh, how's the oul'one, man? Jaysus, I nearly forgot. (*To* PADDY.) Fuckin' oul'one in hospital. (*To* HUGHIE.) C'mere. Puppacat says to tell you he's sorry for askin' you to do this while… You know, felt a bit bad about it. (*To* PADDY.) Complimented me there on me perm, she did.

PADDY. Yeah?

KILBY. Thought it was fuckin' dapper. How *is* she?

HUGHIE. I'd rather not talk about it, man. (*Short pause*.) 'F you don't mind, like.

KILBY. You'd rather not talk about it?! Jays, don't talk to Kilby, who the fuck can you talk to?

HUGHIE. 'Preciate that, man. You know?

KILBY. Ah, sure…

HUGHIE. Do. 'Preciate your interest. '*But…* ' (*Beat*.) You know…? Have to say, now, '*But…* '

KILBY (*to* PADDY). Bit offensive that, whatsay, Paddy? Lack of confidence in Kilby?

HUGHIE. It's not, man, it's just that…

KILBY. Lack of trust an' all? Find it a bit hard to reconcile meself to that now, Hughie. But, all right, man. Fuck it. You don't wanna tell me, don't. (*Beat*.) '*But…* '

HUGHIE. Well…

KILBY. '*But…*' (*Beat*.) You know what I'm sayin'?

Pause.

HUGHIE. She's still in intensive care, all right? She's there, she's stable, they're monitorin' her, like, she hasn't gotten any worse, but…

PADDY. Still an' all.

KILBY. Right. Still…

HUGHIE. …It's fuckin' intensive care.

Pause.

KILBY. Empathy, man. You know? Seriously. Sympathy. (*To* PADDY.) She never cusses.

PADDY. That's right.

KILBY (*to* HUGHIE). Does she?

HUGHIE. No.

KILBY (*to* PADDY). Never fuckin' cusses. (*Long pause*.) So she's in there, safe, anyway, bit of tender lovin'…?

HUGHIE. Yeah.

KILBY. She'll be all right. Don't worry about it, for fuck's sake. (*To* PADDY.) Paddy?

PADDY. She will, she'll be fine.

KILBY. An' what about this dirtbird?

HUGHIE. Which?

KILBY. Dirtbird crashed her.

HUGHIE. What *about* him?

KILBY. I don't know… (*Beat*.) You know? You tell *me*.

HUGHIE. Tell you what?

KILBY. *I'm* askin' *you*, man. (*Pause. To* PADDY.) D'you get me, Paddy?

PADDY. What?

KILBY. You not spottin' where I'm headin'?

PADDY. Well, I'm *tailin'* you. But, eh…

KILBY. You don't know where I'm bound.

PADDY. …Didn't spot that, no.

KILBY. Payback, man.

> PADDY *coughs*.

> Gallopin' consumption. (*To* HUGHIE.) Taste of the lash, whatsay, Hughie?

> PADDY *coughs*.

> That's gallopin' consumption, man. (*To* HUGHIE.) Grind the fucker up like he ground… (*Short pause*.) Em…

PADDY. Dolly.

KILBY. I know her name, man. (*To* HUGHIE.) Whatsay? Cook him in a pot. Mangle the cunt like he mangled Dolly. (*To* PADDY.) See? No need to tell me. (*To* HUGHIE.) Like he mangled your *oul'*one.

HUGHIE. Listen. Kilby…

KILBY. Your mother.

HUGHIE. …Grateful's I *am*, man. Your interest, concern, all that. Empathy…

KILBY. Sympathy.

HUGHIE. All that… Thankful's I *am*… (*Short pause*.) I've no interest at the moment. No offence. She's still in the critical, you know? I've more on me mind than…

KILBY. All right…

HUGHIE. …than fuckin'…

KILBY. …right. No need to reproof me, man. Jaysus. Just tryin' to offer me help. (*To* PADDY.) D'you hear him reproofin' me?

HUGHIE. I'm not reproofin'. She's old, she's broken to bits. I haven't a clue what parts'll be workin', she gets out, what parts won't, if she *makes* it out 'cos there's a big chance she won't. Find it hard to separate me mind, you see, me emotions from what's goin' on with her, d'you understand me? Sure, I'm not too gleeful 'bout doin' *this* thing.

KILBY. What?

HUGHIE. This Denk shit. I've more on me mind the night that's fuckin' *in* it.

Pause.

KILBY. Well, d'you want *me* to go up an' do it?

HUGHIE. Right.

KILBY. No. Hughie...

HUGHIE. What?

KILBY. *Do* you?

Long pause. PADDY *coughs.*

(*To* PADDY.) Cancer, man.

PADDY (*coughs again*). Fucksake!

KILBY. Tuberculosis, that is. (*To* HUGHIE.) Get up there, Hughie...

PADDY. Fuckin' *flu*, I think.

KILBY....All right? Break Bernie's pins an' make Puppacat proud. An' the Kilby. (*Winks.*) Goes without sayin'.

HUGHIE *finishes his tea, goes to* PADDY, *stands over him.*

PADDY. What?

HUGHIE. You finished?

PADDY *gives him the cup and he exits. Silence.* KILBY *picks up videotape again.*

KILBY. What's this *Eight Diagram Pole Fighters* about?

PADDY. 'Bout these eh...

KILBY. Pole fighters?

PADDY. Yeah.

KILBY. They baldy?

PADDY. They are, yeah. Monks.

KILBY. Think I seen it.

Silence. HUGHIE *enters with baseball bat, goes over to window, looks out.*

HUGHIE. Lend us your brolly, Kilby.

KILBY. Sorry, man. Might wanna go out, get treats or somethin'. Goodies.

PADDY. You can borry me snorkel if you want.

Pause. HUGHIE *gives him a look.*

Ah, fuck you!

HUGHIE (*grabbing one of his own jackets, putting it on angrily*). Fuckin' snorkel! I'd rather get up on Obboe the fuckin' Abo... You know Obboe?

KILBY. Ooh...!

HUGHIE. ...On O'Connell Street or somethin'.

KILBY. ...Fuck! In public?

HUGHIE *exits, slamming door.*

Nasty, man. (*Pause.*) Cheek of the fuck, huh?

PADDY. Fuckin' Obboe the Abo!

KILBY. Don't mind him, man. (*Goes over to the window.*) Cheeky cunt *like* him. (*Looks down at the street.*) There he goes, look? The fuckin' eejit. (*Pause.*) Paddy.

PADDY *joins him.*

Drowned, he'll be. Any grub here?

PADDY. Dunno.

KILBY. Bit of hunger, I have.

KILBY *exits to kitchen.* PADDY *looks out the window once more.*

(*Offstage.*) Ever have Nik Naks, man?

PADDY (*returning to his chair*). Which're they?

KILBY (*offstage*). Crip things. You suck them. (*Enters.*) Suck all the flavour out, then chew.

PADDY. No.

KILBY. Taste of spare ribs. You like crips?

PADDY. *Some* crips.

KILBY. Right. You'd think he'd have somethin' gourmet in stock all the same; some veg or the like. (*Sits down*.)

PADDY. Whatever happened that Chink-writin' jacket you used to have, Kilby?

KILBY. Dragon Fist.

PADDY. That what it said?

KILBY. It's a northern system. Shaolin.

PADDY. Kinda had a feelin' it said somethin' karate, now.

KILBY. Fuckin' thing was stroked on me. You know…? Nah, you wouldn't.

PADDY. Who?

KILBY. …CopperDolan.

PADDY. I *do* know him.

KILBY. Stroked it off me thirty year back.

PADDY (*going over to snorkel*). See this?

KILBY. How *d'you* know him?

PADDY (*of rip*). See that?

KILBY. …Paddy!

PADDY. I'm tellin' you, man. See how it's ripped, it's wrecked?

KILBY. Yeah.

PADDY. CopperDolan fucked me in a puddle tonight. Beset me me way over.

KILBY. The fat fuck! He *beset* you?!

PADDY. Hughie reckons it's 'cos I was seen with him…

KILBY (*simultaneous with 'seen with him'*). …Seen with him. Prob'ly right. Prob'ly thought you were an echelon. Hates Puppacat…

PADDY. Yeah?

KILBY. …Hates, *oh*, yeah. Hates us all, the fuckin' menace! But with the agreement an' all, the treaty…

PADDY. An' he stroked it on you.

KILBY. You know Delgado's over the Gook Nation? Down there one night, coupla games. Took a shine to it, he did, liked the cut. Stuck it on his back an' sauntered out the door, guffawin'…

PADDY does CopperDolan's laugh.

Fuck could I do? Not bad, man.

PADDY. Cheers.

KILBY. Not *great*, now. But, fuck could I do?

PADDY. He's a copper.

KILBY. That's it, an' he's mad.

PADDY. The fuck d'you do?

KILBY. Keep your mouth shut an' your eye on the black 'cos it's bait. You get me?

PADDY. He wanted to rile you.

KILBY. To bait me for a batterin'. Same reason he beset yourself, man.

Pause.

PADDY. Used to think that jacket was great, you know that…?

KILBY. It *was* great.

PADDY. …See you walkin' down the street, think, Jaysus! I wish I had a fuckin' Chink-writin' jacket.

KILBY. That jacket was a one of a kind, man. Hand*made*, hand-*stitched*…

PADDY. Who stitched it?

KILBY. Who d'you think?

PADDY. Well *done*, man.

KILBY. Bit of craftsmanship for you. (*Indicating his own jacket.*) That one there's the same make, now, same leather an' all, but it's *not* the same, you know? I'd me Dragon Fist yonks.

PADDY. Same here.

KILBY. Your snorkel?

PADDY. Donkey's, man.

KILBY. See, Hughie knows nothin'. He's gonna come back pissed on, now. An' why? 'Cos he wouldn't… wear… the functional… item. Got the values of a woman, he has. Woman'd walk six miles nippy through a blizzard, you know? Give herself frostbite on the buds to show off a ring in her pissflap. He's the same. Stop buyin' jacks roll if muck was in fashion, do his day-to-day, dirty brown between his legs. Fuckin' designer shirt…

PADDY. John Rocha.

KILBY. That a Rocha?

PADDY. So he said.

KILBY. Fucksake. See, this is what I'm talkin' 'bout. I mean, you ask me 'bout clothes, I'll tell you… You know, if you *ask* me. Say about… (*Pause*.) What?

PADDY. I dunno, jackets?

KILBY. You askin' me?!

PADDY. Yeah.

KILBY. Same as yourself, man, same as meself. Snorkel, a good leather… You *know* jackets. What else?

PADDY. Pants? Trousers?

KILBY. 'Bout trousers, I'll tell you. Combats. All right? Combats. Strong. Baggy. Style an' function. Now. Baggies… Right? Why baggies?

Short pause.

PADDY. They're baggy?

KILBY. Zactly. Function. Room. Movement. Jeans, now. Jeans, the same thing.

PADDY. I… Well…

KILBY. What?

PADDY. …I wouldn't've thought…

KILBY. 'Cos they're tight? Constrictive? That what you're sayin'? (*Hand on crotch*.) 'Cos they bind your packet?

PADDY. Yeah.

KILBY. Not Action Jeans, man.

PADDY. What?!

KILBY. Not Chuck Norris Action Jeans. Chucks've a hidden gusset in the packet area so's you can get your leg up high, get that kick action goin', you know? (*Bends over*.) See it? Little gusset in there under me bollox?

PADDY. Oh, yeah.

KILBY. Chuck wears them on his ranch. I mean, I couldn't do a high roundhouse in a normal pair, for instance, spinnin' hook kick...

PADDY. Right.

KILBY. ...No gusset, man. Can't get the leg up. But with the Chuck jeans... Think about it. Function. Room. Movement. (*Modelling*.) An' they *look* good as well. So it's style in harmony with em...

PADDY. Practicality.

KILBY. That's it.

PADDY. Well, that's what I'd be interested in.

KILBY. I've order forms at home. Have to send away the States. D'you wanna couple?

PADDY. Yeah.

KILBY. See what I can do, man. Jaysus, the oul' belly's gettin' a bit leppin'. Might have them Nik Naks, calm it down. (*Short pause*.) Ungourmet's they are.

PADDY *coughs*.

Whoopin' cough, is it?

PADDY. Fuckin' *flu*, man.

KILBY. 'Flu'! Spoonful of Veno's's all that needs. (*Short pause*.) Bit of a hoopman, Paddy, aren't you.

PADDY. I am in me hole a hoopman.

KILBY. No wonder Hughie's reluctant to do the business, the likes of you gayin' him up. Hate to see you get a dig, now, you'd fall down, prob'ly *stay* down.

PADDY. I'd get up.

KILBY. Would you, now?

PADDY. Get up an' walk tall, I would. Hit back hard.

KILBY. A big man? Not CopperDolan, like, but someone else big?

PADDY. If he hit me.

KILBY. ...Like Bernie Denk, say. Reckon you could lick a heifer like Bernie? Huh? Break his pins for a penny or two? (*Pause.*) I'm not askin' you to *do* it, man. I'm just askin' if you think you've the fibre, the sand for that kinda fuckin' *activity.*

    Pause.

PADDY. I reckon so.

KILBY. Reckon so too, man.

PADDY. Do you?

KILBY. Well, let's say I've reason to believe. Have that hunch about you, I do. So, d'you know any moves?

PADDY. Headbutts an' shit?

KILBY. Fuck headbutts. Techniques, man. Karate, fucksake, put your man down, disempower the cunt.

PADDY. Not really.

KILBY. You should. That's somethin' Hughie never learnt, he'll regret. Coupla lessons with Kilby if you want, set you straight. (*Short pause.*) Fuck this, man.

    KILBY *exits. Pause. Re-enters with Nik Naks, stands at doorway, opens packet, puts one in his mouth, sucks.*

PADDY. You actually know the arts, Kilby? (*Pause.*) Kilby.

    Pause. KILBY *still sucking.*

    Kilby, man.

KILBY (*starts chewing*). Fuck d'you think I know the lingo, man? *Or* the moves. Can't know the lingo an' the moves without knowin' the fuckin' art. (*Puts another one in his mouth, sucks.*)

PADDY. An' what like... belt would you...?

    KILBY *shakes his head. Pause. Sucks five or six seconds, chews.*

KILBY. Black. Second dan. Goin' for me third. D'you want one? (*Short pause.*) Go on. Taste of spare ribs.

PADDY. What do I do?

KILBY. Suck them.

> PADDY *takes one, puts it in his mouth and sucks*. KILBY *likewise. Pause, seven or eight seconds. They chew,* PADDY *nodding.*

> Get all the flavour?

PADDY. Jaysus.

KILBY. Savoury, aren't they?

PADDY. Salty.

KILBY. Yeah... That's what savoury fuckin' *means*, man. (*Short pause.*) Think I feel somethin' brown brewin', now. (*Short pause.*) Shotokan.

PADDY. Huh?

KILBY. That's me school, man. Me discipline. Thirty per cent fists, seventy legs. Hence the fuckin'... me Chuck jeans. Me gusset. Weapon of choice is the pole.

PADDY (*of Nik Naks*). Delicious.

KILBY. You listenin'?! An' not *this* fuckin' pole. (*Grabs crotch.*) A longer pole for fightin'. But not *much* longer, think you know what I'm sayin'. (*Winks.*)

PADDY. An' can you smash bricks an' shit?

KILBY (*holds out his hands*). See them calluses?

> PADDY *looks*.

> Make no mistake, man. (*Of Nik Naks.*) Might have some of them after for durin' the film, huh? Might send you out. (*Pause, sucking his fingers.*) Time you.

PADDY. Give us another one.

KILBY. One more. (*Giving him one.*) Make the most of it.

> *They suck seven or eight seconds before chewing.*

> Don't know will I go up yet.

PADDY. Where?

> KILBY *lifts his buttocks slightly off chair. Pause.*

KILBY. It's approachin' the lips of me hoop. (*Pause. Considering, then sitting back down.*) Fuck it. What d'you think of this place?

PADDY. Nice.

KILBY. I think it's a hole.

PADDY. You know what you are, Kilby? Have to say…

KILBY. What's that?

PADDY. You're the Deputy Sheriff of fuckin'… of Crip.

KILBY. You clever cunt.

PADDY. Aren't you?

KILBY. That's *exactly* what I am. (*Short pause.*) Of crip an' of batterin'. (*Takes another from the packet, holds it in front of his mouth.*) Sorry, man. Rest are for Kilby.

> KILBY *puts it in his mouth, sucks five or six seconds, scrunching the bag closed, then, chewing.*

That's really pissed me off now, you know that? 'Bout your snorkel an' all. Kind of ingrained on me brain.

PADDY. Ah, he's always at that.

KILBY.…Branded in there. I know he's under pressure, but there's ways to talk to your mates. (*Pause. To himself.*) 'The Deputy Sheriff of Crips.'

PADDY. Crip.

KILBY. '…Of Crip.' Even better. (*Pause.*) Class fuckin' phrase, that. (*To* PADDY.) 'Cos I *like* crips, I do. (*Pause.*) *Like* savoury. (*Pause. Fidgets a little on chair.*) That's it, now. (*Beat.*) Is it? (*Half stands up.*) Yep. It's touchin' cloth. (*Stands up, exiting.*) Gonna flush me quarry, man.

> KILBY *exits.* PADDY *goes over to his trousers and turns them. Goes over to* KILBY*'s jacket, feels it, admires it. Takes jacket off coat rack. The toilet flushes. Quickly puts jacket back on coat rack. Jacket falls on floor. Picks it up again and hangs it up just as* KILBY *enters.*

Fuck're you doin'?

PADDY. Just admirin'.

KILBY. Go easy! (*Sits down.*)

PADDY (*running his hand along back of jacket*). Was downwards, wasn't it.

KILBY. That's the way Chink *goes,* man. Downwards or backwards.

PADDY. Dragon Fist.

KILBY. Northern Shaolin school. Now get away from it.

PADDY (*sits down*). An' it was pre*cisely* fuckin' stitched, wasn't it?

KILBY. Took a month an' a half.

PADDY. Jaysus! (*Pause.*) An' would you not ask Puppacat to get a few echelons together, like, yourself, Hughie an' all an' just, you know, *do* somethin'.

KILBY. 'Bout CopperDolan?

PADDY. *To* him.

KILBY. He's a copper, Paddy. There's rules, man, the treaty. We can't fuck with him.

PADDY. But he can fuck with us.

KILBY. Outs...

PADDY. *Youse.*

KILBY. Outside the boundaries he can do what he wants. An' I know Puppacat's talked to him 'bout goin' easy in general, but yeah, he's still there, man. Causin' hassle, fuckin'...

PADDY. Like *Serpico.*

KILBY. Who?

PADDY. The film.

Pause.

KILBY. Karate film?

PADDY. Pacino, man. Coppers.

KILBY. Didn't see it. An' why's he like him?

PADDY. Bit of a righteous cunt.

KILBY. CopperDolan's not righteous.

PADDY. Well, I know, but…

KILBY. Sure how could he be, cahootin' with wicked cunts like us, makin' villainous treaties an' all? CopperDolan's a half-rogue fuckin' maverick, spends half his beat down Delgado's playin' pool an' gettin' his billy club sucked gratis by hooers.

PADDY. He's into that, yeah?

KILBY. Which?

PADDY. That kind of act.

KILBY. *Oh*, yeah. Pig in shite, man. See, the Gook Nation's his beat so no one keeps an eye on him. Get them to come in, he will, one or two a night. He'll have a couple of games, few pints an' a hooverin'. An' *dogs*, man…

PADDY. Yeah?

KILBY. …*Jaysus! But*… You know? Long's they're a mouth an' a tongue an' some power of good suction…

PADDY. …He's a happy copper.

KILBY. Zactly. (*Pause.*) Like to give him a spankin', I would.

PADDY. Like to meself.

KILBY. Good buggerin'.

PADDY. What?

KILBY. An' not in a sexual way, now. Not in a way he'd like it, pansy an' all's he is, but in a violent way. Disable him with a Wing Chun flurry, stun the cunt, I would, then stick it up there, snap his hoop for him, bugger him with a tearin' forceful motion. Powerful motion he wouldn't like. Bugger resistance out of him. Then I'd sit him down with a needle an' thread, make him sew Dragon Fist onto *that* jacket.

PADDY. Good idea.

KILBY. Have me lob out like this, I would. He'd be bent over bareholed, beaverin' away an' every time he made a mistake, I'd – Uuh! – slide it up a bit, there, just an inch or two, maybe three. As a threat, you know?

PADDY. Of the *full* bugger, yeah?

KILBY. Full-length an' horn-spread, man. As a taster. Unh! An' I'd be sayin'… Give his arse a little spank, there, too – (*Mimes a slap on CopperDolan's arse with sound effect.*) bit of a shamin' spank an' I'd be sayin'… The fuck'd I be sayin'?

Pause.

PADDY. You want *me* to…?

KILBY (*simultaneous with 'to'*). I'm askin' you, fucksake.

PADDY. I don't know. Em…

KILBY. No?

PADDY. Em…

KILBY. '*Get* that fuckin' thing done.'

PADDY. Right.

KILBY. 'Now!'

PADDY. 'An' no mistakes.'

KILBY. 'Or it'll be the full hog an' rim-strain'.

PADDY. Rim-strain. *Ring*-sprain.

KILBY. …Fuckin', *yeah*. Unh! 'You feel it, CopperDolan?' Unh! 'You feel the potential, there, man?'

PADDY. Potential for anguish.

KILBY. 'You feel it? (*Mimes arse-slap.*) Huh? Gonna stop you destroyin'. Treaty or not, man. Treaty or none, gonna make you create.'

PADDY. 'Or suffer.'

KILBY. Yep.

PADDY. 'Create or suffer, man. Create or endure. *Your* choice.'

KILBY. 'Vicious full-length buggerin' or, or…'

PADDY. '… Sewin'.'

KILBY. '*Sewin'!*' Fuckin' *needle*craft, man.

PADDY. 'Buggerin' or needlecraft, CopperDolan.'

KILBY. 'One or the other.'

PADDY (*self-consciously*). Unh!

KILBY. Unh! *Oh*, yeah.

PADDY. 'That hurt, CopperDolan?'

KILBY. 'That hurt, man?'

PADDY *and* KILBY (*simultaneously*). 'Well, it's meant to.' (*Slight laugh.*)

KILBY. ''Cos playin' with Kilby, you're playin' with fire...'

PADDY. Uh-huh...

KILBY. Like it?

PADDY. I do.

KILBY. What else?

PADDY. '... So you're gonna get burnt.'

KILBY. Nah, that's a continuation.

PADDY. It is. Of...

KILBY. Go on.

PADDY. ...Of the other...

KILBY. Go on. Somethin' else.

PADDY. Em. 'You were nasty, man.' Yeah?

KILBY. Unh! '*Yeah*, man. Nasty to Kilby. (*Mimes arse-slap.*) To his jacket.'

PADDY. 'So now Kilby's gonna be nasty.' (*Mimes arse-slap.*)

KILBY. Unh!

PADDY. Yeah?

KILBY. Go on, man.

PADDY. '... Nasty to the CopperDolan.' (*Mimes arse-slap.*) Unh!

KILBY. Unh! (*Mimes arse-slap.*)

PADDY *mimes arse-slap.*

(*Mimes arse-slap.*) Unh!

PADDY. Unh!

KILBY. Fuckin' unh, man!!! You've more style in your... (*Mimes arse-slap*.) in your little fuckin' *finger*!

PADDY. Thanks.

KILBY. ...In your *flute* than Hughie has!

PADDY. Give us another one of them Nik Naks, will you?

KILBY. Sorry, man. Nik Naks stay with Kilby. See, Hughie's clothes have style, you can't dispute that, polly an' all's it is, but the man *inside* the clothes...? Sorely lackin' I reckon. An' I'm not puttin' him down, now, I know he's your mate, what I'm doin's questionin'. I mean, who am I to say straight out he's an arse or a fuckhead or, I don't know, a shitpoke, when he's got, you know, people like yourself really like him, Puppacat an' all...?

PADDY. Puppacat?

KILBY. *Weell*, he's *fond* of him. But what I'm sayin's just 'cos he thinks one thing, doesn't mean I can't observe an' question, me own self, does it?

PADDY. Course not.

KILBY. ...Follow me *own* hunches. That's me way, man. (*Standing up*.) C'mon. Show you a few moves.

PADDY. What?

KILBY. You said you wanted a lesson. Let's go. Get up there an' take the stance.

PADDY *stands up*.

All this mimin' of buttfuck has me riled up. (*Takes out Nik Naks*.) Here. (*Gives one to* PADDY.) Fortify us for the session.

KILBY *takes one himself and they suck, six to eight seconds, then chew.*

PADDY. Hang on a sec, man. Sorry... Just to go back...

KILBY (*doing stretching exercises*). What?!

PADDY. You said about the Puppacat bein' fond of Hughie an' all?!

KILBY. Mmm-hmm.

PADDY. Yeah?

KILBY. *Yeah*, man.

PADDY. Well, if he feels that way, then why's he makin' him go up an' break Bernie Denk's pins when he knows he's all fucked up over his oul'one?

KILBY. *Ah...*

PADDY. ...You know?

KILBY (*stops stretching*). ...*Well...* Maybe he doesn't *have* to. Maybe all's not what it seems an' Hughie's gonna get a surprise when he gets up to Bernie's. Puppacat works in wondrous ways, man. Don't underestimate his power to go all corkscrewy, lep off the beaten track, know what I'm sayin'? Go the less travelled.

PADDY. What's the surprise?

KILBY. Surprise, man.

PADDY. Huh?

KILBY. It's a surprise. (*Heading towards toilet.*) Goin' for a shite. Get ready.

PADDY. Again?!

KILBY. Once you break the seal, man. An' shut the fuck up! You countin'?

PADDY. No.

KILBY. Had *half*, man.

> KILBY *exits.* PADDY *goes over to his jacket, puts it on, gets a feel for it. He tries a karate kick, admires himself, tries a different kick. His cock falls out of his boxers. He puts it back in. The toilet flushes. He takes the jacket off quickly, hangs it up, sits down.* KILBY *enters.*

> Right. Take the stance.

PADDY. Ah, you're all right, Kilby.

KILBY. What...?

PADDY. You're grand.

KILBY. Did I *say* there was somethin' wrong with me, Paddy?

PADDY. No.

KILBY. Then shut the fuck up… *get* up… an' take the fuckin' stance.

Pause.

PADDY. Can you not just *tell* me?

KILBY. Can you *tell* someone how to swim, Paddy? No. You've to fuck them in the water. So… Actually, hang on. You mind puttin' your trousers on first? Don't want your flute fallin' out when we're in close contact. D'you mind?

PADDY *gets his trousers off the radiator and begins putting them on.*

Dirty, wriggly thing. Don't get me wrong, man. I'm sure certain birds like it, possibly Hughie, whatever. Just that compared to me own… in me own *opinion*, like… it's a bit fuckin' wriggly. (*Short pause.*) D'you take that personal?

PADDY. No.

KILBY. Good. Take the stance.

The door opens and HUGHIE *enters, soaking wet. He walks by without even looking at them.*

Well…?

HUGHIE. Very clever, aren't you?

HUGHIE *exits left. Pause.*

PADDY. What's he on about?

KILBY. None of your business. C'mon an' I'll show you the one 'fore he comes back in.

PADDY. Aah, now…

KILBY. …C'mon. Show you a lock, I will. An arm-lock you can do with one hand an' keep the other one free to inflict damage, pull your lob or whatever. (*Beat.*) All right?

PADDY. Why's he sayin' you're clever?

KILBY. 'Cos I *am*, man. Now, c'mere an' try an' grab me.

Pause. PADDY *goes to grab him.*

Wait. No. Wait. Try an' hit me a dig.

PADDY. Hit you a…?

KILBY. That's right. Try an' hit me a wallop. (*Pause*.) I won't hurt you, Paddy.

PADDY. You swear?

KILBY. Don't doubt me precision, man, me control. All right? Have faith in me skill as your sensei. Now go.

Pause. KILBY *takes a defensive stance.* PADDY *gets ready to attack.* HUGHIE *enters, interrupting them. He wears dry trousers and a T-shirt, carries a towel.*

Did you wreck your Rocha, man?

PADDY. Should've wore me snorkel, Hughie.

HUGHIE *sits down in an armchair.*

The offer was there.

HUGHIE *begins drying his hair.*

KILBY (*to* PADDY). Do it after, yeah?

PADDY. Which? Oh, right.

KILBY. The *moves*, man.

HUGHIE *finishes drying his hair. Silence.*

Well…? (*Pause*.) Hughie.

HUGHIE. What?

KILBY. Tell.

HUGHIE. Nothin' *to* tell, man. Who left stink?

KILBY. Stink?

HUGHIE. In me jacks.

Pause.

KILBY. I think if you go back in, Hughie, take a good sniff, you'll discover you're mistaken there. It's not a stink, it's a hum.

HUGHIE. A hum?

KILBY. A sweet, healthy hum. My stools don't stink. Now tell us about up Bernie's.

Pause.

HUGHIE (*to* PADDY). D'*you* know about this?

PADDY. What?

HUGHIE....No?

KILBY. 'Bout what, Hughie?

HUGHIE. You *know* what. The bloke up Bernie's. The fuckin' driver.

KILBY. *Aaaah*, right. Driver in the chair...

PADDY. Who's this?

KILBY....Tied up.

HUGHIE. Tied up in the chair, minus *teeth*, you cunt. Fuckin' Bernie Denk in leather fuckin' gloves, isn't that it.

KILBY. Work gloves.

HUGHIE. Me thinkin' *he's* the one whose pins I'm s'posed to be breakin' an' there he is, workin' your man over, leather gloves an' brass knucks, smackin' him round, he's after knockin' half his teeth out. An' *that* mad cunt, that peg-legged cunt, hoppin' round.

PADDY. Who's it, Nancy?

HUGHIE. Nancy *an'* Bernie.

KILBY. The lovers.

PADDY. Huh?

KILBY (*to* PADDY). *Oh*, yeah.

HUGHIE....Hoppin' round behind me like a pogo stick, hasn't the common fuckin' manners to wear her prosthetic. Up an' down, up an' down, over me shoulder, talkin' in me fuckin' ear, 'I predict this, I predict that...'

KILBY. What'd she predict?

HUGHIE. A batterin'. Fuck d'you think?

KILBY. Receivin' or givin' ?

HUGHIE. You *know*, givin'. Predictin' me gettin' in there, Paddy, givin' your man one 'sif he wasn't in a bad enough state already.

PADDY. Who, man?

HUGHIE. The driver. (*Pause*.) Me oul'one, Paddy, the driver who…

PADDY. Aaaah….Who crashed into her.

HUGHIE (*to* KILBY). A dirty fuckin' trick to play on someone. (*Pause*.) It's not on.

KILBY. Bit ungrateful, man…

HUGHIE. Yep. It's too much.

KILBY….Aren't you?

HUGHIE. It's not fuckin' on, Kilby. Too much, you've gone *too* far.

Pause.

KILBY. So, you didn't do it.

HUGHIE. No, I didn't.

Long pause.

KILBY. That's bad, now. Took work, that. Detective work an' dog work. Puppacat did business for you…

HUGHIE. Puppacat did?

KILBY….An' Puppacat doesn't do business. *Yeah*, the Puppa. But Kilby had foresight said, 'Fuckin', man. The fucker's no grace, he'll throw it back in your face, won't recognise it for the gesture it is.'

HUGHIE. I'm not throwin' an'thin' back fuckin' anywhere. I'm declinin' participation in Puppacat's fuckin'…

KILBY. *An'* Kilby.

HUGHIE….You an' Puppacat's fuckin' surprise.

Pause.

KILBY. You're declinin' participation.

HUGHIE. Much as I'm moved, man.

KILBY. Yeah?

HUGHIE. Touched as I am.

KILBY. Kilby stood back, man. Kilby observed. Puppa was the one smacked.

HUGHIE. What?!

KILBY. On the *head*, man. That's right. Dragged the fuck up to Bernie's, set up the Puppa-surprise. Surprise took time an' thought, took plannin' out of goodness, the benevolent Puppacat, magnanimous cunt *like* him, helpin' out his *man*. Givin' him justice an' payback an' the chance of some righteous batterin'.

HUGHIE. An' I 'preciate the gesture, man... You know? Respect to me, to me oul'one...

KILBY. Then why can't you accept it in good grace? Bit of bone-breakin', fuckin' show you're grateful. 'Cos the Puppacat won't like it. Say that *now*, I will. Puppacat'll be upset, not to mention Kilby. May be some major tin-star throwin'-down, you know what I'm sayin'? (*Mimes throwing down star.*) Caution to the wind an' layin' fuckin' in. Be some Shotokan head-stomps takin' place this particular night, this very address!

Pause.

PADDY. So did Bernie Denk not cripple the peg leg?

KILBY. Everything *but*, man. 'Costed her, broke in, wrecked her gaff...

PADDY. Why?

KILBY. They're lovers. What d'you expect? They were lovers an' they had a tiff, she dumped him an' that's not the issue.

PADDY. An' why'd he wreck her gaff?

KILBY. 'Cos she dumped him, didn't I say?

PADDY. Why?

KILBY. He ca... (*Beat.*) Fuck off. He called her 'Ma' in the sack, all right? Now somethin's gonna have to...

PADDY. He *what*?!

KILBY. He called her 'Ma'! They were in... (*To* HUGHIE.) I'm not finished with you. (*To* PADDY.) They were in the sack saddlin' an' just as he was shootin' his muck in her...

PADDY. No way.

KILBY....He shouted it out. Yeah, freaked the peg leg to fuck, an' peg legs don't freak easy. Usually been through the mill when they get the fuckin' thing chopped off, they become impervious to *lesser* freakin's. Anyway, she dumped him, he hounded her, they made up an' all's lovey-dovey again. They're doin' favours for Puppacat, so's he can do favours for you, Hughie, not that you give a fuck, throwin' it back in everyone's fuckin' face!!!

Pause.

HUGHIE. You don't know what the fuck you're talkin' about. *You* understand, don't you, Paddy?

PADDY. Your reasons, like?

HUGHIE. Yeah.

PADDY. Have to say, man.

KILBY. *Now!*

PADDY. ...I don't see the problem.

KILBY. *Now*, man!!

HUGHIE. Your man didn't mean it, Paddy. For all we know it was me oul'one's fault, you know? She's an oul'one, she...

KILBY. Oul'ones don't crash, man. Oul'ones drive careful, fuckin' six miles an hour; check both sides 'fore fartin'... *an'* the fuckin' rear-view. It was his fault, man, piss positive.

HUGHIE. Kilby...

KILBY. So you're gonna have to go back up there.

HUGHIE. But...

KILBY. That's it, man, no. (*Short pause.*) The decision's made, the gavel is pounded.

Long pause.

HUGHIE. Well, I'm not.

KILBY. Sorry?

HUGHIE. I'm not gonna, Kilby.

Pause.

KILBY. Would that be in your dreams, now?

HUGHIE. No.

KILBY. Where'd it be?

HUGHIE. Be somewhere else.

KILBY. That right?

HUGHIE. Be in reality, man. I'm not fuckin' doin' it. (*Pause*.) It's me oul'one. D'you not understand? Oul'one, mother whose fuckin'… whose vagina I came out of, day one.

KILBY. I know where you came out of, man.

HUGHIE. Who bore me to fuckin' *term*, man, raised me up. Who wouldn't say feck 'stead of fuck, wouldn't even say flip. Have youse no concept of me torture, the loss I'm facin'?

KILBY. Potentially.

HUGHIE. …Of an'thin' beyond batterin'?! Fuckin' hell!

Pause.

KILBY. Think I'll talk to Puppacat, get him to take *you* on, Paddy, huh? What d'you think? *This* touch-hole's on his way out.

HUGHIE. *I* am?

KILBY. Yeah.

HUGHIE. *You* are.

KILBY. On me way out?

HUGHIE. A touch-hole.

Pause.

KILBY. That's in there, now, Hughie. All right? That's carved on me brain, now, permanent. (*To* PADDY.) Paddy. (*To* HUGHIE.) Won't be forgotten. (*To* PADDY.) Paddy.

PADDY. What?

KILBY. Get Puppacat to take *you* on, huh?

Pause.

PADDY (*quietly*). Yeah.

HUGHIE. Fuck're you sayin' 'Yeah' for?

PADDY. Just… (*Short pause*.) *because*, man. I'm only…

HUGHIE. '*Yeah*', for fuck's sake?!!! (*To* KILBY.) An' Puppacat'd take him?!

KILBY. He might.

HUGHIE. His gee, man. Over me?! No offence, Paddy, but you couldn't hack it. (*To* KILBY.) What makes you think he could hack it?

KILBY. A hunch.

HUGHIE. 'A hunch'?! A *guess*, man. (*To* PADDY.) No offence, Paddy... (*To* KILBY.) Guess of a *dirt*burger.

KILBY (*indicating his head*). I'm markin' all this in here, Hughie.

HUGHIE (*to* PADDY). An' when did you decide you wanted to work for Puppacat?!

KILBY. Did he say that?

PADDY....I never said that.

KILBY. He said he *could*.

Short pause.

PADDY (*to* KILBY). *Well... You...*

KILBY (*to* PADDY). I said. Fine! (*Beat*.) Did you agree, man?

PADDY. Yeah.

KILBY. Then you said too.

HUGHIE (*to* PADDY). On Kilby's hunch...?! Guess?! (*Beat*.) Paddy!

KILBY. *Hunch*, man.

HUGHIE. On Kilby's just decidin' out of the blue?!! (*Pause. To* KILBY.) What did you do while I was gone?

KILBY. Did nothin', man. Kilby was Kilby.

HUGHIE. A turkeyburger, yeah?

Pause.

KILBY. Bit of carvin' goin' on, Hughie. Touch-hole, dirtburger... On me brain, man... Turkeyburger. 'Proachin' puppyness, gonna have to *be* one. Be a puppy, you won't like it. Paddy's not your man. Paddy's his own man. You don't dictate. (*To* PADDY.) Does he?

PADDY. No.

KILBY (*to* HUGHIE). See?

PADDY. But, same time, man, have to say, I'm not *against* you or an'thin... You know? I'm not sidin' or an'thin', I'm wonderin'.

HUGHIE. Wonderin' what?

PADDY. Why you can't just do your job, man.

KILBY. Zactly.

PADDY. ...Get it done. Don't get me wrong, man.

KILBY. Fuckin' zactly.

Pause.

HUGHIE. Who the fuck are you to...? No, wait, now.

PADDY. Hughie.

HUGHIE. ...To fuckin'... Wait a sec. All a sudden, *you*... Someone who never went out, broke a finger, let alone a pin or a head... are tellin' me... Am I hearin' this or what?... are tellin' me I can't do my job proper? (*Indicating* KILBY.) 'Cos this...?

KILBY. Ah...! Ah...!

HUGHIE. 'Cos this fuckin'...?

KILBY. Ah...! Don't say it. Have to pinch off your bronchis.

Pause.

HUGHIE. ...'Cos Kilby has a hunch?! You're tellin' me how to handle head-breakin', you can't even dress yourself, can you? Fucksake, smackin' advice from someone...

PADDY. Don't... Hughie!

HUGHIE. ...who wears...

PADDY. ...Don't slag me fuckin' snorkel!!!

Pause.

HUGHIE. ...a filthy dirty, ugly, rubbish-lookin' oul...

KILBY *grabs him by the throat.*

Urk!

KILBY. Don't slag Paddy's snorkel, man. You're slaggin' stools, you're slaggin' snorkels an' it's not fuckin' 'preciated. That thing has served him well an' faithful. Paddy?

PADDY. Ten years.

HUGHIE. Urk!

KILBY. It's kept him dry in the torrent, warm in the gale an' if you say any more, I won't just pinch off your bronchis, I'll tear out your gizzard. D'you understand? Just say 'Urk'.

HUGHIE. Urk!

KILBY *lets him go. He falls to the floor clutching his throat and coughing.*

KILBY. Don't think the badge came off there, 'cos it didn't. That was controlled discipline, not mayhem. Badge comes off, you'll know it.

PADDY (*to* HUGHIE). Sorry, man.

KILBY (*to* PADDY). What're you…? (*Sighs. Picks up* PADDY*'s videotape.*)

PADDY (*to* HUGHIE). You all right?

KILBY. Can I borry this thing off you, Paddy?

PADDY. What? If you want.

KILBY. 'Cos I don't think we're gonna be watchin' it here, now. (*To* HUGHIE.) Hughie? Sorry I had to do that, man. (*Takes out Nik Naks.*) Here, d'you want one? (*Holding packet out.*) They're *yours*, like. (*Pause.*) Don't be a little fuckin' sulk, now. I'll get you back for them. (*To* PADDY.) Paddy? Just one, now.

PADDY *takes one.* KILBY *puts packet away.*

PADDY. You not havin' one?

KILBY (*holding up videotape*). Savin' them.

PADDY *puts a Nik Nak in his mouth. Sucks.*

Bit in this where he…? (*Remembers that* PADDY *is sucking.*) Oh. (*Short pause.*) Fuck it.

KILBY *takes the packet back out, has one himself. Sucks.*
PADDY *begins chewing.*

PADDY. What're you sayin'? (*Remembers that* KILBY *is sucking.*) Oh.

Pause. PADDY *waits.* KILBY *begins chewing.*

KILBY. Bit in this where he does his mad battle-cry?

PADDY. Which one, man?

KILBY. What d'you mean?

PADDY. Does various.

KILBY. Does he?

PADDY. Yep. Various tones, frequencies…

KILBY. Hunky, man. They're funny noises he makes, aren't they?

PADDY. Mm.

KILBY. Funny but deadly, like. (*Putting on jacket. Pause.*) Just use your jacks 'fore I go, Hughie, yeah? Conclude me epic.

KILBY *exits.* HUGHIE *and* PADDY *looking at each other. Silence.*

HUGHIE. Paddy…

HUGHIE*'s pager goes off.*

PADDY. Who is it, man?

HUGHIE *looks at him.*

End of Act One.

ACT TWO

The same. A week later. Daytime. KILBY *and* PADDY *enter,*
PADDY *carrying an umbrella. Both are formally dressed, although*
PADDY *still wears his snorkel. There are a few sandwiches on the*
table, several cans of lager. They proceed to take off jackets, etc.
PADDY *shakes out the umbrella.*

KILBY. That *Eight Diagram* shit's shit, man. That muck about
scratchin' an eight with your pole durin' a ruckus. Figure eight on
the floor? Bollox, man. An' a pole fighter never fights that
flamboyant. Their movements're too wide, too circular. Suppose
that looks good on film an' all, looks graceful, but real life it's
short, jerky, straight lines; keep it tight in here, you know?
Protect your body. That monk shit's just madness. An' you
don't… Paddy!

PADDY *stops shaking umbrella.*

You don't just walk out of the temple like that either. You have to
heft the urn, man, receive your tats. Well, not your tats…

PADDY. The urn?

KILBY.…Your *brands*. Fuckin' giant urn blockin' the exit, man.
Filled with white-hot coals, have to heft it with your forearms
like that; dragon an' tiger get branded in there.

PADDY. No way!

KILBY.…Seared in permanent. Yeah an' the fuckin' *pain*, Paddy.

PADDY. Yeah?

KILBY. 'Scrutiatin', 'parently.

PADDY. I'd imagine.

KILBY. So. You know… Bit lackin' in authentics.

PADDY. Mm. (*Short pause.*) Good, though.

KILBY. Oh, yeah.

They sit down.

Fuckin' excellent otherwise.

Pause.

PADDY. What'd you think of Nancy an' Bernie?

KILBY. Fuckin' disgrace, man.

PADDY. Weren't they?

KILBY. The moans of her!

PADDY. *An'* him.

KILBY. What?

PADDY. Could hear it all the way 'cross the church. 'Nah.' Like that.

KILBY. Not '*Nah*', man.

PADDY. What, then?

KILBY. '*Ma*', he was sayin'.

PADDY. Oh. (*Pause.*) She let him?

KILBY. They came to an agreement.

> KILBY *attacks* PADDY. PADDY *blocks and counter-attacks, pulling his strike short.*

On'y way he can get off, man.

PADDY. Jaysus! An' how'd she fall out of the pew?

KILBY. He put his hand in her nik-niks, man, cold paw on her privates, she got a shock, jumped, wasn't wearin' her fuckin'…

PADDY. Ah.

KILBY.…You know…

PADDY.…Her prosthetic, right, so she'd nothin' to balance her.

KILBY. Into the aisle, man, nik-niks exposed. I'd a great view; purple, couple of stragglers.

PADDY. What?

KILBY. Pubes, man. Creepin ' out the side there like moss.

> KILBY *attacks*. PADDY *blocks and counter-attacks, pulling his strike short.*

Good stuff, Paddy.

PADDY. Yeah?

KILBY. You're blossomin'.

PADDY attacks. KILBY blocks and counter-attacks, hitting
PADDY in the stomach, winding him.

Sorry, man. Shouldn't attack the Kilby like that. To strike back's
me nature. You all right? To attack, to counter-attack's Kilby's
instinct. Get up there.

PADDY. I'm all right.

KILBY. Toughen you up anyway. What doesn't kill you. That right?

PADDY. Makes you stronger?

KILBY. That's right. Conditions you.

KILBY goes over to window. Looks out. Pause.

PADDY. C'mere, when you gonna show us you smashin' somethin'
barehanded?

KILBY. When I've somethin' to smash.

PADDY. I'd love to see it.

KILBY. Somethin' worthy of me fist. Fuck is he, now? (*Pause.*
Looking out.)

PADDY. I hate that fuckin' church.

KILBY (*moving away from window*). The steps, man?

PADDY. Thought I was gonna collapse.

KILBY. This is what I'm sayin' 'bout conditionin'. You need a
regime.

PADDY. I mean...

KILBY. You listenin'?

PADDY. I *know* I do.

KILBY. I'll start you on one. Go on.

PADDY. ...I mean, the on'y ones go to mass regular're fogeys an'
how the fuck're they supposed to, every day of the week, you
know, negotiate those...?

KILBY (*going back over to window*). *I* don't know. Should find another church or somethin'. Stay at home. (*Short pause. Looking out.*) Fuck that fogey shit, man. Fuckin' *hate* them cunts.

PADDY. Why?

KILBY (*to himself*)....Fuckin' stinkholes! (*Beat. To* PADDY.) 'Cos they stink, man.

Pause.

PADDY. C'mere. When Hughie comes up, right? Will you not mention an'thin 'bout me, you know...

KILBY (*coming away from window*)....Gettin' in there?

PADDY....Joinin' the, yeah, the echelons. Wanna break it to him slowly; gentle. Wanna ease him the info. An' a day like today...

KILBY. I get you. Be wrong, would it?

PADDY. Be inappropriate. Solemn an' all's it is.

KILBY. It is, it's solemn. It's mournful.

PADDY. It is. Today's a day of support. (*Pause.*) Can't wait all the same, man. What d'you think he'll think?

KILBY. The Puppa?

PADDY. Of me, like.

KILBY. Be impressed, man. Big bloke such as yourself; strong, smart, vicious-lookin' – don't smile – fuckin' capable...? Don't smile front of him. I'll give you an attack, you defend. When he's here, like... Defend, do a technique, say nothin'. Might do it again, couple of times, put it in his head, 'Jesus, this fucker's good...'

PADDY. This *him*, now?

KILBY. '... Good in the arts 'f he can counter the Kilby.' This is Puppacat.

PADDY. Right.

KILBY. What he's ponderin'. So be diligent.

PADDY. Vigilant. (*Beat.*) Diligent.

KILBY. Vigilant. No, you're right. Be ready.

Pause.

PADDY. Why shouldn't I smile?

KILBY. Well, does he wanna see how nice you are? How sweet?

PADDY. No.

KILBY. What's he wanna see?

PADDY. How fuckin'… how vicious I am.

KILBY. That's right, so don't worry. You worried?

PADDY. A bit.

KILBY. Fuck that. (*Returning to the window*.) Be hunky monkey with me to vouch. Get you in now, get you workin', man…

PADDY. Hunky.

KILBY. …Get you a *wage*.

Pause.

PADDY. Wasn't too happy, was he?

KILBY. Hughie?

PADDY. With Nancy an' Bernie.

KILBY. He wasn't. (*Short pause*.) Ah, sure. (*Beat*.) Kinda lightened it, though.

PADDY. Which? The…

KILBY (*simultaneous with 'The'*). The service. Gave it an element of levity.

PADDY. Did.

KILBY. …You think? As opposed to gravitas.

PADDY. Would you get up on her, Kilby?

KILBY. Nancy?

PADDY. Yeah.

KILBY. I *would*, yeah.

PADDY. D'you reckon it'd be hard with the stump an' all?

KILBY. Be like any other bird, man. Just grab a pawful of satchel an' pull your way in. I wouldn't run a *mile*, though.

PADDY. Ah no.

KILBY. ...Or eat Nik Naks out of her nik-niks. Or if I did I wouldn't suck them. But a jockey, now...

PADDY. Zactly.

KILBY. Good saddlin' for the experience of it. The novelty.

PADDY. Speakin' of Nik Naks.

KILBY. Huh? Sure, have a sambo.

PADDY. Ah, fuck that.

KILBY. Not good enough now, that it? You fuck, see once you've had a taste...

PADDY. This is it, man. ...You're hooked.

KILBY. See's he any, sure.

> PADDY *exits to kitchen.* KILBY *looks out window. Pause.*

> Here he is now. (*Pause.*) Fuck's he holdin'?

PADDY (*offstage*). A brolly?

KILBY. *No!* Well, *yeah*, but...

PADDY (*entering*). None there, man.

KILBY. The fuck is he heftin'? (*Beat.*) Quick, man.

> PADDY *joins him at window.*

> (*To himself.*) Misses it...?

PADDY. Where's he?

> *Buzzer sounds.*

KILBY. ...Course. (*Buzzes* HUGHIE *in.*) There none?

PADDY. I'm gaggin', man.

KILBY. You junkie.

PADDY. I am. (*Short pause.*) The Echelon Junkie of Nik Nak.

KILBY. Class, man.

PADDY. Yeah.

KILBY. Class-*ic!* 'Cos you *are* a fuckin' echelon.

> KILBY *attacks.* PADDY *blocks and counter-attacks, pulling his strike short.*

An' a Fist of the Dragon to be.

PADDY. Sensei.

KILBY. Pupil.

> HUGHIE *enters, carrying an umbrella and Nancy's fake leg, wearing a suit.*

The fuck are you doin'?

HUGHIE (*taking off coat, etc.*). Fuck her.

PADDY. That her prosthetic?

HUGHIE. Fuck *her* if she wants to heavy-pet in church front of me dead oul'one. Huh? She wants to expose her dirty nana, fuckin' mockerise the ceremony, me time of mournin'. *Fuck* her. See how far she gets now.

KILBY. You didn't just rief it off her stump, did you?

HUGHIE. She left it down... No.

KILBY. Good.

HUGHIE. ...An' I picked it up. Sittin' on Bernie Denk's lap, she'd her tongue in his gullet...

KILBY. Still?

HUGHIE. ...Fuckin', *yeah* still; tongue in his gullet, hand on his jockey, fuckin' prosthetic was left there, leanin' against the wall, so I sauntered by furtive, swiped it an' moseyed off. (*Sits down, fake leg on his lap.*) Price of lust, man.

PADDY. Mustn't've predicted that.

KILBY. Huh? She mustn't've.

HUGHIE (*to himself*). ...Price of bein' a slut.

KILBY. Did you hear that, Hughie?

HUGHIE. I did.

KILBY. She mustn't've predicted that. (*To* PADDY.) Nice one, man.

HUGHIE (*coughs*). Fucksake. (*Coughs. To* PADDY.) Think I got what you had, man.

KILBY. Bit of a tickle, yeah?

HUGHIE. More than a tickle, man. Bit of a bark.

PADDY. Mine's gone.

HUGHIE. Bit of a *hack* in me. *Top* of me fuckin' belly.

KILBY. Here's your keys. (*Throws them to* HUGHIE.)

HUGHIE (*catching them*). Puppacat not here yet?

KILBY. He should be. Prob'ly doin' the usual…

PADDY. Chattin'…

KILBY. …thing, yeah. Givin' an audience. Was good all the same, Hughie.

PADDY. Wasn't it? Very poignant.

KILBY. Still. Better place, man.

PADDY. Where?

KILBY. Better place, Hughie. (*To* PADDY.) *Heaven*, you fuckin'…

PADDY. *Oh*.

KILBY. Fuckin' 'Where?'! (*To* HUGHIE.) An' what happened last time, man; shit done, gullet grippage an' all, shit said…?

PADDY. That's right.

KILBY. Heat of the fuckin' moment, man. *Course* there's understandin'. *Course* there's respect. Sure, aren't we here to show that? Even Puppacat, busy an' all's he is, huh? Takes time out? Come up, he will now, we'll have our private, our *echelon* wake. Little adios, send her on her way, you know?

Pause.

HUGHIE. She was good, she was.

KILBY. Your oul'one?

HUGHIE. Dolly, yeah.

KILBY. She was.

HUGHIE. Whatsay, Paddy? Bit of history there with yourself an' herself.

PADDY. *Lot* of history. Good times. Good days…

HUGHIE. The best of days.

KILBY. Dug me perm she did. Did I tell you that?

PADDY. Oul'ones love perms.

KILBY. So? Doesn't take from the compliment.

PADDY. No.

KILBY. ...The intention.

HUGHIE. Many a time she gave Paddy his dinner.

PADDY. An' many a time I gobbled it up, fuckin' *licked* the plate.

HUGHIE. Didn't you?

PADDY. Licked it clean, man. Asked for more. 'Little Ollie Twist', she'd say.

KILBY. MORE?!!!

PADDY. 'Little Orphan Paddy', huh?

KILBY. MORE?!!!

PADDY. Never said that, Kilby. *Gave* you more 'cos she always had plenty. Growin' lads. That it, Hughie?

HUGHIE. Strappin' lads.

PADDY. That's it.

HUGHIE. An' that time you called up...

PADDY. Jaysus. Me complete nip, man.

KILBY. What?

PADDY. Was battered by the knackers.

HUGHIE. Mugged. (*To* PADDY.) An' what did they take?

PADDY. Everything. Money, me wallet, me watch...

HUGHIE. ...Your clothes...

PADDY. ...Me shoes... Thought I was in for a rapin', I did. Your oul'one opens the door, clicks me there all cockadangle.

HUGHIE. What did she do, but?

PADDY. Took it in her stride, man. Sure it wasn't as if she'd never seen one in her time...

HUGHIE. No.

PADDY. ...was it? Your oul'fella's, your own...

HUGHIE. It wasn't.

PADDY. Took care of business, then. Jesus, bathed me wounds… Eye out to here, I had.

HUGHIE. …Ran you a bath…

PADDY. Bubble bath. Fuckin' healin' salts, herbs, dose of Radox, the works; little bathrobe there, bit of talc…

HUGHIE. Good as fuckin' new, huh?

PADDY. Good as new.

HUGHIE. …Fuckin' woman! I'll miss her.

KILBY. We'll *all* miss her, man. (*Short pause.*) We'll all miss Dolly. (*Silence.*) You cryin'?

HUGHIE. No.

KILBY. It's all right to.

HUGHIE. I'm not.

KILBY. …'F you're a faggot. That right, Paddy?

PADDY. Ah, Kilby!

KILBY. I'm messin', man.

PADDY. Cry if you want, Hughie.

HUGHIE. Nah, fuck that. (*Beat.*) Find me own time, you know? Mourn private. I will. Unhindered, unwatched…

PADDY. That's the best way, suppose.

Silence.

HUGHIE. Ask you somethin', man?

KILBY. Go ahead.

HUGHIE. Am I out?

KILBY. What, of the echelons?

HUGHIE. Yeah. (*Pause.*) I am, amen't I.

KILBY. Dunno.

HUGHIE. Yeah, you know I am.

Pause.

KILBY. We weren't gonna tell you till after.

HUGHIE. No, that's all right, man. That's hunky. (*Pause*.) New beginnin', huh? A life change, sure fuck it. (*Pause*.) Fuck it.

KILBY (*jumps*). *Jaysus!* (*Takes a pager off his hip*.)

PADDY. You got a beeper ?!

KILBY (*looking at it*)....Frightened the fuckin'... Down the Windsor. How much was yours, Hughie?

HUGHIE. Ten.

KILBY. You were robbed, man. Seven. Bargained him down, I did. (*Checks number*.) Puppacat. (*To* HUGHIE.) Bit of Sellotape there, but it's perfect. Didn't even have to threaten a batterin'.

HUGHIE. Very good.

KILBY. Skills of the barter, man.

PADDY. Any Nik Naks, Hughie?

KILBY....Gift of the haggle. Know what I'm sayin'? Where's your fuckin' phone till I...? (*Looking around*.)

PADDY. Hughie.

HUGHIE. What?

PADDY. Any Nik Naks?

KILBY....Only you haven't fuckin'... *Bollox!* The fuck's wrong with me? Have to go all the way, now, down the fuck...!

PADDY. Hughie.

KILBY....The fuckin'... He's *none*, man!! (*Beat*.) Fucksake. No *phone*, no...

PADDY. Mellow.

KILBY....no *Nik Naks*... I'm *in* me fuckin' mellow.

PADDY. Should've got yourself a mobile.

KILBY. What, an' be a melanoma-head like the rest of them? (*To* HUGHIE.) There shops near here?

HUGHIE. On the corner.

KILBY. I'm no tool, Paddy.

PADDY. Get Nik Naks.

KILBY. Maybe it's fuckin' Nik Naks you want. Fuckin' 'mobile'! Where's the…? (*Picks up umbrella.*) Be back in a minute.

HUGHIE. Take the keys with you.

KILBY. *Buzz* me in. (*Going to door.*) Lazy prick, you!

KILBY *exits. Silence.*

PADDY. Mad cunt, isn't he?

HUGHIE. Mm. (*Beat.*) Fuckim!

PADDY. Huh?

HUGHIE. Hear him commiseratin'? Fuckim! Meets her once, you'd swear he knew her all his life, fuckin' fake. Talkin' 'bout understandin', fucksake, fuckin' respect as if he had any.

PADDY. He's plenty.

HUGHIE. What?

PADDY. Kilby's sensitive, man, you take the time, get some dialogue goin'. Fact, he's vulnerable, I'd say…

HUGHIE. Bollox.

PADDY. …insecure. Tellin' you, Hughie. All the fucker needs is patience, bit of understandin', whatever, you get *behind* the exterior, the mask, get the *real* Kilby. 'F people on'y made the effort…

HUGHIE. Fuck the effort.

PADDY. See?

HUGHIE. An' he didn't come here for the wake, Paddy, either. He came to see me expelled, the little satisfaction he'll get from it. (*Short pause.*) Betcha he hoped there'd be more, sure.

PADDY. More what?

HUGHIE. Punishment, the fuck! Betcha he'd other plans for today. Betcha behind me back he was houndin' Puppacat, huh? Gimme a goodbye batterin'. 'Come on, the Pup, he deserves it.' Can just imagine the cunt.

PADDY. Well, what happened, man?

HUGHIE. Huh?

PADDY. To make him want to. It can't be just…

HUGHIE (*simultaneous with 'just'*). So he was?!

PADDY. He… Well, he…

HUGHIE. Doesn't fuckin' surprise me, Paddy. An' nothin' happened. Least nothin' I'm aware of. Maybe it's me threads, he's jealous? I don't know… Me style?

PADDY. I don't know.

HUGHIE. It's mutual, anycase. (*Beat.*) An' what did Puppacat say?

PADDY. Said 'no', man. What d'you think?

HUGHIE. Did you see this?

PADDY. He told me.

HUGHIE. Well, fair play to Puppacat. Although, fuck it, fuck him, too. Fuckin' behaviour!

Pause.

PADDY. How's your belly, man?

HUGHIE. The pains?

PADDY. Yeah.

HUGHIE. Bad. Worse than before. Fuck, before it was like grease in me grill, now when it comes it's like chip oil in a chip pan on full, man, you know that way?… Fuckin' *sears* me innards.

PADDY. Should see a doctor, man. Get some prognosis.

HUGHIE. Mm. (*Pause.*) The fuck d'*you* care?

PADDY. Course I care. I'm sorry what happened.

HUGHIE. Me oul'one?

PADDY. The echelons. Well, her as well, course, but…

HUGHIE. I bet you are. An' who's me replacement, I wonder, huh? Someone not too far? 'Sorry' me hoop! Some fuck name of Paddy?

PADDY. No.

HUGHIE. Don't 'no' me, man. You an' Kilby all cosied up, now, couple of buds, sure what's the logical step? Petitionin' of Puppacat, I reckon. The lickin' of his hole, get you echeloned up. Am I right?

PADDY. Hughie, don't…

HUGHIE. Am I right?

PADDY. …Don't… *Yes*, you're right, but don't start actin' all betrayed, man. This is *outside* you, *outside* us.

HUGHIE. No, it's not…

PADDY. It is.

HUGHIE. …It's *about* us. It's *all* about us. The fuck happened you, Paddy? (*Pause.*) Huh?

PADDY. I bloomed if you *must* know.

HUGHIE. You 'bloomed'?!

PADDY. …Got out from, yeah, from under you an' blossomed. I stopped listenin' to you to me detriment, started listenin' to someone else to…

HUGHIE. Kilby?!

PADDY. …to me whatever. *Yeah*, Kilby.

HUGHIE. Advantage.

PADDY. …To me fuckin' advantage, man. Traded up, I did. Minion to echelon. 'Cos that's all I was with you. Keepin' me down all the time, fuckin' *stuntin'* me. You haven't a fuckin' clue what I'm capable of!!! (*Pause.*) All me fuckin' life!

Pause.

HUGHIE. What did the oul'one say that time you called up, Paddy?

PADDY. When?

HUGHIE. That time you were mugged, man, you called up nippy.

PADDY. Dunno.

HUGHIE. You do. 'F you remember what she did, then you remember what she said. Somethin' important. Somethin' we talked about since.

Pause. PADDY *shrugs.*

Paddy!

PADDY. Sorry, man.

HUGHIE. You fuckin' liar. You traitor.

PADDY. 'Traitor'?!

HUGHIE. After all she fuckin' did for you. You're betrayin' her beliefs, man!

PADDY. An' what've you been doin' these past years?

Short pause.

HUGHIE. Ah, yeah, but...

PADDY. ...Huh? Swear you never smacked in your life.

HUGHIE. ...but have to tell you, man. Been ponderin' this *last* while. Realisin', re-evaluatin'... Somethin' happens, then, you know, a stressful, a cathartic... occurrence or couple of 'currences, you get a new perspective an' I've got one. What happened last week put a stamp on what I suspicioned, Paddy. Gave me sight to see me for what I've been an' those cunts for what they are.

PADDY. An' what are they?

HUGHIE. Cunts, man. Cunts to stay away from. Glad I'm out.

PADDY. Yeah, right!

HUGHIE. ...Happy. No, I am, Paddy.

PADDY. Hang on. You spend...

HUGHIE. Didn't realise, but...

PADDY. ...Wait now. (*Beat.*) You spend years tellin' me how great they are, how cool, then soon's...

HUGHIE. I know.

PADDY. ...As...

HUGHIE. I fooled meself into thinkin' they were, *it was*, into believin', but the oul'one's kickin' clarified me perceptions an' I feel a need, now, to, I'm serious, a duty to caution you. All right? The last thing you wanna do is work for Puppacat. I could *tell* you shit. Shit that'd change your mind, man... right quick.

PADDY. So tell me.

HUGHIE. Can't.

PADDY. Yeah, right!

HUGHIE. Don't wanna get battered. That's *right*, right. Tell I'll get head-smacked, so I'm… Or fuckin' *worse*, man, so I'm not *gonna*. Suffice to say but. Shit you can't hack. *Know* what you can hack an' you can't hack this.

PADDY. An' why's that, now? 'Cos I don't polly up?

HUGHIE. Polly what?!

PADDY. …Like you, man? This isn't polly-polly land, Hughie. This is seat-of-your-pants land an' pollyness is moot.

HUGHIE. 'Moot'?

PADDY. …Is a moot way of life, man. Live your life polly, you do, always have, *judge* things polly on a fuckin'… a polly-polly scale. Well, I'm not on that scale. All right? That's not how you judge me any more. (*Short pause.*) Just 'cos I don't wear a Chief shirt, whatsis…?

HUGHIE. John Rocha.

PADDY (*simultaneous with 'Rocha'*). …A John Rocha shirt like yourself, polly pants…

HUGHIE. *Trousers!*

PADDY. *Pants*, I says!! Or *any* of that polly shit, you think it fuckin' behoofs you to…

HUGHIE (*simultaneous with 'to'*). …'Hoofs'?

Pause.

PADDY. Huh?

HUGHIE. Think it '*behoofs*' me? Like a dunkey?

PADDY. Fuck is a dunkey?!

HUGHIE. I mean a…

PADDY. Fuckin' dunkey!

HUGHIE. …a *don*key. Fuckin' be*hoofs*, sure, fucksake!

PADDY. An' I'll tell you what style is. *Guru* style. It's a durable Dragon Fist, a long-lastin' snorkel…

HUGHIE. 'Dragon Fist'?

PADDY. ...Shit like that. (*Beat*.) The jacket, man! Kilby's jacket that Dolan stroked, you fuckin'...

HUGHIE *bends over in agony, holding his stomach.*

...You know what I'm talkin' 'bout.

The intercom buzzes. HUGHIE *recovers, goes over to door, buzzes* KILBY *in, puts it on the latch. Pause.*

HUGHIE. Paddy.

PADDY. What?

HUGHIE. What did me oul'one say that time?

PADDY. I don't know.

HUGHIE. You do, you lyin' fuck! What'd she tell you, your hour of need?

PADDY. Hughie? Fuck your oul'one.

HUGHIE. What?!

PADDY. ...An' fuck you. You heard me. You're out an' I'm in. It's over. I'm an echelon, you're not an' never the fuckin' twain, man. (*Beat*.) *Never* the twain.

KILBY *enters. Pause.*

What's the jack, man?

KILBY. I ever tell you about the tin star, Hughie? (*Approaching. In his face.*) When that's thrown down, I'm gonna scratch a jangle on you, take you over me *knee*, I'm gonna, an' break bits...

PADDY. What happened?

KILBY (*shouting*). ...Break them *choppin'*. (*To* PADDY.) What? Be another hour or so. We've to stall here till then.

HUGHIE *coughs.*

I better not catch that, Hughie. D'you hear me?

HUGHIE. It's on'y a tickle, man.

KILBY. Tickle me hoop!

PADDY. Where is he?

KILBY. Down in James's Street, fuckin'...

PADDY. Hospital?

KILBY....fuckin' yeah. Nancy's after havin' a mishap, havin' a tumble down steps, she's after. Steps of the Sacred Heart.

PADDY. How the fuck did...?

KILBY. She's missin' a leg, Paddy.

HUGHIE. Fuck her.

PADDY. But was she not...?

KILBY (*to* HUGHIE). '*Fuck* her'?! (*To* PADDY.) Not what? (*To* HUGHIE.) That's lovely.

PADDY....Watchin' what she was doin'.

KILBY (*to* HUGHIE)....So *considerate*, man. (*To* PADDY.) She was upset, Paddy. Her attention was on other things.

HUGHIE. Like what? Bernie Denk's flute?

KILBY. Funny, man. How 'bout a five-grand prosthetic?

PADDY (*of leg*). That?!

KILBY....She thought was gone for ever. Could be more, Paddy. Tried to get her to calm down, they did. Tried to get her to *sit* down, but she insisted on standin', hoppin', weaker-sex shit, fuckin' wailin' an' all, 'I'm gonna have to save for a new one!' Hysterical. 'It's gonna take me years!' She didn't see, hoppin' backwards, the top step... pogoed off the edge an' down she tumbled. Thirty-six of the concrete fuckers. *Steep* fuckers. Head over hogans, she went, smacked damagous off each an' every one.

HUGHIE. For someone can see the future, she's not very good at... fuckin' seein' the future.

PADDY. *I* said that, man.

KILBY. So what we do is... He fuckin' did *too*.

PADDY. *What* do we do?

KILBY....Cheatin' cunt, you. (*To* PADDY.) We stall. (*To* HUGHIE.) Said to tell you, man...

PADDY. 'Stall'?!

KILBY. That too difficult?

PADDY. No.

KILBY. Cunt strokin' your gags, man, huh? (*To* HUGHIE.) Said to tell you it *was* on'y gonna be a talk, man. You an' Puppacat jaw-jigglin', him expellin' you verbal. Asked me to relay to you, he did, inform you it's gone up, now, 'cos of your boldness. Now he's expellin' you *corporal* 's gonna snap bones various an' sundry.

HUGHIE. Himself?

KILBY. He's bringin' her true love to avenge her on you. Bernie Denk up to do what he will in his grief. Purgin' an' shit, you know? Says you're fucked 'cos he's gonna give Bernie free rein, an' distraught an' frenzied's he's gonna be...

HUGHIE. Motherfucker.

KILBY. An' he is, man.

HUGHIE. What?

KILBY. He *did* fuck his mother.

HUGHIE. I'm talkin' 'bout Puppacat, not Bernie. (*Short pause.*) Cunt, *like* him.

KILBY. Shut the fuck up.

HUGHIE. Fuckin' mule!

KILBY. ...You hear me?

HUGHIE. Make me.

Pause.

KILBY. I will if you test me. Tin badge comes off, then...

HUGHIE. Sure you're allowed?

KILBY. ...then... What?

HUGHIE. Don't think you're allowed, some reason.

Pause.

KILBY. Paddy. Somethin' you're gonna have to learn. All right? Keep your fuckin' mouth shut.

KILBY *attacks for real.* PADDY *defends and counter-attacks, pulling his strike short. Pause.*

You fuckin' with me?

PADDY. No, man.

KILBY. Huh?

PADDY. That was instinct.

Pause.

KILBY. The apprentice learns fast.

PADDY. Well…

KILBY. Paddy. Textbook.

PADDY. Cheers.

KILBY. Proud of you. (*Gives* HUGHIE *a slap*.) Wasn't let *then*, Hughie. When Paddy told you, I wasn't. But *now*, maybe the situation's changed. Maybe I'm let give you a warmer-upper like your man mangled your oul'one was warmed up, brass knucks an' broken teeth. You 'member? Maybe that's Kilby's instructions.

PADDY. *Is* it, man?

KILBY. Huh? 'Fraid not, Paddy, no. Can't slap major, much to me fuckin'… chagrin. Though get ready yourself, man, yeah? Do your share if the Puppa demands it.

PADDY. Of batterin'?

KILBY. 'Cos he might.

Pause.

PADDY. How bad'll it be?

KILBY. Dunno. Stand you good stead, but.

PADDY. Bad, but?

KILBY. Depends on Puppacat, man. On Bernie. I'd imagine bad, yeah. You on? I *hope* bad. You on?

PADDY. Well…

KILBY. Course you are. This'll be your chance, see. Your audition piece. Audition for Puppacat, demo first hand in *person*, man, your focused viciousness, willin'ness to inflict. You with me? Get you in this very day. 'I want you,' he'll say. 'I want Kilby's apprentice paid a wage. Steve Lynch owes me money, needs a smackin'. Send the Deputy Sheriff of Crip, man, his sidekick, the Nik Nak Kid.' Am I right?

PADDY. The Nik Nak Kid.

KILBY. Am I learnin'?

PADDY. You are.

KILBY. Here. (*Throws him Nik Naks.*)

PADDY. Oh, *wild*, man!

KILBY. 'Who's that fuck?' They'll say. Think I'd leave you without?

> PADDY *begins sucking and chewing.*

> 'Who's that fuck with the Kilby, swaggerin' all cocky an' earnin' himself a rep? I hear he likes the Nik Naks,' they'll say. 'In Nik Naks as it is in batterin', I hear. As it is in his victims. Sucks them dry, then crunches, chews them.' That right, Paddy?... Swallies them down. That right, man?

PADDY (*sucking a Nik Nak*). Mm?

KILBY (*to* HUGHIE). Fuckin' loves the Nik Naks.

PADDY (*begins chewing*). D'you want one?

KILBY. Nah, man. Paddy an' Kilby, partners bonded, tin badges unclipped an' woe betide they don't get thrown down, huh? Woe betide the non-echelon. Ah, sure, go on. (*Takes some Nik Naks.*) 'Cos there'll be double the reckonin'. Won't there?

PADDY. There will.

KILBY. Reckonin' times two, man.

> KILBY *puts Nik Naks in his mouth. He and* PADDY *suck six or seven seconds, then chew.*

> Mm.

PADDY. Yeah.

KILBY (*to* HUGHIE). Where's your keys?

HUGHIE. There.

KILBY. Feel a behemoth brewin'.

> *He grabs the keys, goes over to the door and locks it, puts the keys in his pocket.*

> (*To* PADDY.) So's he doesn't bolt, see.

HUGHIE. Wasn't *gonna* bolt.

KILBY. Have to empty me gulley trap.

>KILBY *exits to toilet. Pause.* HUGHIE *stands up, goes over to* KILBY*'s jacket.*

HUGHIE. So, Paddy's made his choice, yeah?

PADDY. Yeah.

HUGHIE. Even though Hughie's in peril. Fair enough, man.

PADDY. Just doin' me job.

HUGHIE. Fair enough. (*Bringing* KILBY*'s jacket to* PADDY.) Have a look at that. (*Shows him inside label.*) That familiar?

PADDY. Which?

HUGHIE. The writin'. That say 'Dragon Fist'?

PADDY (*reading*). 'Dry clean only as…'

HUGHIE. The Chink, man!

PADDY (*reads. Pause*). 'Made in China.'

HUGHIE. How sage is that? Huh? (*Hanging jacket back up.*) Copies it off the label. How fuckin' guru is that? An' sells it to CopperDolan? '*Nother* fuckin' chunkhead.

PADDY. He told me he stroked it.

>KILBY *enters.*

KILBY. You've no fuckin' jacks roll, Hughie.

>HUGHIE *searches.*

>(*To* PADDY.) Squattin' there, spotted, man. Gettin' ready for me first heave, fuckin' perceived. Fuck's wrong with you?

PADDY. Nothin'.

KILBY. …Huh? There fuckin' *is*.

>*Pause.* HUGHIE *stops searching.*

PADDY. You told me it said 'Dragon Fist'.

KILBY. What did?

PADDY. Your jacket.

KILBY. That's what it *does* fuckin'… (*Pause. To* HUGHIE.) You low-stoopin' supergrass, Hughie. Know what that's gonna get you?

HUGHIE. Nothin' I'm not already gettin'.

KILBY. Says whatever I want it to say, Paddy. That's the best thing *'bout* Chink writin'.

HUGHIE. Not to some people, man. Not to CopperDolan.

KILBY. Where's your jacks roll? An' shut the fuck up!!!

HUGHIE. None left.

KILBY. Well, tissues, then! Fuckin' kitchen roll! C'mon, you cunt, I'm burstin'!

PADDY. What'd CopperDolan do?

KILBY. Nothin'.

HUGHIE. But Puppacat, now. Huh? What your boss-to-*be* did…

PADDY. *What'd* he do?

HUGHIE. …to the little Kilby. What'd he *do*, man?! (*Looks at* KILBY. *Long pause.*) Gonna tell your legend.

KILBY. You're dead, man.

HUGHIE. …Tell it to Paddy. Dead *any* case.

KILBY. By *me*, but.

HUGHIE. That right?

KILBY. …By the Kilby. You tell him, man…

PADDY. Sure, fuck it.

KILBY. …an' I'll… What?

PADDY. I don't wanna know.

KILBY. Ah, no, Paddy. No. Hughie'll tell you an' you know what I'll do to him? (*To* HUGHIE.) You know what I'll fuckin' do to you?!! I'll fuckin'… I'll… Where's your fuckin' jacks roll?!!! (*To* PADDY.) Paddy. Find me tissues. (*To* HUGHIE.) After me fuckin' shite!

KILBY *exits.* PADDY *begins searching for tissues. Pause.*

HUGHIE. See, CopperDolan saw the writin' there, Paddy, thought it looked alpha. An' it *did* look alpha. Fuckin' *stitch*work? (*Appreciative whistle*.) Stool-boy in there…

PADDY. Who?

HUGHIE. Stool… Scutter-boy.

PADDY *stops searching. Short pause.*

Kilby, man. The fuck's he doin'?

PADDY. Takin' a shit. (*Beat*.) Ah…

HUGHIE. …Was short of cash, okay? Needed money, send away the States for these jeans. Don't know if…

PADDY. He did.

HUGHIE. His Chuck jeans?

PADDY. With the gusset.

HUGHIE. …Needed money, so they bartered a bit; hundred, hundred an' twenty-five, Kilby needed two-fifty so he told CopperDolan it said, the *writin'* like, said 'Brotherhood of the Guard', hiked the fuckin'…

PADDY. 'Brotherhood of'…?

HUGHIE. *Gards*, man. D'you get it?

PADDY. Coppers.

HUGHIE. …Hiked the price up. Zactly. Told him he could impress them all down the Gook Nation, as if he wouldn't find out eventually. Huh? As if the Chinks couldn't read what the Chink writin' writ. An' that's the fuck you wanna folly, wanna be your Yoda in batterin'?

PADDY. So, what happened?

HUGHIE. D'you get that fuckin' stink? Phew!

Beat.

PADDY. I…

HUGHIE. Don't tell me you don't, now.

PADDY. I *do*! (*Beat*.) Fucksake!

HUGHIE. How many shites did he have the other night?

PADDY. Three. One.

HUGHIE. Three or one?

PADDY. One. They were three parts of the same shite.

HUGHIE. No they weren't, they were separate.

PADDY. Fine. What did CopperDolan do?

HUGHIE. Dolan did nothin'. *Puppacat*, but.

PADDY. Well, what did *Puppacat* do?!

 Pause.

HUGHIE. *Caused* that stink.

KILBY (*offstage*). Hughie!

HUGHIE. One day, see, Dolan's down Delgado's havin' his billy
 club sucked by Minnie Pearl P'au… You know Minnie?

KILBY (*offstage*). Paddy!

PADDY. No.

HUGHIE. Call her the Yellow Pearl.

PADDY. Don't know her, man.

KILBY (*offstage*). You fuckin' deaf?!

PADDY (*shouting, to* KILBY). What?!!

KILBY (*offstage*). C'mon with the fuckin' tissues!

PADDY. Hang on!!

HUGHIE. Gook bird down Delgado's. Hooer, like.

KILBY (*offstage*). I *won't* hang on.

HUGHIE. …CopperDolan blows muck in her gob after sayin' he
 wouldn't, she goes apeshit, right? 'Cos he's done it before many
 a time an' she's sick of it, can't abide the taste of fuckin' paste.
 Minnie reveals somethin' in her wrath this night, somethin' many
 a gook knows, an' *has* known, but few gooks'll say for fear of
 Copper*Dolan's* wrath. That what he's been wearin' proud,
 struttin' all boastful an' thinks says 'Brotherhood of the Guard'
 actually says…

PADDY. Right.

HUGHIE. ...'Made in China.'

PADDY. I fuckin' adored that jacket.

HUGHIE. So poor CopperDolan, mockery of gooks all over, loses face, so, see, loses honour, the place of his beat, needs somethin' to restore it. Meantime. His boys an' the echelons're about to make their deal...

KILBY (*offstage*). I'll fuckin' burst you, Paddy!!

HUGHIE. ...The Parish Treaty, on'y...

PADDY (*shouting, to* KILBY). I'm lookin'!

HUGHIE. ...On'y the jacket embarrassment's queerin' things up. All right? CopperDolan wants a certain thing done 'fore he'll commit.

PADDY. What's that? Come on.

HUGHIE. ...An' Puppacat needs him to commit. Hang on.

PADDY. Hughie!

HUGHIE. ...I'm gettin' there. Wants somethin' done by Puppacat, show he's sorry. Wants some kind of punishment meted out to Kilby, give him satisfaction. Otherwise it's not gonna happen. Echelons'll end up bein' the lower 'stead of the higher. So we all meet down Delgado's this night, night of the treaty; CopperDolan, few goons, Puppacat, meself, couple of echelons. Puppacat gives the nod – I'm nearly finished, man – gives the nod, we all go for Kilby. Echelons *an'* goons. An' adept an' all's he is at the arts, now, skilled's he *is* – got a whack or two meself – we grab an' restrain him...

PADDY. You helped?!

HUGHIE. I had to... bend him over table six... I was ordered, man, sure. Same's you'll be. Puppacat leans down an' looks him in the eye, man, says, I'll never forget, says, 'I'll make this up to you, Kilby.' Then another nod an' we rief, as per Puppacat's instructions, down Kilby's strides, tear *off* his understrides. Puppacat goes up behind him, fuckin' pool cue in his paw, there, hefts, holds it, gives the end an oul' chalkin' an'...

PADDY. Oh, Jaysus!

HUGHIE. ...Yep...

PADDY. Up his dirty dirt road?!!!

HUGHIE. 'Bout two fuckin' *foot* up his dirty dirt road.

PADDY. Ah, *fuck!*

HUGHIE. *Three* foot, maybe.

PADDY. *Fuck*, man! He never told me this shit.

HUGHIE. Well, he wouldn't.

PADDY. ...This horrid shit. *Fuck*, an' his own boss?!

KILBY *enters and sits down.*

HUGHIE (*to* PADDY). *Your* boss-to-*be*, man. Welters of gore, there was, fuckin' *geysers* of blood spurtin', *sprayin'* out of both ends of him, hole *an'* mouth. That right, Kilby? Gurglin' like a blocked drain.

PADDY. Jesus Christ!

HUGHIE (*to* KILBY). Speakin' of blocked drains. (*To* PADDY.) I *know*, man. (*To* KILBY.) You never hear of flushin'?

KILBY. I'm enjoyin' me bouquet.

HUGHIE. Your...

KILBY. Bouquet of me creation. (*Inhales deeply.*) Relishin', I am.

HUGHIE. Fucksake! (*On his way out.*) An' how the fuck did you wipe your hole?

KILBY. Clothes in your basket.

Beat.

HUGHIE (*in doorway*). What?! (*Runs out.*)

KILBY. Strips of John Rocha.

HUGHIE (*offstage, shouting*). Oh, you cunt!!!

KILBY. A smooth moppin' of crevice.

HUGHIE (*offstage, shouting*). You dirty, dirty cunt!!!

Silence.

PADDY. Kilby?

HUGHIE (*offstage, shouting*). You fuckin' scumbag!!!

PADDY. Have to say, man...

KILBY (*of* HUGHIE). You hear this?

PADDY. ...All this new shit, you know? I do.

KILBY. Desired effect.

PADDY. What he just told us, man? Kinda givin' me pause, it is.

KILBY. Fuck're you talkin' 'bout?

PADDY. Pause for thought, man. Think I might leave it for today, catch Puppacat again, I think, whatsay? Do the oul' technique thing an' all the next time, huh? Reckon I need to mull a bit if you know what I'm sayin'. On this info, like. (*Pause.*) So will you open the door for us?

KILBY. You're not gonna join, you fuck, are you? Now that you've...

PADDY. No, man, I am. Fuck. Just the situation's not what I thought it was before, so I can't lep into it lightly.

KILBY. Stay, man.

PADDY. ...Have to *look* before I lep. 'Fer not to, Kilby. 'Fer not to, will you give us the key? 'Fer to split, so will you give us it?

Pause.

KILBY. Gonna keep you here a while, watch Kilby get personal with Hughie.

PADDY. But...

KILBY. ...All right? Dance a tango, think you follow. No, you're part of this now. Fucker's no business.

PADDY. An' what about Puppacat?

KILBY. ...None a-tall! What?

PADDY. ...An' Bernie. You're not allowed touch him till...

KILBY. *Wasn't*, Paddy. *Wasn't*. But the release of that story's justification, man. D'you not think?... Is a personal attack on me, an' Puppacat gives me sanction as the Deputy Sheriff to supersede the avengin' of Nancy by Bernie. An' I'll leave him the dregs, like.

PADDY. Well, fair enough, man. 'Fer to leave it *to* you, but. Whatsay? Just eh... retreat. You know? 'Vaporate...

KILBY. Paddy...

PADDY. ...Come back when the aggro's over.

KILBY. ...Paddy. Sit down an' have a Nik Nak. Give us one.

PADDY *gives him one.*

Gonna sit here, all right? Sit down!

PADDY *sits.*

Gonna suck. (*Sucks five or six seconds.*) Mmm. Chew. Swally. (*Takes chewed up Nik Nak from mouth.*) *Not* swally, should say. (*Puts it on table.*) Recline back an' *wait*, should say.

PADDY. Right.

KILBY. ...Cultivate me rage.

The toilet flushes.

PADDY. But, listen...

KILBY. D'you hear me? Me fuckin' *rage*!

HUGHIE *enters with John Rocha shirt.*

HUGHIE. Been cultivatin' mine as well, man. So, Paddy, so...

KILBY. How's the shirt?

HUGHIE. ...The cue stick did... (*To* KILBY.) *Wrecked*, you cunt! (*To* PADDY.) ...Did damage up there, see... (*To* KILBY.) You destructive *cunt!!* (*To* PADDY.) Whenever an'thin' not veg or fruit enters his body it sets off his bowels, 's you can see. (*Holds out shirt.*) He becomes incapable of clutchin' his filth. (*Dumps shirt in bin. To* KILBY.) Don't you. (*To* PADDY.) Doesn't usually stray from the veg, but...

KILBY. Couldn't resist the oul' Nik Naks...

HUGHIE. ...Could you?

HUGHIE *sits down.* KILBY *stands up.*

KILBY. Not the rib 'n' saucys.

HUGHIE *stands up.*

What're you standin' up for?

HUGHIE (*backing away*). Readiness.

KILBY (*approaching*). What're you backin' up for?

HUGHIE. Tactics.

KILBY. Retreatin'?

HUGHIE. Manoeuvrin'.

They circle the room. KILBY *advancing,* HUGHIE *retreating.*
Continue this until stated.

KILBY. Me rage is up there, Hughie. The highest of planes.

HUGHIE. So's mine, man. (*To* PADDY.) So Puppacat's finished
rootin', Paddy. (*To* KILBY.) Just to wrap up. (*To* PADDY.) He
takes the cue stick back out... You listenin'?

PADDY. Yeah.

HUGHIE....Kilby's hole an' he's not too, what's the word? Lucid.
So, there's all fuckin' stuff on it, an' Kilby says, 'What the fuck is
that?!' You know? Asks what all this muck on the cue stick is.
Guess what Puppacat says? (*Short pause*.) Paddy!

PADDY. What?

HUGHIE. 'It's your shite an' your guts.' An' you'd wanna hear
CopperDolan.

KILBY. C'mon.

HUGHIE....The guffaws of him.

HUGHIE *does CopperDolan's laugh.*

KILBY. You're wastin' time.

HUGHIE. I'm bidin' time.

HUGHIE *does CopperDolan's laugh.*

KILBY. An' that's not how he guffaws.

HUGHIE. How, then?

KILBY. Not tellin' you.

HUGHIE. 'It's your shite an' your guts', Paddy. Then he...

KILBY *does CopperDolan's laugh; angrily.*

That's not fuckin' it. (*To* PADDY.) Then CopperDolan puts his
right hand in it, smears it all over, gives Puppacat a little look
like that. Kinda sly an' evil, not to be biblical, now, Puppacat
does the same an' they shake...

PADDY (*to* KILBY). In your shite?

KILBY. Huh?

PADDY. They shook in your shite?!

KILBY. Shook symbolic, they did, all ceremonial, made the pact legit an' bindin' on the sufferin', the martyrdom of Kilby. An' that *is* his fuckin' guffaw!

HUGHIE. I pre...

> KILBY *does CopperDolan's laugh; very angrily.*

> I presume that's why he hates me. (*To* KILBY.) Is it? (*To* PADDY.) 'Cos I was witness to his shame.

KILBY. Because you helped, you fuck!

HUGHIE. I was ordered.

KILBY. You could've said no, man! (*Pause.*) Or...

HUGHIE. Kilby comes out of a coma three days later... This right, man? This bit true?

KILBY. What?

HUGHIE. You woke up an' you'd a perm?

> KILBY *stops advancing. Pause.*

> Ordeal harrowed your hair up so curly no one can straighten it, you've gone to everyone in town, keeps curlin' back?

> *Pause.* HUGHIE *has manoeuvred himself in front of the baseball bat.*

KILBY. That's a real fuckin' paid-for perm, man, groomed an' styled an' you're a liar. You're an insidious little fuck, have to conquer with lies an' shit-stirrin'. The badge is down now, you hear me? (*Mimes throwing down badge.*) The tin star is well an' truly on the floor an' Kilby's fuckin' ragin'!! Ragin' like a beast an' ready to fuckin' maim!!!

> KILBY *attacks.* HUGHIE *picks up the baseball bat and hits him in the arm.*

HUGHIE. C'mon, then, you permy fuck, you.

> *They circle.*

KILBY. I'll let you have that one, Hughie.

HUGHIE. Which? The whack? Or…

KILBY. The whack, man.

HUGHIE *feints*.

The whack I'll grant you. The perm comment's another fuckin' tale.

HUGHIE *feints*.

Not one more blow'll penetrate me defences. (*Pause*.) Ready for you, I am.

HUGHIE *feints*.

Me mind is focused. (*Short pause*.) Me wrath is channelled. (*Pause*.) Gonna inflict.

HUGHIE *attacks,* KILBY *on the defensive, avoiding strikes with skill, before knocking the bat out of* HUGHIE*'s hands. Pause. Circling.* KILBY *throws a less-than-waist-high side kick.* HUGHIE *dodges it easily.* KILBY *tries again with a roundhouse kick. This too is less-than-waist-high and easily dodged by* HUGHIE.

The fuck? Where the fuck's me high-leg action? (*Tries a spinning back kick with the same result*.) These fuckin'… See this, Paddy?

HUGHIE *picks up Nancy's fake leg*.

'F I had me Chucks, now, bollox! Me Action Jeans.

HUGHIE *gives the distracted* KILBY *a whack with the leg, dropping him*.

HUGHIE (*ready to strike again*). You lackin' your gusset, Kilby?

KILBY. Ah! Ah! Don't! (*Pause*.) Don't fuckin' use that. That's five grands' worth of prosthetic, man. That's Nancy's fuckin' savin's. Don't break it. (*Pause*). Think of *her*, Hughie. (*Pause*.) Think of poor Nancy, spite of her faults, man.

Pause.

HUGHIE. Fuck Nancy.

HUGHIE *raises the leg again to strike, but suddenly lets out a howl, drops the leg and doubles over, holding his stomach*.

Aagh! Fuck! Fuck!

KILBY *gets up and grabs him*.

KILBY. Need some medicine, do you? (*Getting behind him*.) Take your pick man. (*Punches him in ribs with left*.) Castor oil? (*Punches him in ribs with right*.) Or milk of magnesia? You fuckin' muckhole, you. Paddy! (*Picking up umbrella*.) Get over here, do me a job. Take this brolly.

PADDY. Ah, you're all right, man.

KILBY *looks at* PADDY. *Pause*.

KILBY. I fuckin' *know* I'm all right. C'mon. Want you to expand the girdle of Hughie's ringpiece. (*To* HUGHIE.) Take your trousers off.

HUGHIE. Me hole!

KILBY. That's what I'm tryin' to get to, man. Take them off, save me boxin' your head to get them off. (*To* PADDY.) Paddy! (*To* HUGHIE.) Gonna show you what it's like to be a cue stick's whore. (*To* PADDY.) C'mon, man. Bit of impalin'. Well within your powers.

PADDY. Em...

KILBY. ... Your skills. I'll hold him for you. All you've to do is press it against the pink little star an' thrust. (*Pause*.) *C'mooooon!!!* Sober dialogue, Paddy, you don't. Now, get over here 'fore I scold you.

PADDY *approaches*.

Good man. (*Gets* HUGHIE *into a one-handed arm-lock*.) See this lock, man?

PADDY *picks up the baseball bat*.

Incapacitate your opponent single-pawed, leaves the other free for whatever you want. (*Opening* HUGHIE*'s belt. Pulling down his trousers*.) It's popular with faggot rapists an' berserk sodomites. (*Slaps* HUGHIE*'s arse*.) Bit of a slap, there, Hughie, shame you. You like that? (*Slaps his arse*.) You ashamed? (*Slaps his arse*.)

PADDY. Kilby!

KILBY. Just relax the oul' sphincter, now. Don't clench, man, be easier for one an' all. (*Holds umbrella out*.) You right, Paddy, here. You know where to aim. (*Pause*.) Will you *take* the fuckin'...!!!

PADDY *whacks* KILBY *over the head with the baseball bat.*

Oh! Oh, good fuck! (*Reeling, dropping umbrella.*) I'm all dizzy an' all.

PADDY. Fuck that buggerin' shit.

KILBY. You knocked me for six. The fuck's wrong with you? After skullhaulin' me, you are. Gimme that bat.

PADDY. Gimme the keys.

KILBY (*approaching*). I'll take it off you.

PADDY. Gimme the fuckin' keys so's I can get the fuck…

HUGHIE. Paddy!

PADDY. …*out* of here!!!

KILBY *makes for Nancy's leg.*

HUGHIE. He's goin' for the fuckin'…!!!

HUGHIE *goes for the leg himself, trips over his trousers, falls on his face.*

Ouch!

KILBY (*picking the leg up*). Out on your snot, Hughie.

PADDY. You all right, man?

HUGHIE. Fuck!

Over the following, HUGHIE *gets back up and pulls up his trousers, buttons them, etc.*

KILBY. So come on, Paddy.

KILBY *and* PADDY *circle.*

See if you can get your keys off the Kilby.

PADDY. I'll beat you down.

KILBY. Not in me fury, man. Gonna…

HUGHIE (*standing with umbrella in his hands*). Kilby…

KILBY. …Gonna nab you, I am. (*Sees* HUGHIE.) Oh.

HUGHIE. That's right.

HUGHIE *and* PADDY *circle* KILBY. *All three have their weapons raised.*

KILBY. Two against one.

HUGHIE. That's right. Drop the prosthetic.

KILBY. ...I like the odds.

HUGHIE. Drop the prosthetic or we'll pound down upon you, Kilby!!!

They continue to circle. KILBY *looks at* HUGHIE. *Looks at* PADDY. *Pause.*

KILBY. Pound ahead.

They engage. After several exchanges, KILBY *having the upper hand, they stop and circle,* KILBY *spinning the leg above his head.*

Think youse can duel me? Youse're rubbish, man. Can youse not feel me ease?

HUGHIE *coughs.*

No? Feel me toyin' with youse all devil-may-care?

HUGHIE. Prosthetic as pole.

KILBY. That's right, man.

HUGHIE. Very MacGyver.

PADDY. Pole's your weapon of choice.

KILBY. That's right. Feel me nonchalance, now?

Pause. They continue to circle. HUGHIE *coughing.*

Attained a knowin' state that day, I did, day I was impaled. Somethin' youse cunts'll never understand. Mastery was attained; understandin', balance... State a monk of Shaolin reaches when he lifts that giant urn, you get me, Paddy? When he brands himself in white fire; the torment, the pain, I reached that state. Bear the marks, I do. Damage to me bowels within, the curls on me head without. They're *my* dragon an' tiger, see, 'cos I *am* Shaolin. I'm the treaty, I'm echelon incarnate.

HUGHIE *coughing.*

I am alpha male of youse fucks 'cos I can take it an' have *took* it to the fuckin' hilt, man. Youse're on'y twopenny strong, twopenny true. Your convictions're twopenny. I took cue stick…

HUGHIE *coughing*.

I took…

HUGHIE *coughing*.

Shut the fuck up!! Fuckin' barkin' like a mutt! I took fuckin'…

PADDY. Some Veno's, Hughie.

KILBY. Zactly. The fuck was I…?

PADDY. …Sort you right quick.

KILBY. I took cue stick stoic an' acceptin' an' me will was forged tenfold stronger in, yep, in shite an' guts! Thick, ripe shite, too. Black shite. Your will's forged in piss, man, the pair of youse. Weak fuckin' watery piss, not even yellow, an' that's why youse'll never beat me. (*Short pause.*) Gonna take you out first, Hughie, hew a gorge in you.

KILBY *feints at* PADDY. PADDY *jumps back*.

Youse ready to re-engage?

KILBY *feints at* PADDY. PADDY *jumps back*.

You jumpy cunt, you, Paddy.

PADDY. Kilby.

KILBY (*spinning leg*). Youse ready, now?

PADDY. Don't be mayhemic.

KILBY. Let's go, then.

KILBY *attacks. They fight.* KILBY *hits* PADDY *in the leg, dropping him with a scream.* KILBY *versus* HUGHIE. *A short exchange, followed by a vicious pummelling from* KILBY. HUGHIE *drops and doesn't move. Pause.* KILBY *throws the leg down, goes over to* PADDY.

PADDY. Me leg's broke. Fuck. I know it. Agh!

KILBY *takes the baseball bat off him*.

KILBY. Broke?

PADDY. I'm tellin' you.

KILBY. Well, there's another one.

> KILBY *whacks* PADDY*'s other leg with the bat*. PADDY *screams*.

> …Keep it company.

> KILBY *sits down. Pause.* PADDY *moaning*.

> Not too often that happens, Paddy. Tell you that. A hunch doesn't play for the Kilby? Bit disappointin', man. 'Cos you *couldn't* hack it, could you?

> (*Touches* PADDY*'s leg with bat*.) Could you?

PADDY. Agh! No! No, I couldn't!

KILBY. …After sayin' you could.

PADDY. I *thought* I could. (*Short pause*.) Unh. I *thought* I could.

KILBY. *I* thought so too, man. (*Pause*.) Fuck it. Faggots like yourself don't belong in the echelons, anyway. Weak-willed fucks.

PADDY. I am.

KILBY. Huh…?

PADDY. I *am* a weak-willed fuck.

KILBY. Don't tell *me*, man. *Very* disappointed, I am. You coulda been the Nik Nak Kid, coulda been me 'prentice, man. Two of us all buddy-buddy vicious, fuckin' *legends*. S'pose I'm destined to journey solo, so, without partner or companion, alone in the echelon. S'pose that's me fate, man. (*Pause*.) Still. 'Preciate the skullhaulin'. Stopped me buggerin' Hughie at least. Could've got into trouble for that with Puppacat, fucked him up *too* bad there, denied Bernie his vengeance, you know? Could've set meself up for a disciplinin'. So thanks for that, man. Gratitude. (*Pause*.) Still an' all. Still have me rage-horn…

PADDY. Your what?!

KILBY. …between me legs. Me rage-horn! Need to douse the flame, man, drain the blood from me cock 'fore Puppacat comes, clear me head an' calm me down for focused explainin'. Still too tumescent in me fury, I am. (*Short pause*.) You wanted to see me smashin' skills, Paddy? Me barehanded skills?

PADDY. Ah, no.

KILBY. Well, now you're gonna. Ah, no, I'll show you, now.

PADDY. Kilby.

KILBY. You ready? This'll bring back me balance.

PADDY. Kilby!

KILBY *now on his knees, begins deep meditative breathing with arm movements, eyes shut. His breathing gets faster and faster, becomes more intense.* HUGHIE *has recovered consciousness. He gets up, picks up the baseball bat and approaches* KILBY *from behind.* KILBY*'s breathing, now louder, reaches a crescendo, his right hand raised for the fatal strike.* PADDY *repeats 'Kilby, Kilby', over and over, pleading.* KILBY *lets a final shout and* HUGHIE *smacks him viciously in the head with the bat. He topples over and is still. Pause.*

PADDY. Oh, Jesus! Oh, Jesus!

HUGHIE. You all right?

PADDY. Me fuckin' legs! (*Tries to get up without success. Lets out a shout of pain.*) Oh, fuck, man! *Fuck!* Fair *dues*, man!

Pause. HUGHIE *begins rushing around the apartment, packing clothes, etc., into a bag. Continue until stated.*

Me fuckin' legs! Fuckin' *animal*! (*To* KILBY.) We got you, you *cunt*, you! We *slew* the goliath. (*To* HUGHIE.) Didn't we? Defeated him *wicked*, me fuckin' *leeegs*!!! (*Short pause.*) Agh…! The fuck're you doin'?… *Je*sus!

HUGHIE. Splittin'.

PADDY. Off?

HUGHIE. …The fuck out of here, Paddy. Yeah.

Pause.

PADDY. What about me, man? You givin' me a jockey?

HUGHIE. Sorry, man. Have to be nimble for me 'scape. You made your bed…

PADDY. Me legs!

HUGHIE. …Lie in it. Your what?

PADDY. I took wallops for you.

HUGHIE. An' thankful I am, Paddy. Saved me a brolly up me dirty dirt road. I'm 'preciative. But you deserted me, me hour of need, man. Sided 'gainst me, 'gainst me oul'one.

PADDY. Your oul'one?

HUGHIE. …Sided 'gainst us proper. Name's Dolly, man. She was buried today, case you forgot.

Silence.

PADDY. I remember now… Hughie!

HUGHIE. What?

PADDY. What she said was…

HUGHIE. Oh, you *remember* now?!

PADDY. Yeah, it just came to me. We were in the sittin' room… Ah, shit! We'd, we'd hot whiskeys an' dry roasters, am I right? Peanuts, an' I started… I spilt my whiskey, started, cryin' 'cos of the stress of the day, man, the events that were in it… Started cryin' an' she hugged me, I remember, man, an' said it was okay. It was okay because she'd be… (*In pain.*) Agh!

HUGHIE. Go on.

PADDY. Don't know how I forgot. Said she'd be me mother…

HUGHIE. Yeah…?

PADDY. …long as you were my brother. (*Pause.*) Isn't that it? Long as…

HUGHIE. No.

PADDY. No?! *Yes*, man!

HUGHIE. Long as you were mine, Paddy. Long as you were mine, an' as of today, man…

PADDY. You fuck!

HUGHIE. …you're Kilby's, aren't you. Tell *him* your problems.

PADDY. I can't. (*Pause.*) Hughie! (*Pause.*) The fuck am I supposed to do?

HUGHIE. Tell you what. If the cunt's no more, all right? If he's kicked, you can tell Puppacat it was me battered the pair of youse. Might get you off the hook if you're convincin'. But if he's alive, now...

PADDY. He'll tell them I helped you.

HUGHIE. That's right.

PADDY. They'll scalp me.

HUGHIE. That's right. Among *other* inventive shit.

Long pause.

PADDY. Check for us.

HUGHIE. Hm?

PADDY. ...If he's dead, man. Will you?

HUGHIE. Sorry, Paddy. Fugitive has to be scabby with his time, 'cos he's *got* none. Surely you can crawl that far. (*Puts on his jacket.*)

PADDY. You fuck!

HUGHIE. Well...

PADDY. ...Why're you doin' this?

HUGHIE. ...Somethin' I've learnt today, Paddy. (*Picks up bag and a can of lager, looks out window, then going to door.*) Somethin' you helped teach me.

PADDY. What's that?

HUGHIE. You *an'* the oul'one. (*Opens door, turns to* PADDY.) You do what's right for yourself, man.

PADDY. Hughie...

HUGHIE. ...Long as you're able to hack it. That right?

PADDY. ...Give us a jockey.

HUGHIE (*opens the can, holds it up*). So here's to youse both. Can't, man.

PADDY. Hughie.

HUGHIE. ...Or rather won't. (*Drinks whole can.*) Aahh! (*Throws can in corner.*) Adios, partner.

PADDY. Hughie!

The door shuts. HUGHIE *is gone.* PADDY *tries without success to get up. He lets out a shout of pain. Pause.* KILBY *groans.*

Oh, no...

KILBY *groans again.*

No, fuck! Fuck! Fuck!

PADDY *crawls over to* KILBY, *very slowly, shouting in pain as he goes, sits beside him, picks up the baseball bat. He starts crying, stops abruptly, composes himself, looks at* KILBY. *Long pause. He raises the bat. Hold. Brings it down to his lap, begins weeping again as the lights fade down to darkness...*

The End.

CRESTFALL

Crestfall was first performed at the Gate Theatre, Dublin, on 20 May 2003 (previews from 15 May). The cast was as follows:

OLIVE DAY   Aisling O'Sullivan
ALISON ELLIS   Marie Mullen
TILLY McQUARRIE   Eileen Walsh

Director   Garry Hynes
Designer   Francis O'Connor
Lighting Designer   Rupert Murray
Sound Designer   Paul Arditti

The play received its UK premiere at Theatre503, London, on 27 November 2007. The cast was as follows:

OLIVE DAY   Pauline Hutton
ALISON ELLIS   Niamh Cusack
TILLY McQUARRIE   Orla Fitzgerald

Director   Róisín McBrinn
Designer   Paul Wills
Lighting Designer   Philip Gladwell
Sound Designer   Sarah Weltman

Characters

OLIVE DAY

ALISON ELLIS

TILLY McQUARRIE

ONE

Olive Day

Dressed up,
pressing forward,
feel my body's workings working
beneath my garb, my Sunday best.
The sun is high,
today we're blessed.
For once it's dry,
and I have to confess
it allows my mind to open a bit,
my senses to savour surrounding shit,
the muddy bank, the green,
the water on the river curve,
which curve I follow, trace,
till I'm faced
with certain images unforeseen.

Kiddies' heads bob about rambunctious,
hear their crazy high-pitched ruckus.
Bank-to-bank racing, some mutual splashing,
a boy dunks a girl, she goes down thrashing.
Others call from the bridge for space,
then dive or cannonball in. The place
is as merry,
although, as always, the feeling is only momentary.

Watch as laughter lilts,
then tilts
toward moans
as a pissing of heavens means
the children have to shoreward flounder,
clamber out and hoof for shelter.

I hoof myself,
my shelter also my destination –
The Burning Bell,
to which I fly post-haste,
though, fucking hell,

by the time I get to the place,
I'm soaked to the skin.
Who cares? I'm in.
All right,
so, who've we got?
A couple of frightful-
looking hags at a table, fucked,
a furtive fogey corner-tucked
– there he is –
the Bru at the bar.
I'm surprised he even came *this* far.
Approach and belly up beside him.
'We doing this?' I ask. 'We riding?'
Course, he says
and kills his whiskey,
heads for the door
and exits. I folly,
keeping my distance up to the Green,
where it's safe to join him under his brolly.

He's keen.
He practically drags me through the wasteland
behind the old slaughterhouse, the Boneland,
where bits of cow lie scattered, decaying,
and the odd hound laps at bone in vain
for any remaining
bits of meat
as we exit the Boneland,
cross the street
to The Vanguard, a hotel,
or so called.

Kit Rankin's the man on the desk.
He's bald
and pretty fucking thick.
Behind said desk is a hurley stick,
nail-studded to counter minor grief.
For major, it's what Kit calls his 'Enforcer-in-Chief'
a pump-action shotgun.
It's Kit's belief
we all should have one.

He probably thinks I'm some kind of ho,
but he signs us in and up we go,

me clutching the key, the Bru clutching me,
all the way to the room which we enter and see
what we've got. A shower, a single bed,
a lot of dried-in stains on the sheets – they're red.
My God, it's a dump,
but, look it:
You don't need a presidential suite to hump,
so fuck it.

And so we begin,
committing maybe the oldest sin.
(Or old enough in any case.)
He grabs me roughly by the face,
and licks my neck, and bites my lip,
then tears my ninnies off and flips
me round and pulls me to him quickly,
entering me fairly slickly
from the rear
and commencing to pump,
his belly bouncing on my rump,
my flank,
every now and again
(I don't mind.)
he gives me a little spank.
(Sure, whatever he's in to.)

But now I find,
in this fuck, I begin to
mull on fucks gone by, and I grin to
think of Daddy always broaching
furtive but always failing,
settling always for lap-sat stroking.
Or Uncle Christopher succeeding,
a little pain, a little bleeding.
A little more determined than Daddy,
he was the one to pop my cherry.

And in the years that followed,
I became a righteous sexual fiend, and wallowed
in my many filthy rendezvous.
Come one come all, I thought. I wasn't choosy.
Jesus, half a cockeyed look'd get you entry
to my cockeyed coozy.

What the fuck is going on here?
The Bru's emitting moans of despair.
He stops his thrusts,
withdraws, and busts
out crying, saying, 'My wife! I can't…'
'Your wife?'
'…My son! I'm really sorry,' he says. 'I can't go on
with this.'
'Are you fucking kidding?!' I hiss.
(My arse is still in the air.)
'I'm not,' he says. And with this,
he's out of there,
half-dressed.

And am I pissed? You'd fucking best
believe it.
On top of which,
I have a serious carnal itch,
needs dealing with.
And so I linger
just about long enough to relieve it
with my finger.

Then I'm gone.

And, passing through the lobby,
I come upon
Kit Rankin, sitting slouchy,
giving his 'Enforcer-in-Chief' a clean,
(His shotgun. *You* know what I mean.)
which he suddenly pumps and points at me,
and, as he gleefully
pulls the trigger,
I holler, 'Stop!'
before I hear a hollow 'Pop!'
and tell him I figure
I've never come across a bigger
prick in all my days,
which doesn't faze the fuck at all.
'Still made you shit your fucking pants!' he calls
as I leave.

And my heart is still in my mouth,
my ego still pretty tender,
as I retrace my initial route

through the rain,
my once-clean finery rendered
bedraggled and stained.

And I curse the Bru and Kit,
and more than either man, I curse the stupid shit
who adores me, Jungle Day,
my husband, who in a way,
I adore as well,
though, I know, you couldn't tell
from my tale so far.

But let me take you back to clarify
that declaration,
and tell you that our early days
were full of love and consideration,
and me a brittle jewel treated so gently,
gentle as Jungle's nature was,
a disposition at odds
with where we were,
you know what I mean? With here.

And, who cared?
They were happy days and I loved him for it,
stopped my fucking around and reciprocated
his fidelity with my own;
a monogamy which, instead of growing
stronger like it should have, finally weakened,
and it wasn't long before I started seeking
out some cock to suck,
some guys to get to fuck me,
(In a sense, to re-corrupt me.)
which is what they did.

And the man I wed
became, in time,
a man I was deeply ashamed
to call mine.

He doesn't belong, you see.
He's wrong
for this wicked place.
An anomaly.
And my bond with him makes me equally weak,
something I despise to be thought of as, and so I wreak

erotic carnage on this town,
to show that I'm in no way bound
to him.
(Or at least no way that shows.)

And, of course, the fucker knows
what I do, sure how could he not?
And of course you can see how much it's got
to be fucking him up,
the tears he often squirts,
it's obvious how much it hurts.

And, though it's hard, I push him further,
mocking in an effort to murder
the meek in him,
to bring out the strong, the mean.
But it's always the fucking same.
He runs to his room every fucking time,
and locks himself in
with some bottles of wine,
some gin,
which is actually what he's been doing
these last few days, and still is.
Though not over me for once, but some business
down in The Probable.

'Jungle?'
No answer. I knock on his door.
(This is this morning.) 'Back about four,
okay?'
There's a hesitation
before he tells me he reckons
he won't be here.
'Why not?'
''Cos I'm going to kill myself!' he cries,
and I laugh at the way his voice goes high
and shrill.
'Okay,' I say,
dismissing this routine as overkill.

And yet. Insane as it seems,
a seed has been sown.
What the hell is that about?
Something in his tone,
there, making me doubt.

That very misgiving growing
in my mind
as the day goes on. Even now I find
myself a bit beset by thoughts of this,
which, I must admit,
are particularly difficult, at times, to dismiss.

Jungle was taking a drunken piss
in The Probable and his aim went awry
and the piss ricocheted
and sprayed
on the legs of the guy
beside him,
a one-eyed
man with a patch,
and this was big enough an affront
that the man called Jungle a stupid cunt
and dragged him back outside to the bar
and forced him onto the floor
on his belly,
then whistled and shouted 'Billy!'
And out from under a table appeared
a hideous-looking three-eyed mutt,
I swear,
who came and rubbed his junk, his gear
off Jungle's butt,
and came again,
but in the messier sense,
leaving a glutinous stain
all over Jungle's pants.

And the shame
I felt as I watched him leave,
cock-java dripping off the arse of his britches,
every single person there in fucking stitches,
was the reason I had to find a man
(Like who? Well, that night, it was one you've met. The Bru.)
and seize him,
take him out the back,
and squeeze
him all about the sack
and suck his cock,
but not allow him to jip,
oh, no,

telling him that'd cost him a trip
to The Hotel
Vanguard, which was around where we came in.
(You and me, like, not me and him.)

But only, see,
by showing myself as fancy-free
and not attached to Jungle, could I begin to reclaim,
if only in my fucked-up mind,
a little bit of my self-esteem,
my dignity, you know what I mean?
My cachet.
And, today…

What the hell is this?
A crowd is coming my way,
about forty strong,
who follow three men
who are dragging a bellowing
horse along.
(As you do.)

Dennis and Daniel Deegan are the two
up front.
Twin brothers,
try and tell one of them from the other,
you can't.
A couple of fucking freaks
in the sack,
you ever take them on,
you'll ache
for as long
as whatever wounds they make
remain.
These men are really into pain.

Benny 'The Mule' Drumgoole's the third,
the truth of whose name exceeds the word.
And this isn't something I've only heard,
but know,
having had all three.
(Though not in a row. Ha-ha.)

I say 'Hello,'
and they wave and wink.

(At least, I think
that's what they did.)
And then a kid
runs up and kicks the horse's
flank with force
and flees,
and another couple of urchins seize
a couple of stones,
the little shits,
and throw them,
getting a couple of hits.

Then Benny lets go of the rope
and enters a garden, leaving the Deegans to cope
alone,
and rings the bell,
and, fucking hell,
the door is answered by Ali Ellis,
who, by the way, is the Bru's fucking missus.
Oh! And this is
exactly what I expected,
she spots me and gives me a look as if I'm infected
with, I don't know,
the pox or whatever,
the pious fucking cow.
'Have you any idea where your husband's been till now?'

She stands aside as Benny enters,
disappears as the front door closes.
And I suppose it's
tougher being only two,
because it's all the brothers Deegan can do
to hang on to the rope.
Except they can't.
A hit with a massive brick
to the ear,
causes the horse to kick
and rear
back just a bit too far,
and it topples over against a car,
destroying the passenger door,
and setting off the alarm.

And whatever more
goes on,
whatever other harm
is done,
I couldn't say,
'cos I'm gone by then
on my merry way.

But it's short-lived merry.
'cos two streets later,
I bump into Tilly fucking McQuarrie,
a junkie,
and of course she's gonna ask me for money.
A punter was supposed to appear,
but didn't.
Yeah, she's a whore
as well,
and, I say, 'Couldn't
you just crawl
away somewhere
and die?'
But, instead of replying,
she grabs my hair
and pulls back my head,
and says, 'You say
any shit like that to me
again, you're dead.
You hear me, you whore?'

Now that's a word I just won't endure.
I've never charged a man for sex and, what's more,
I only fuck who I want,
(Unlike this cheeky junkie cunt.)
and my skills in the sack and my reputation,
and every fucker's hope of selection
gives me position
and prestige above the rank and file.
And so they'll smile,
and wink in the street,
and give me welcome, and treat
me as equal.
The woman's better,
the match of the men,
a kind of queen of this fucking hole.

And then,
of course,
there's Inchy Bassey, pimp of her
and all the whores
around,
each of whom he found
and made,
trading
on his allure
to ensnare
the formerly pure,
to deprave them
with his carnal bent
and make them crave him
to the extent
that they'd succumb
to whatever whim you want,
and what Inchy wants is a lot of money,
made by dealing in quality fanny.

He tried with me.
(Now, when I say 'tried',
what I mean is, he got the ride.)
But I was strong.
I stood aloof.
The thing that went wrong
(Or right. Or both.)
was an irrefutable proof
of our beautiful sin
dropping in.
(Or by. Or out.)
The Poppin'eye,
our baby
son,
who made me
Inchy's number one
in a way,
who he has for an hour or two today,
unbeknownst to you know who,
of course, to Jungle.

Jesus, could you imagine?

That's a question
I wouldn't go near,
(Such is his love for the child.)
for fear
that, seeing him revealed
as the issue of Inchy Bassey,
Jungle'd probably kill himself.
If he hasn't already.

Jesus, that isn't even funny.

Anyway.
Fucking Tilly should know better.
Actually, she does,
but, with her need for a certain buzz,
she forgets exactly who I am. So let me remind her.

Remember?
She has me by the hair.
So I merely
take a handful of crotch
and squeeze,
(Like so.)
and it hurts the bitch
so much
she lets go
and I tell her, 'You know
what Inchy's gonna do
when he hears about this?'
And I slap her pissy
face and slap it again,
first with the front, then the back of my hand,
and there's a puddle behind where she's standing,
so I throw her in, her landing
hard on her skinny arse
with a curse,
and, of course,
before she can make it any worse
by speaking any further,
I give her that pointy finger you often see,
the one that says, 'Don't you fuck around with me.'
And she keeps it shut,
which is smart for the slut,
and off I strut

with what you might call a conqueror's comportment,
heading, in my victory,
for the very same Inchy Bassey's apartment.

I arrive there, knock, he opens the door,
and, I swear
I moisten a little bit beneath his allure.
Some men just seem to have it, you know?
He stands aside and in I go.

'Am I bit early?'
'No, you're cool.'
'How was he?'
'I wasn't able to change his nappy.'
'You fool,'
I say, and go in
to the kitchen,
and seeing Poppin'eye's gleeful grin
of recognition,
my heart does a spin
and a flip and I find my condition
lifted to the level of delight,
that level remaining completely consistent,
even as I clean his shite,
then rising yet another notch
as I take him into my arms, saying, 'Gotcha!'
and hold him there,
and he reaches out and grabs my ear
and gives it a pull,
and does it again,
and I may be full
of shit for being proud of something so,
I don't know,
inconsequential,
but, he hasn't ever done it to anyone else
(Not Inchy, not even Jungle)
and that feels pretty special to me.
That I'm the only one.

Inchy, now in the sitting room,
chats with someone on the phone.
I tell him we're going,
he ends the call,
comes in, and asks if I'm all

right for cash, which I am,
and I tell him this.
He says, 'Fine,'
gives Poppin'eye a kiss
on the top of his head,
then asks (Get this.)
if I want to come to bed
for a bit of a bout,
and swears he'll do his best to turn me inside out.

And I do,
my God,
or should that be, I will,
'cos two minutes later, his beautiful cock is filling me,
Inchy drilling me
hard, though with consummate finesse,
Poppin'eye distracted by a kids' cartoon
on TV,
though I guess,
as I moan,
I see
over time,
that it's a little less
with ecstasy
than distress,
inexplicably
afraid
as I've become
that the declaration Jungle made,
the one
about suicide,
has come
to pass.

And isn't that just gas
that both me and the Bru
should have our passion
rudely doused
by nagging feelings
regarding our respective spouses?

Inchy senses something's up,
so he stops
and asks me what it is.

I tell him there's some business
I forgot to take care of and need to go.
And, as I dress,
he says, 'Fuck!
Do you know
how close
I was to blowing my muck?!'
I apologise…
'This close!'
… And again,
as I rise
and get into my things,
and he's about to complain
some more
when his mobile rings,
and then he's berating some whore
about enduring
a client's 'peccadilloes' or something,
and I'm hunting
down Poppin'eye's gear,
saying, 'See you soon,'

and then we're out of there,
zooming
from one street to another,
me presuming
he's dead,
yet hoping
he's not,
when from around a corner
come loping,
a hell of a lot
of fucking hounds,
twenty or so,
and I hunker down
in front of the buggy, throw
my arms around Poppin'eye
to protect him, and as the dogs go by,
one stops for a second and stares,
and the fucking hairs
go up on the back of my neck
as I clock
the extra eye which, along with the other two,

looks into mine, as if seeing through
to something elemental in me.

And then he's gone,
joining the pack,
moving on
as if they're tracking
a scent,
the episode
only adding to my sense of portent,
of premonition,
serving only to keep me pushing
on, then, when I get to my house, pushing
in, then calling Jungle and getting no reply,
then calling again and hearing, 'Hi'
from the kitchen,
in which
I find him sitting at the table.

And I see that his face
is transforming,
a trace
of baseness
adorning
his features.
No, not that at all.
Of hate.
Which even seems to change his smell.
No, wait...

'Fucking hell!'
I shout, when he slaps me across the face. 'Go easy.'
'Whose is he?'
'What?'
'The baby.'
Shit. 'He's yours.'
'You're all the fucking same, you whores,'
and I think, How the hell did he find out?
before his fist connects and a tooth
is ricocheting around my mouth.
I spit
and he throws another punch.
Another hit
and I hear a crunch

and think, Oh, shit!
My nose is broken!
'Jungle! Jungle, listen,' I shout,
and start to explain to him about
the fact that duty is the only truth
of who's a father and who's not,
and not who came in whose vagina,
and not who fertilised which egg.

'You pig,'
he interrupts. 'You sow!'
And it really is amazing how
he's changed his face,
as if he's thrown
away his own
and replaced
it with another.
Stone-like. Steel-like.
And I feel like,
This is the man I longed for him to become,
so why am I sorry now? So dumb!

And so, when he starts his barrage of blows,
I lean forward into the punches he throws
and accept them,
thinking, Fine, then.
This one time
I'll play the prey
and endure the pain,
the destruction,
in order to assist in your evolution,
your gaining of strength,
of resolution,
of the will
to be vile
and, in being
so, to belong,
to fit.

(I mean,
what the hell could be wrong
with that?)

I look to the side,
see Poppin'eye staring,

eyes wide open,
at our display.
I attempt to tell him it's okay,
but I can't.
My eyes are closed
as Jungle's blows
bind them up
beneath bruising,
swelling
fireworks blinding,
flashing.
Explosions.
Eruptions.
Inside there, behind there.

TWO

Alison Ellis

Out in the street,
moving beneath
little spits
which, bit by bit,
become sheets.
And soon,
I'm soaked to the bone,
as I head down a lane,
in search of my son,
who one minute was in the front
garden, the next minute gone.

I exit the lane
looking left and right,
surveying
Beacon
Street, while praying
that my seeking
isn't fruitless.
I mean, defeatist
as that may sound,
this place abounds
in menace and risk,
the threat of reprobates
and miscreants,

like the fellow who locates
himself at a fence
not far from the takeaway,
the Thai,
and awaits a boy
who approaches, holding something out,
and, Jesus, it's Philip, whose name I shout
as I run to him,
or them,
getting there and taking my son by the hand,

and asking the man,
(Who has a patch on his eye
like Captain Hook
from *Peter Pan*,
or one of those pirate guys.)
what it was he took.
'This,' he says,
and holds out Philip's Def-Con Des,
this robot of his.
'He was showing it to me, weren't you, son?'
Philip nods, says, 'See his gun?'
'I do,' says the man,
and I don't understand
how Philip,
normally so anti-
social,
so remote
has opened up to this guy,
this suspicious man, who says, 'Why…?'
(To me, this is.)
'…Did you think I was gonna grab his business
or something? Or fondle his little butt?
Jesus, missus, all I'm doing's
asking him if he's seen my mutt,
you know?
He's easy to single out,
has an extra eye along his snout
to make up for the one *I'm* missing.
Ah, no,' he says. 'I'm only messing.'
I tell him this description
doesn't ring a bell,
and he shrugs, 'Ah, well.
In that case, before you vamoose,
can I tell
you, it isn't boys I like to abuse
but their mammies,
and so,
if you have any
kind of itch
for something of serious length and girth
in your hairy twitch,
then I'm your guy.'
And, full of mirth,

he opens his fly
and reaches in
and takes out his thing,
and lets it hang,
and it's long
and it's thick,
and he lets out a filthy bellow,
and I pick
up my son
and, turning away from the fellow,
his penis,
trying to put a bit of distance between us,
run,
all the while Philip calling, 'Goodbye!'
and trying to pull my hand away from his eyes!

Back to the house and out of the rain,
in and up to Philip's room to change
him, chancing, having arranged
myself at that angle,
to spot, in the mirror, the mangled-
looking part of his head,
that ragged hairless scar
that curves from temple to ear
and causes tears
to pool
in my eyes, fearful fool
that I am, whenever I see it.
You see, to me, it's
a kind of
reminder
of a period before
his stepping inside
himself and shutting the door
on the world and cutting us off,
and how fucking awful
that his only words of late
would be to a dirty reprobate.
And how disturbing.

Anyway, curbing
my urge to cry,
I explain
to the boy

that he can't be talking to strangers.
'Ever. Okay?
And never stray.'
He nods at me in his distant way.

I take him down to the kitchen for lunch
fish fingers and beans,
which he munches
on with what seems
a fairly healthy appetite.
(He ignores
me when I ask for a bite.)
And as I pour
myself some tea,
I hear my husband's key
in the door,
and enter the Bru,
dripping rain all over the floor,
and passing through
without speaking,
gone upstairs to change his clothes since he's soaking,
returns
and turns
on the television, sits,
his back to us.
Ah, this is the pits.

For months, he and I
have been this way.
Ever since Kelly Keegan's party in Bray,
when looking through
her mobbed and swarming house for the loo,
I opened a door I shouldn't have,
and caught the Bru
with Kelly's sister Beverly.
They were on a bed, you see,
and he was licking her out.
(I know. That's a horrible phrase,
but it's hard to watch your mouth,
your Ps and Qs,
after you've caught your husband right
in the middle of going down on
some filthy cooze.)

And so, I shut him off
and thought about some awful
ways of getting back at him,
which I never followed up on,
though we never spoke again,
except for, I suppose, that awful fight
we had in the kitchen one awful night
when he put his hand
on my breast
in a manner
that suggested
all was okay,
or would be
should we
just make love, and I went crazy,
throwing the whiskey
he'd been drinking in his face,
stinging his eyes,
thinking that'd teach him that feeling frisky
isn't something that nullifies
or even lessens his offence.

And then we went to town
on each other,
every other
word an insult or a recrimination,
a put-down or a description
of some failing
or deficiency,
our division
from that night till now
persisting
even through
what happened to Philip,
support uncalled-for and, hence, unheeded,
each of us failing to provide the comfort the other needed.

A commotion outside,
then a yell
or two,
then someone rings our front doorbell
and, noticing the Bru
doesn't move to answer, I do it myself, spying,
as I open the door,

the Deegan brothers trying
to pull a horse along,
a crowd of others
cheering them on.
Though, here on the porch is Benny Drumgoole,
who I tell to come in,
(He says, 'Cool.')
and as he passes me, grinning,
and calls to the Bru,
and the Bru says, 'Benny! Hey!'
I spy
across the street that slapper, Olive Day,
Jungle's wife,

and whatever way
a person wants to live their life,
that's fine by me,
but, Jesus, the manner in which I see
that horrible bitch abuse and betray
that man is a fucking disgrace.
I've seen her call him a girl to his face,
a queer,
goad him with hateful,
hurtful slur
after slur
in front of one and all,
and act the whore
with such appalling
regularity,
and him made such a figure of hilarity,
I reckon it'd be an act of charity
if someone ensured
that she endured
some shame
and humiliation,
see how she enjoyed
a bit of fucking pain
and degradation.

I decide
I'd better go back inside,
which is what I make to do,
closing the door behind
me and turning to find

that the Bru
and Philip are wearing their coats
and that they and Benny are heading out.
A car alarm begins to wail
in the street.
'Where are you going?'
I ask, failing,
even when I repeat
the enquiry,
to get a reply. He
just passes,
guiding Philip out the door,
followed by Benny, who tries to ignore
my imploring
glance, but can't.
He likes me too much to,
and so, I'm granted
the truth
which hits me like a punch in the mouth.
'That's Philip's horse,'
he says, and he's out
the door.

And I stand there a moment more,
perplexed,
before
returning to the kitchen,
the table, at which, in
the next,
twenty minutes or so,
I must smoke six
or seven
cigarettes,
I don't know,
or even eight.
And if you figure that's
a lot, you're right.
My disquiet's
causing me
to light
one after another
while I consider
the horse's fate

and its crime,
and what it indicates
that its punishment will be done
in Philip's name.

See, he and his buddies
found the horse one day
and brought it down to Mick McGillacuddy's
field and had a blast,
mounting one by one and riding fast
to the end of the field and back,
till, spooked
by something or other, it bucked
and Philip got thrown,
and it kicked
as he hit the ground,
and struck
him around
the back of the head
with a resounding
'Thwack!'

And later on they said,
his friends,
that they were sure he was dead,
so lacking
in any movement was he,
so copious the blood he shed.
But he wasn't. And he lived
of course,
but the horse
had taken something from him;
joy or a simple sense of accord
or common communication,
though I love him all the more
for what he's lacking,
which is why I'm out in the rain now, tracking
them by trailing horseshit piles,
souvenirs
of the fear
the creature's endured,
thus far,
which, I'd imagine,
is nothing compared

to the pain, I reckon,
it will.

Up on Marais Hill,
as I pass St Matthew's,
my attention is drawn
by the Son of Man,
his statue,
whose hands
are broken off,
the sight of which evokes two thoughts.
How symbolic of a loss of hope,
is the first.
(I know. Pretentious.)
The second is,
what kind of fucking dope
would want to pinch his
hands?
Unless the symbolism *was* the reason.
The loss of hope the point,
the meaning.

Putting this out of my mind,
I move on,
the mounds
of horseshit chaperoning
me all the way
to the Boneland,
where,
before me, I observe
a throng
in a ring,
which I approach
and reach
and broach
and make a breach
in and advance
to the front
and try to make sense
of what the cunts
(If you'll pardon my French.)
are doing.

They've bound the horse
to a burnt-out van
with barbwire, which cuts into its skin
as, mouth agape
in a scream of pain,
it tries to escape
from the blows being rained
down upon it,
by a bunch of pricks
in the centre, with their bats and sticks,
with which they strike and poke
and belt
and smash,
the strokes
all causing welts
and gashes,
several beaters red with blood which splashes
as the barbwire tears
into the horse's throat.
And it foams at the mouth,
and continues to scream,
and its belly swells
and contracts, and it seems
just like a ceremony,
so fucking solemn is everybody,
Jesus,
so austere.

And here
is where my angst increases
as enter
my husband and my son,
and one second later,
I understand
what's going on
when one of the brothers Deegan,
Dennis or Daniel,
meets them in the middle,
and the rain relents,
becomes a piddle, .
then stops altogether
as whichever
one it is

hands Philip an axe
and leads him to the horse.

But seeing it, he backs
away, of course,
saying, 'No,'
his pleading
mocked by the crowd,
who all about me, goad
him and chide
him for ducking
his duty in providing
them with an end
to their escapade,
a fitting one,
which might have made
the work they'd put in
of some account.

But, wait.
Their fitting end
may happen yet,
because, right then,
the Bru gets
down on one knee
and whispers something in Philip's ear,
(What the hell could it be?)
and Philip nods and says, 'Okay,'
and suddenly he's there,
the crowd all cheering
again,
as he raises the axe in the air,
it's blade a-gleam.

And then I'm steaming
toward him,
taking it, throwing it down
and lifting him up,
doing my utmost to ignore them
as they tell me to stop
and call me a cunt
and a fucking bitch
and any other name you want,
and I touch his scar

and kiss his hair
and try to carve my way from there
to the other side of the crowd,
the epithets still flying loudly,
some of these people trying to grab me,
grab my boy
– 'Get the fuck away!'
And then I'm through,
but no sooner
am I than
I'm grabbed by a Deegan
– Daniel? –
who says,
'Man, who the fuck do you think you are?!'
and the other one is also there
– Dennis? –
and, I swear,
I can barely
hang on to Philip as they try
to pull him away,
me saying,
'Stop!'
me saying,
'Leave him alone!'
as I'm thrown
to the ground,
me saying,
'Please!'
as Philip is seized,
then staying silent
as a sudden, violent
punch from the Bru,
(Who's just appeared from out of the blue.)
sends the Deegan who
had hold of Philip to the ground.
Then he's turning round
and jumping back
to avoid a kick
from the other Deegan,
then attacking
with a left
– what is it, a hook? –
then a right, and look

at them both in the grass now,
noses bleeding,
telling the Bru
as he's leading
us away,
that they're gonna make him pay
next time they see him.

'Keep going,' he says,
as several people start throwing stones,
and we do,
passing out of the Boneland now,
then through
the green,
where Philip suddenly stops and exclaims,

'My Robot!'
'What?'
'My Def-Con Des!
It's gone!'
And the Bru just frowns
and says,
'We'll get you another one
tomorrow,
okay?'
and this redresses
his oddly inexpressive
sorrow,
or dismay,
and we continue on our way,

up Burton Lane, then Rowney Street,
then home. (Or almost, at any rate.)

We're accosted
at our gate
by Emily Frost,
a gossip, who boasts
of news she has of a heist
which occurred
only moments before,
at The Vanguard Hotel.
Its lobbyman, Kit Rankin, felled
by his own nail-
studded hurley stick,

having been tricked
by the fact that the thief had a child in tow,
a baby, really, and so,
had seemed pretty inoffensive.

'He's on his way to the A and E,'
she says, 'to receive some surgery,
I'd presume,
for a pretty serious wound
to the head, maybe even the brain,
his face torn right away from the skull
from forehead to chin.

'But stranger still,'
she goes on,
'was the fact that the tally was left alone
by the thief,
and that all that was stolen
was Kit's "Enforcer-in-Chief",
his shotgun, as well
as some shells.
My belief
is he's going to make poor Olive pay.'
'Poor who?'
'The thief was Jungle Day.
And considering how
much he was disrespected,
ridiculed
and treated like crap,
it was only to be expected
that, one day, the stupid fool
would snap.'

She turns to go,
then turns back around
and asks us if we've just returned
from the Boneland.
We reply that we have,
and she asks if the horse was still alive
when we left.
We reply that he was
and she says, 'That's all right. Because
I'd hate to arrive
and discover I'd missed, you know,
the most exciting bit!'

And with that,
she hits the road
with a hurried stride,
and we open our front door and go inside,
and just seat ourselves around the kitchen table,
each of us, it seems, unable
to do much more than that.
Just sit
in the quiet,
the hush,
the calm,
all three of us lost in thought,
or at least I am,
my mind caught
up in today's events,
my husband's offence,
my own
in keeping this silence between us going
for so fucking long.
And, though I want
to say 'thank you' or apologise
or just start a simple conversation,
a chat,
I realise
I can't just yet.

Even after Philip rises
and heads to his room,
leaving us to our gloom,
the silence sustains.

I get up and dump the remains
of lunch in the bin,
clear the table and clean
the dishes at the sink,
until, amid their clink
and jangle,
the Bru, in an almost inaudible mumble,
says, 'Poor Jungle.'

And, why?
I really couldn't say,
but I reply,
'Poor Olive,' the Days

having actually been on my mind
at that exact minute.

I wait for the Bru to go on,
but he's done.
He moves to the telly, switches it on
and I resume
my washing up.

Later, I enter Philip's room.
He sits at the window, looking down
at the street.
I join him to see what he's looking at,
my God,
and see a pack of dogs
surging about
in a kind of confusion,
while one, standing out
from the general mill,
stands still,
looking up at me and my son,
and I see that he's the one
that one-eyed man was looking for.
The one with three.
But, why the hell is he staring up at my son and me?
What brought him here?
And why do I feel such fear
beneath his gaze?
And why does Philip raise
his hand and say, 'Hi,'
something he won't do to me or his father?

The dog holds his look a moment longer,
then turns and scampers
up the street,
his comrades chasing him out of sight,
and I realise I'm shaking in fright,
but I don't know why.

I look at my boy,
then take him in my arms
and, as always, his lack of response alarms
me a minute before I remember
again that he's not the child he was
and relax.

But only a little bit, because
something now gnaws
at me like a rat,
something important I've forgotten,
though, caught
up in this misbegotten
embrace,
I'm happy to let it go for now.

I offer up a prayer
in any case,
a request, that we be taken care of,
given grace
or protection
in the event of catastrophe encroaching
upon us in this insidious vicinity,
this savage quarter,
this perpetual… whatever.

Do you hear me trying to be clever?

THREE

Tilly McQuarrie

Soaked with rain
from my ramble,
stained with mud
from my fucking tumble,
enraged
at its hateful agent,
Olive Day, who slung me,
flung me,
sent me into a puddle, the cunt,
all on account
of a minor affront
not severe enough
to warrant that rough
a rebuke.

Man, I could fucking puke
right now.
I'm cursed.
And, all right, I know
I'm the one who got violent first,
but I was out of my mind with my need
for the scourge,
my thirst,
so the deed
was done in a surge
of rage,
of fucking despair,
which is why I called her names
or whatever,
grabbed her hair.

Still.
The shit I know and could tell.
The strife I could incite as well,
if my quest was that, but it's this.
Obtain

that ever-elusive strain
that'll bless
me with bliss,
ease my pain
for a time
at least,
maybe for the rest of the day,
though, Christ,
how to procure without payment,
how to earn any cash
without anybody wanting to buy any gash?

This day two of a drought,
the only potential john about
being one who, in the end,
didn't show,
and left me standing,
slowly
increasing in frustration, in fury,
as the relentless rain soaked through me,
till at last, I left the meeting place,
saying, 'Fuck it!'
and, since, I've been moving pretty much apace.
(Apart from my confrontation with Olive.)

But now I stop, suddenly clocking,
huddling under the butcher's awning,
four more
scourge-addicted whores,
each of who I appeal to, see,
and each of who refuses me.
Even Ciara McFee,
who I supplied
a time or two when she was in need
and I wasn't,
though she does say
that she's had the seed
of the core
of an inkling
that she might be able to procure
some that evening,
and if she does, she swears
she'll drop around and give me some.

And that right there's
about as good as I'll do
for now,
so I thank her kindly and bid adieu
to the other three and leave them,
heading, then, across the Hyland Bridge,
and up the rise at the Dripping Ledge,
where I stop to see,
beneath a slide
at the centre
of the green,
a couple of youngsters
hiding
from the rain,
making me chide
myself my own
self-pitying nature,
the tears brought on
by this pretty melancholy picture,
which I wipe away,
though, as I move along
I find I'm unable to keep at bay
the memories rushing in
(Which happens every now and again.)
of my own almost maternity.

Puking announcing my pregnancy,
my only certainty
that the father was Inchy,
my pimp,
simply
because he deferred
the wearing
of a contraceptive
the night he took me,
a prophylactic,
something a john was never allowed to do,
and so fucking apoplectic
was he at my lack of care,
(Though, of course, it was actually his.)
he bawled me out
and boxed my ears,
then, having paced about

a bit, declared,
(First sitting down beside me,
stroking my hair.)
that he'd take care
of it,
that, it was only fair.

But, shit,
what he meant
was that a drunk incompetent
named Derek Dawson
would perform a cheap abortion,
which, with his greasy paws and his whiskey breath,
he did, my baby's death
and disposal
carried out in the most loathsome
way you could possibly think of.

Then, after another drink of
Bushmills Red Label,
he told me I wouldn't be able
to get out of bed for a while,
which suited me fine,
because Inchy agreed to mind
me, and did,
those couple of days of care and attention
also ridding
me of most of my sense
of bereavement,
maybe not so great an achievement
when you understand
just how in love I was with the man.
(And I suppose still am
and will always be.
Such is the effect the fucker has on me.)

Anyway, that wonderful stay
didn't last beyond the second day,
when, turning off the television,
he revealed that the actual reason
he couldn't let me keep my child
was that he already had one
with that mad one
Olive Day,

and that this complicated his life in so many ways
he just couldn't afford to have another.

He was drunk when he told me this
and, the morning after, he confessed
that he'd made an error in doing so
and so he had to make the threat
that, if I ever revealed what he'd disclosed,
he'd make me wish I'd also been disposed
of at birth.

And, How on earth,
I often think,
could Inchy Bassey sink
so low
as to associate
himself in any way
with a piece of fucking shit like Olive Day?

A car pulls up beside me,
a voice says, 'Hi!'
I look to see a man with a single eye,
a patch on the other,
who says, 'Are you Tilly?'
And here, I shudder
with joy,
knowing now that he's the guy
who didn't show,
who, as we pull away
in his car, lets me know
why he was delayed.
'It's silly,
but my dog,
a mutt who goes by the name of Billy,
ran away.'
'And did you find him?'
'No.
So maybe
you can keep an eye out as we go?'
'Of course,' I tell him,
then a question:
'How the hell will I recognise him?'
'Well, he has more eyes than normal.
Three all together,

the third on his snout.'
He bangs on the wheel
and lets out a squeal,
'Man, isn't that a fucking hoot?
You know what some people say once they've seen us?'
'No.'
'That we have the requisite four between us,'
he says, and he slaps his thigh,
then fixes me with his remaining eye
and says, 'Before I ride you,
answer me this:
what are the types of things you've had inside you?'

'What do you mean?'

And the sky continues to piss
down rain
as, later, I lie, doubled over in pain,
bleeding
from my vagina,
my arse,
alone in a kind of sparse
little clearing near to what we call the wood.
And my mouth is filled with blood
as well,
my teeth are loose,
but, fucking hell,
what makes me really confused
is why somebody would choose
to do those things.
I've been abused
before by johns,
and badly.
It goes with the territory,
but, God, I'm sorry.
Whatever it is I've done,
surely I deserve just one
fucking break.
The fucker didn't even pay, for Jaysus' sake.

I spot a toy right there on the ground,
which I take in my hand
and wipe on my jacket,
and try to get a decent look at

what it is.
Some kind of robot.
Or, what does it say?
A 'Def-Con Des'?
And on my way back home,
I muse
on the boy
who disowned
this toy
and render him in my mind,
and imagine him mine,
then, finally, finding
I'm on the verge of breaking down,
I quit these thoughts
and switch to ones of retribution,
which I'm able to entertain
without any untoward emotion
interfering,

until, spying
a phone box appearing
up ahead, I put them into action,
approaching it at a limp,
entering, calling my beloved pimp,
and telling him who this person was
and what this person did,
and bidding him get this person back,
and he says, 'Kid,
you're forgetting the fact
you're a whore,
and as such, you have to endure
your clients' peccadilloes.'
'What?'
'You heard me.'
'Do you know what the fellow
put inside me?!'
'You already said,
now I'm busy.
Ring again and I'll break your fucking head.'

And, just before the line went dead,
did I hear what I think I did?
The voice of Olive Day? The cry of her kid?

How fucking convivial, eh?
How cosy for the cunt,
who only has what I should, but don't
because, of the two of us, she was the first
to be impregnated. Reverse
the order
and I would have had a son or a daughter,
and I would have been the one
who was doted on
and held dear
instead of just a useless scourge-addicted fucking whore,
and I abhor
the bitch,
I hate her,
and so I commit a manoeuvre
which,
later,
I know I'll regret, but for now seems proper
and right and justified.

I dial the operator,
ascertain a number,
dial the number ascertained,
tell the picker-upper
in a timbre feigned
to sound like a man's,
that the child he thinks is his is not,
that everyone knows who baby Poppin'eye
was begotten by.

He says, 'Who?'
I say, 'Guess.'
He says, 'Inchy Bassey.'
I say, 'Yes.
Did you already know?'
He says, 'It only just occurred to me now.
Thank you,' he says.

And, now that he knows,
I start to have qualms, I suppose,
about the potential effect
of what I've done,
Though not, in fact,
for very long,

because, soon, I find
that any thought of any kind
is overcome
by my yen
for scourge,
my desire
tormenting
me, my nerves on fire,
my marrow
attacked
and me with nothing to ease
my pain,
and harrowed
and wracked
to the bone,
I go home.

And my bad luck changes
(Who could have known?)
to good, once I get to the door of my room,
outside of which
my friend Ciara sits,
who, seeing me, stands
and holds out her fists
says, 'In one of these hands
is the answer to all your prayers, bitch.
Try and guess which.'

I lie in the bath in a kind of nirvana,
the water red from my earlier trauma,
the memory of which, right now, is nothing
in this pacifying serenity,
this peace,
this tranquillising divinity,
this release,
before, Christ,
my hair is seized
and I'm pushed beneath the water,
then raised again
to come face to face with the Deegan brothers,
Inchy's friends.
'Where's Ciara?' I say,
and receive a slap.
'We sent her on her way.'

Then they have me up
and dressed and in a car,
the weather nicer than before,
the streets now dry,
a bit of blue in the sky,
'Jesus. It's really picking up,' I say,
which comment the brothers ignore,
stopping the car
now as they are,
then dragging me into The Probable bar,
in whose absence of light,
Inchy Bassey and Olive Day await,

though, oddly, my attention is taken
by the great-
looking ashtray Inchy's using,
a hand with a nail in,
one of two,
symbolic of the crucifixion
of you know who.
I won't say his name.
Why should I acknowledge the one
I've been disowned and forsaken by?

Anyway, voice breaking, I
ask Inchy what's going on,
and only then
do I notice Olive's face,
my God, how devastated
it is
with cuts and welts and bruises
and there and then is where Inchy chooses
to knock me down
with a punch to the chin,
then proceeds to beat me,
the Deegans joining in,
Olive refraining,
though bitterly grinning
at the kicks and punches raining
down upon me.

A rib snaps.
I hear it.
Then another.

I fear it's
gonna be a day to remember. If I survive it,
which, fuck,
beneath the blows I'm receiving,
is looking
increasingly uncertain.

One of the Deegans
lifts his foot for a kick,
I see a ragged purple sock,
hear a 'Thwack!'

then I'm coming to out the back
of the bar,
among the bins and the garbage,
body wracked,
wrecked,
barely able to affect
a movement.

I lie there a moment,
staring up at a passing jet,
when the sun's blocked out by the silhouette
of a man who squats
atop the wall,
then drops
says, 'Hey,'
his identity explaining all
to me now. It's Jungle Day.

He reaches up to the wall again,
takes down a shotgun,
racks it and grins,
then, reaching up with his other hand,
takes down Poppin'eye, says, 'Grand,'
then shoots me a wink,
enters the bar with the child and the gun,
and, in that moment, what I think
is, 'What the fuck have I done?!'

Then a 'Boom!' and I somehow
crawl to the door for a peek
at what harm
a shotgun shell has wreaked
on a Deegan's arm,

Daniel's, I reckon,
hanging off as it is by a piece of fucking gristle,
some tendons,
a second shot sending
him over a chair,
bits of brain and hair
on the wall behind him.

And, once again, the shotgun booms
and Deegan number two
takes one in the chest
which blooms
a sudden crimson flower
before his body comes to a rest,
such was the shotgun's power,
against the bar.

Then silence ensues,
except for a residue
of ringing in my ears
from the barrel's roars,
and Jungle leers
at Olive and Inchy
and approaches them. And it's a cinch he's
gonna blow them away,
but wait, he stops instead,
and places the baby on the floor
then puts the barrel to its head.
And when Inchy asks him what it is he wants,
he says, 'For you two cunts
to watch me make your fucking baby dead,'

and Olive says, 'No,'
and Olive says, 'Please,'
and Olive says, 'I love you, Jungle,'

and, Jesus,
her head erupts, as the trigger
is pulled, with a bang, a spatter,
as pieces of matter
hang in the air a moment,
then descend
as her body drops and lands
with a clump.

And Inchy tries to jump
the bar
to get to Jungle,
though he doesn't get far
as, with another rumbling
boom,
more
gore
is added to the room.

Then Jungle goes around
behind the bar
and pours himself a beer
and downs
it in one,
watching what he once believed was his son
as he does.

And he cries as he puts
the empty glass back down on the bar
and approaches Poppin'eye
and sits on the floor,
and lifts him into his lap,
the baby looking up
adoringly at him.

Grinning.

Ruby motes ascend in a sunshaft spinning.
Time suspends. All's in stasis.
What seems like a millennium passes.

Then, at last, his
time-out done,
Jungle kisses his never-was son
on the top of the head
and smells his hair,
then, having put him back down on the floor,
a look of remorse
comes over his face
as he places
the barrel under his chin,
changing to one of surprise
as he spies
me lying
like a dog in the doorway.

'Hi Jungle,' I say.
(I know. Kinda silly.)
He smiles in a wistful way.
'Hey Tilly.'

Then he's a man without a head,
nothing above his neck which gushes red
upon the baby,
who, oddly, passive until now,
goes crazy
as he's drenched beneath
his would-be father's blood.

And, badly beaten
as I am,
and though I shouldn't
be able to stand,
on my second attempt, I do,
accompanied by a couple of truly
piercing screams of pain,
and I go to Poppin'eye and groan
as I pick him up
and say 'Fuck,'
and 'Shit,'
and sway a bit,
nearly passing out,
and swearing
some more,
as I manage to regain
my bearings
and open the door
and go through,
Poppin'eye covered from head to toe
in Jungle's grue.

And, my God. Who knew
how nice a day it would be?

And, as I approach the river, I see
kiddies abounding,
dressed in their undies,
sounding
as if they're having fun, these
creatures,

as they splash and swim
and shout,

and Poppin'eye and I go in
about
a hundred metres
away, and once the water's up to my waist,
I dip him in and the face
he makes is just delicious,
it's like, 'What the hell are you doing, you vicious
cow?!'
But he's getting into it now,
you can tell,
he's making gurgling sounds
and splashing about
as well.

Then a shout,
then shrieking,
and we look to see the kids upriver freaking
out,
clambering up the bank, wide-eyed,
aghast,
in an effort to avoid
the form which floats on past,
a horse in barbwire bound,
its sockets empty of eye,
the sickening sight
of its head and body utterly destroyed.

I move to my right
to get out of its route,
and as it goes by,
I see,
on the bank, a pack of dogs in pursuit,
the leader of which,
(Surprise surprise.)
is the one that man was looking for,
you can see its three eyes.

And at the awful sound of their baying,
their snarling,
Poppin'eye starts crying,
so I take out the toy
I found, saying, 'Darling,

look?'
Its shiny appearance
calming the child,
allaying his fears
arresting his tears
as the horse's body disappears
around the bend,
then the dogs, and now we're grand
again.

And the kids upriver jump back in,
and the sun shines on,
and the splashing and squealing recommences,
and I frown at the child,
'cos common sense is
saying he'll soon be taken away from me.
And, of course, it's true.

But, live for the moment.
Live for the now.
Isn't that what they always say?

They do.

And so, I play
with the toy,
the Def-Con Des,
and with me supplying the voice, he says,
'Where's your mom?
Is your mommy here?'
And he reaches out and grabs my ear,
and gives it a pull,
the crazy child,
and grins
and does it once again.

Isn't that just fucking wild?

Other Titles in this Series

Howard Brenton
ANNE BOLEYN
BERLIN BERTIE
FAUST – PARTS ONE & TWO *after* Goethe
IN EXTREMIS
NEVER SO GOOD
PAUL
THE RAGGED TROUSERED PHILANTHROPISTS
after Robert Tressell

Andrew Bovell
SPEAKING IN TONGUES
WHEN THE RAIN STOPS FALLING

Jez Butterworth
JERUSALEM
MOJO
THE NIGHT HERON
PARLOUR SONG
THE WINTERLING

Alexi Kaye Campbell
APOLOGIA
THE PRIDE

Caryl Churchill
BLUE HEART
CHURCHILL PLAYS: THREE
CHURCHILL PLAYS: FOUR
CHURCHILL: SHORTS
CLOUD NINE
A DREAM PLAY *after* Strindberg
DRUNK ENOUGH TO SAY I LOVE YOU?
FAR AWAY
HOTEL
ICECREAM
LIGHT SHINING IN BUCKINGHAMSHIRE
MAD FOREST
A NUMBER
SEVEN JEWISH CHILDREN
THE SKRIKER
THIS IS A CHAIR
THYESTES *after* Seneca
TRAPS

Gary Mitchell
AS THE BEAST SLEEPS
THE FORCE OF CHANGE
LOYAL WOMEN
TEARING THE LOOM & IN A LITTLE WORLD OF OUR OWN
TRUST

Bruce Norris
CLYBOURNE PARK
THE PAIN AND THE ITCH

Mark O'Rowe
FROM BOTH HIPS & THE ASPIDISTRA CODE
HOWIE THE ROOKIE
MADE IN CHINA
TERMINUS

Billy Roche
THE CAVALCADERS & AMPHIBIANS
LAY ME DOWN SOFTLY
ON SUCH AS WE
THE WEXFORD TRILOGY

Jack Thorne
2ND MAY 1997
BUNNY
STACY & FANNY AND FAGGOT
WHEN YOU CURE ME

Enda Walsh
BEDBOUND & MISTERMAN
DELIRIUM
DISCO PIGS & SUCKING DUBLIN
ENDA WALSH PLAYS: ONE
THE NEW ELECTRIC BALLROOM
PENELOPE
THE WALWORTH FARCE

Steve Waters
THE CONTINGENCY PLAN
FAST LABOUR
LITTLE PLATOONS
THE UNTHINKABLE
WORLD MUSIC